Now
It Can
Be Told

Now It Can Be Told

A.N. Bali

Published by
PRABHAT PRAKASHAN PVT. LTD.
4/19 Asaf Ali Road,
New Delhi-110 002 (INDIA)
e-mail: prabhatbooks@gmail.com

ISBN 978-93-89982-93-0
NOW IT CAN BE TOLD
by Shri A.N. Bali

Edition
2024

Price
₹ 400.00 (Rupees Four Hundred only)

Printed at
Narula Printers, Delhi

Dedicated to

The hundreds and thousands of unfortunate Punjabis, Sarhadis and Sindhis who, putting faith in the statements that everything will 'stand still', tarried too long behind and perished in the conflagration, unwept, unsung, unhonoured, but certainly not unremembered.

Foreword

Professor A.N. Bali needs no introduction to the Punjabis. After completing a particularly brilliant academic career, he dedicated his life to the cause of education. He is a social worker and a brilliant writer. His interest has been varied and he always takes a practical view of the problems which he studies.

I wish 'Now It Can Be Told' should have been told earlier. The mirage of halo and glory with which some of the political leaders of India have surrounded themselves to cover their errors of policy and their acts of omission and commission which have landed Bengal and Punjab in trouble needs dissipating. Professor Bali has admirably succeeded in this task and by a clever narration of facts. He has shown that our so-called 'strong leaders' are no better than idealists and visionaries who do not know how to face facts.

The Hindus of Punjab in general and Sikhs in particular have a genuine grievance that in their inordinate haste to grasp power, the leaders have thrown them to the wolves. The Sikhs have suffered the most grievous injury. From being rulers of Punjab from the gates of Delhi to Khyber Pass, a little more than a century ago, they have since two years become wanderers on the face of the earth not being able to call a single district of Punjab as their home. Can history cite a single instance where a strong and numerous religious community like the Sikhs has lost the Holiest of its Holies to others? The whole of Christendom united to give back Palestine to the Jews. Why should not the sphere of Hindus of India make a joint effort with the brave Khalsa to undo the wrongs of partition.

Till this is done or till the Sikhs have an independent position in an independent India, Khalsa will never rest.

Professor Bali has given a faithful account of day-to-day happenings in Lahore and other parts of the Punjab in the crucial days of 1947 when the fate of India was being decided by its leaders and when the Punjabi Sikhs and Hindus were undergoing untold miseries and hardships. He has admirably portrayed the hopes and fears that swayed the public mind from time to time as new situation developed and shown how, till the last minute, most of the educated Punjabi Hindus and Sikhs had faith in the statements of their leaders believed that Lahore would be included in India. His description of the Boundary Commission as the greatest farce in history is very apt, and his summing up of the Kashmir situation will appeal to many. I need not agree with Professor Bali on some of the views expressed, but I cannot refrain from paying him a tribute for the frankness and courage with which he has expressed them. There should be no Punjabi home without this book which should be treated more as a Partition Souvenir volume than as a treatise on history.

Amritsar **—(Master) Tara Singh**
18-10-49

Preface

India is free. The dream of centuries has come true, but there are present in the country 7 millions of unfortunates whom nemesis overtook in India's hour of triumph and who, yet reeling under the blow, cannot clearly perceive where freedom is. They say that there is no glow of freedom on people's faces. That is only half true. The glow is there, but it is found only on the faces of the lucky few. The administrative services personnel is happy. Many of them jumped two or three steps higher in as many weeks or months and taking advantage of the inexperience of the new rulers are having all the things in their own way, in fact, in the old way. The ruling classes in the provinces other than East Punjab and West Bengal have joined in the great share out of power and patronage that became theirs for the asking after the 15th of August, 1947. The masses there are also happy. Even if there is no material improvement in their lives, they are at least continuing their life, undisturbed and untrammelled in their own homes and hearths in full expectation of better and better things to come.

Only the lot of the refugees is unenviable. The glow of freedom is certainly not found on their faces. They have lost their everything; their homes and hearths, their kith and kin, their properties, moveable and immovable, their religious shrines and sacred places hallowed by the blood of their martyrs and their accustomed ways of life and living. With their scanty resources dwindling fast, with the snail-like pace of rehabilitation and with the blasted career of their children staring them in the face, they are living in the daily dread of worse and worse things to come.

My object in writing this book is to rouse the conscience of the country, giving it a glimpse of the hell which the prosperous and proud people of North-West Pakistan had to suffer in those critical days and to appeal to the leaders to learn from their past mistakes and take determined and suitable measures in hand to undo the evil effects of the greatest 'wrong' of history.

—A.N. Bali

Contents

Master Tara Singh, who is a noble example of the indomitable. Punjabis, Hindus and Sikhs—the victims of partition—who, though enduring a living death, refused to go under and have not given up the hope of returning what were once their homes and sacred lands.

1
This was Punjab

Punjab before the holocaust was the despair of many political parties of India. The leaders of such parties paid frequent visits to the province to mount propaganda for their parties and win the Punjabis over to their respective causes. The leaders were accorded hearty receptions at the railway station. They were feasted, taken around various sights in Lahore, lodged in the most expensive hotels and given opportunities to unburden their minds on un-receptive audience—but most of them went away disappointed. Caesar could claim *vini, vidi, vici*, but most of these visitors generally wired back to their headquarters *vini, vidi* vanquished. The Punjabis remained Punjabis and their political, social and economic behaviour appeared to be strange to the temporary visitors. The Punjabis themselves realised how strange they were, and what strange anomalies the political, economic and social life of the province was made of. For instance, it could happen only in Punjab that one of the richest landlords should be a Communist who was anything but comradely to his tenants at the time of the realisation of rents; that a gentleman inheriting vast property and accumulated wealth should be a Socialist who was for nationalisation in fields other than those where his own investments lay, where Congressmen hugged the feudal lords and where Sardars of long beards and longer swords professed non-violence with a twinkle in their eyes.

The other provinces of India had a two-fold communal problem; in the Punjab, the problem was three-fold, and yet the trinity was mixed up in a strange sort of unity. The province was overwhelmingly a land of peasant proprietors and yet had not suffered from any acute agrarian problem in spite of the speeches and propaganda of non-agriculturist, non-land-owning, city-dwelling leaders of the South. It was a province where Hindu landlords had Muslim tenants. Muslim landlords had Hindu and Sikh tenants and Sikh landlords had all—Hindu, Muslim and Sikh tenants.

It was a strange land where, inspite of the teachings of economics, tenants in one district after the other, had gone over from cash rents to 'batai' and where they looked upon their landlords, generally belonging to the same caste, as their own kith and kin.

The Punjabi athletes and sportsmen gave a good account of themselves, but the teams winning All-India tournaments held in Lahore used to suffer defeats by Zero to 5 when campaigning outside the Province. And, as several instances showed, people who established All-India records, instead of hugging the trophy, proceeded to marry second wives. It was a land abounding in 'Goonga Pehelwans' (Mute wrestler) and blind singers.

The gastronomic tastes of the Punjabis were also strange. Just imagine the Punjabis eating 'Dumbas' (lamb), hens, brinjals, Bhindi-tori (lady-finger), onions and 'Mash ki dal' with equal relish and drowning everything with 'lassi' in the morning and milk in the evening. A famished-looking socialist leader of Bombay once remarked after seeing his Punjabi host eating a hearty dinner: "Good gracious! Now I understand why we are starving in the South. The entire food of India is being eaten away by the Punjabis."

The political behaviour of the Punjabis was also strange. The political parties carried on the merry old game of creating differences among themselves on petty matters, then settling them among themselves and afterwards having these unsettled once again by carrying these to their respective High Commands outside the province!

Thus, when an outsider visited the Punjab and took note of all these strange happenings in this Land of Five Rivers, he was simply benumbed at this conglomeration of inconsistencies and contradictions and strange behaviour of the people. There was a story going around in Lahore circles about what happened when Mr. Jinnah visited the Punjab a couple of years before partition to win over Sir Khizar Hayat Khan to his own views. After having been closeted with him for two hours and after having explained to Sir Khizar the fullest implications (political, economic and ethnic) of Pakistan and how it would work in Punjab, he was confronted with a retort in colloquial Punjabi "Mainko kai samajh nahin ai" (I have understood nothing). Mr. Jinnah abruptly ended the meeting and told the Muslim League leaders who met him afterwards, "You Punjabis do not understand anything.", to which a reply was given by the Nawab of Mandot, "No Sir, the Punjabis are Yamlas." It was then Mr. Jinnah's turn to exclaim in colloqial Gujarati: "Yamla shu chhe?" ("What is Yamla?")

□

2

Lahore: Before the Partition

In 1913, the city of Lahore consisted of the old walled town, Anarkali, civil area and scattered houses here and there along the Lower Mall. The suburbs of Lahore (not considered Lahore proper at that time) were Muzang, Ichhra, Nawan Kot, Baghbanpura, Badami Bagh and Shahdara. Lahore began to expand in 1914 and this expansion continued unchecked after the war of 1914-18. Construction of houses received great impetus during the worldwide depression of 1929-37. Both the building material and the labour were cheap in Lahore like other towns in India, witnessed development of new settlements all around it. All the open spaces between Central Lahore and its civil area and the suburban areas, like Muzang, Badami Bagh, etc., were built up in the course of few years. Among the new colonies/sectors/settlements populace which came into existence after 1913 were the Ram Gali area between Mochi Gate and the Lahore Railway Station, Gawal-mandi, the Nisbet Road area between the Circular Road and the Mall Road and Rishi Nagar, Sant Nagar, Ram Nagar, Krishan Nagar, Prem Nagar, Chauburji, Rup Nagar, Janak Nagar, Qila Lachman Singh, Qasurpura and Mohd. Nagar. Most of these settlements were situated to the east and west of the Lower Mall, skirting around it from almost Ravi bridge to Nawan Kot. The other new settlements of importance were the New Muzang, Chauburji Quarters, Arya Nagar, Muslim Town, Garden Town, Model Town, Canal Park, Wasanpura, Dharampura, Misri Shah and Raj Garh area. These settlements began from the East of Lower Mall near Chauburji and went up to Badami Bagh, almost in a semi-circle, connecting together the old suburban area of Lahore.

A prominent feature of the new circle of settlements around old Lahore was that its growth had generally been on communal lines and that most of these settlements were predominantly Hindus and Sikhs. The pockets of Muslim settlements in the newly developed Lahore were few and scattered here and there, e.g., Muslim Town, Misri Shah, Wasanpura and New Mozang.

In spite of the great expansion, the area of Lahore, including Lahore Cantonment was only 39.38 miles until August 24, 1939. The building activity had considerably slowed down by 1937 and, on the outbreak of the war, had practically come to an end. If a census of Lahore were taken at that time, it would have shown the population equally balanced, if not a majority of non-Muslims over Muslims. But, with a view to inflating the Muslim population in the area of the then Lahore Municipal Committee, and, later, Lahore Corporation, several villages around Lahore, within a radius of 8 miles, were included within the municipal boundaries by the Unionist Government. Many of these villages were purely agricultural settlements. There were not even roads connecting them with the town and there was no extension of electricity and municipal water supply to them. There was not the remotest chance of these villages becoming a part and parcel of Lahore in the next two decades. The extension of the limits of the corporation area was purely arbitrary and was made only with one end in view which was to give Lahore the semblance of a predominantly Muslim town. The area of Lahore which consisted only of 39.38 square miles, including an area of 13.34 square miles of Lahore Cantonment, was by a stroke of pen, extended to cover 128.75 square miles. In other words, the area of Lahore was more than trebled. It may be interesting to note that the new rural areas included in the limits of Lahore had a preponderantly Muslim population, this percentage being as high as 86.8.

For the purposes of assessing whether the majority of the population of Lahore consisted of Muslims or non-Muslims, we must, therefore, exclude all the new areas which were arbitrarily included into the limits of Lahore. The population of this undeveloped rural

Value and Distribution of Dwellings

	Dwellings ₹	Average Monthly Rent	Total Rent Value	Percentage of Muslim Holdings	Propertyrentearned Muslim	Non-Muslim
Walled City	19,265	7/7/-	1,43,000	50	71,500	71,500
Outer Old Locality	17,287	8/8/-	1,47,000	65.6	96,400	50,500
Predominantly Muslim Settlements	17,447	10/6/-	1,81,000	52.7	95,600	85,400
Civil Lines & Hindu Nagars	2,776	90/3/-	2,50,000	26.1	65,300	1,84,700
Rural Area	10,419	4/3/-	44,000	87.2	38,400	5,600
Lahore Cantt.	3,380	89/4/-	3,02,000	20	60,400	2,41,600
	70,573	10,67,010	10,67,000	58.7	4,27,600	6,39,400
Annual Rent Value		(₹)	1,28,04,000		51,31,200	76,72,800
Total value on the basis of 6¼ of yield.		(₹)	20,48,64,000	8,20,99,200	12,27,64.809	

area was 12.1 per cent of the total population of Lahore. Of this, 86.8 per cent consisted of Muslims. If we exclude this, the Muslim majority of 64.6 per cent, as shown by the census of 1941, is reduced to 53·5 per cent for the developed area of Lahore and it is only the developed areas that should count in such matters.

A survey of Lahore, carried out by the Punjab Government Board of Economic Enquiry, gives the number of dwellings their average monthly rent, ownership by communities and distribution by localities. The word 'dwelling' was used to denote the citizens' residential houses. Shops, commercial buildings, establishments, hotels, etc., were classified separately. The given table gives at a glance the value and distribution of these dwellings. The value was calculated on the basis of a 6¼% return and was arrived at by multiplying the annual rent by 16. The survey showed that the total value of all dwelling houses owned by non-Muslims within the Corporation limits amounted to ₹12,27,64,800. In other words, non-Muslims owned 60% while Muslims owned 40%. The share of the Muslims would be further reduced if rural areas were excluded from calculation.

A complete census of shops and commercial establishments was also taken by the Punjab Government Board of Economic Enquiry. The table shows community-wise distribution of the ownership of these shops. It is clear from the table that Mohammedan owners predominated only on the following roads:

Temple Road, Faiz Bagh, Changar Mohalla, Circular Road, Mozang, Ichhra, Ferozepore Road, Fleming Road and Data Ganj.

The total number of shops on those roads was 711. Of this number, the Mohammedans owned 470, i.e., 66 per cent. As against this, the following areas were overwhelmingly non-Muslim:

Anarkali, Railway Road, Nila Gumbad, Mc'Leod Road, Mohan Lal Road, Ganpat Road, Mall Road, Brandreth Road, Kutchery Road, Nisbet Road, Hall Road, Beaden Road, Multan Road, Naulakha, Shahdara, Moghalpura, Qila Gujjar Singh, Cantonment, Old Anarkali Gawalmandi, Baghbanpura, Badami Bagh, Krishan Nagar, Hospital Road, Nicholson Road, Walled City.

The total number of shops in these areas was 4,621, which were distributed commnity-wise as follows:

NON-MUSLIMS.... 3,260

MUSLIMS................ 1,36I

giving a percentage of 71 for the Non-Muslim shops.

Taken in the aggregate, the city may be divided into two areas—Outer Lahore and Walled City. The percentage of shops owned by the non-Muslims in the Walled City came to 63. The percentage in outer Lahore came to 67. Adding together these figures, the grand total of shops in Greater Lahore came to 5,332, of which non-Muslims owned 3,501. The ownership of these shops community-wise worked out as follows:

NON-MUSLIMS.... 66 per cent

MUSLIMS................ 34 per cent

It would be, thus, clear that Lahore was predominantly a Non-Muslim town from the point of view of shops and commercial establishments. The census of the residential houses shows that 60 per cent of the value of housing property was owned by non-Muslims. The figures given about shops and commercial establishments show that 66 per cent of these were also owned by non-Muslims. A city where the ownership of shops and dwelling houses is overwhelmingly in favour of one community cannot by any stretch of imagination be considered to belong to the other community. The stake of the property owners in a city must be given first consideration in any calculation of this type.

Lahore, though not an industrial town in the accepted sense of the word in which Bombay and Ahmedabad are taken, had as many as three hundred registered factories. In this respect, it had the first place among the cities of the province. This number was more than 1/5th of the total number of registered factories in the British Punjab and more than 1/3rd of the total number of workers employed in all the registered factories in the province were found in this city. In the beginning of this century, the number of factories in the city was exceedingly small. It was only during the last forty years, and particularly during the last fifteen years, including the war period, that the number recorded a phenomenal rise.

Iron and steel engineering industry constituted half the total number of factories in Lahore. The other important large-scale industries were hosiery, oil extraction and flour-milling, chemicals and printing. Ninety per cent of these two groups of factories was owned by non-Muslims. Factories were started during the war period for the manufacture of lathes, oil expellers, machinery for button factory, of spare parts, for cotton ginning, sugar mills, railway carriage wheels, steel billets, electric fans and for repair of aeroplanes. The ownership of this group of industries mainly vested with the Non-Muslims who had provided not only the block capital and finance, but also higher technical direction. It should be remembered that the industries falling in these three groups had come into existence as a result of private initiative and free enterprise of Hindus and Sikhs who, at the time of the partition, ran 80 per cent of these.

A complete survey of the registered factories in Greater Lahore was carried out by the Punjab Government Board of Economic Enquiry and data was collected for the year 1943-44. The survey shows that out of a total number of 218 registered factories working in Greater Lahore in that year, as many as 173 or 80 per cent belonged to non-Muslims. The total fixed capital invested in these factories amounted to a sum of ₹2 crores 40.27 lakhs. Of this, the Muslim investment amounted only to 58.91 lakhs of rupees, i.e., 24.5 per cent only of the total capital invested. If, however, we take the figures of the total capital investment, fixed plus circulating, then the total capital invested in these registered factories amounted to ₹6.29 crores. The non-Muslim share in this total investment amounted to ₹5.12 crores, i.e., 81.3 per cent of the total. As the amount of capital invested by foreigners (other than Indians) amounted only to ₹24.5 lakhs of rupees, it is clear that the bulk of the capital was provided by the non-Muslims. These figures are taken from tables 'A', 'B', 'C' and 'D'.

Table 'A'

Hindu Majority Areas	Number of Shops			% to Total	
	Total	Muslim	Non-Muslim	Muslim	Non-Muslim
Anarkali	216	62	154	29	71
Railway Road	144	38	106	26	74
Nila Gumbad	46	9	37	20	80
McLeod Road	82	34	48	41	40
Mohal Lal Road	68	12	56	18	82
Ganpat Road	33	9	24	27	73
Mall Road	141	23	118	16	84
Brandreth Road	62	15	47	24	76
Kutchery Road	10	4	6	40	60
Nisbet Road	51	6	45	12	88
Hall Road	18	0	18	0	100
Beadon Road	65	14	51	22	78
Multan Road	17	6	13	24	76
Naulakha	208	103	105	49	51
Shahdara	96	29	67	30	70
Moghalpura	136	59	77	43	57
Qila Gujar Singh	170	50	120	29	71
Cantt.	342	95	247	28	72
Old Anarkali	87	26	61	30	70
Gowalmandi	148	10	138	7	93
Baghbanpura	100	13	87	13	87
Badami Bagh	42	5	37	12	88
Krishan Nagar	366	22	344	6	94
Hospital Road	26	9	17	35	65
Nicholson Road	32	11	21	34	66
Walled City	1915	699	1216	37	63
Total	4621	1361	3260	29	71

Muslim Majority Numberof Shops % to Total

Areas	Total	Muslim	Non-Muslim	Muslim	Non-Muslim
Temple Road	67	37	30	55	45
Faiz Road	40	·31	9	78	22
Changar Mohalla	100	76	24	76	24
Circular Road	38	20	18	53	47
Mozang	267	169	98	71	29
Ichhra	39	22	17	56	44
Ferozepore Road	15	9	6	60	40
Fleming Road	94	76	18	81	19
Data Ganj	51	30	21	59	41
Total:	711	470	241	66	34
Hindu Majority Areas	4621	1361	3260	29	71
Muslim Majority Areas	711	470	241	66	34
Grand Total	5332	1831	3501	34	66

Distribution of Industry-Wise Factories in Greater Lahore (As in 1943-44)

Table 'B'

Industry	Number of Registered Factories					
	Indian					
	Hindu	Muslim	Sikh	Others	Foreign	Total
1. Engineering						
(i) Electrical	5	—	—	—	—	5
(ii) General	76	31	5	1	3	116
2. Steel Re-rolling Mills	6	3	1	—	—	10
3. Hosiery & Textiles	5	—	—	—	—	5
4. Chemical Industries	13	—	—	1	1	15
5. Printing & Stationery	27	7	2	—	—	37
6. Class Works	1	—	—	—	—	1
7. Button Factories	2	—	1	—	1	4

Industry	Number of Registered Factories					
	Indian					
	Hindu	Muslim	Sikh	Others	Foreign	Total.
8. Miscellaneous	19	4	1	—	1	25
Total	154	45	10	3	6	218

Table 'C' (Rupees Lakhs)

Industry	Fixed Capital Investment					
	Indian					
	Hindu	Muslim	Sikh	Others	Foreign	Total.
1. Engineering						
(i) Electrical	12.00	—	—	—	—	12.00
(ii) General	68.40	46.91	2.78	1.00	4.00	123.09
2. Steel Re-rolling Mills	20.50	5.00	2.00	—	—	27.50
3. Hosiery & Textiles	11.00	—	—	—	—	11.00
4. Chemical Industries	20.00	—	—	0.26	4.00	24.26
5. Printing & Stationery	12.00	5.00	0.50	0.50	—	18.00
6. Class Works	0.53	—	—	—	—	0.35
7. Button Factories	1.12	—	1.00	—	2.27	4.39
8. Miscellaneous	16.00	2.00	0.50	—	1.00	19.50
Total	161.55	58.91	6.78	1.76	11.27	240.27

Distribution of Industry-Wise Factories in Greater Lahore
(As in 1943-44)
Table 'D'

Industry	Total Capital Investment (Fixed Plus Circulating)					
	Indian					
	Hindu	Muslim	Sikh	Others	Foreign	Total
1. Engineering						
(i) Electrical	28.00	—	—	—	—	28.00
(ii) General	194.56	96.24	5.38	2.00	10.00	308.18
2. Steel Re-rolling Mills	50.00	10.00	4.00	—	—	64.00

Total Capital Investment

Industry	(Fixed Plus Circulating)					
	Indian					
	Hindu	Muslim	Sikh	Others	Foreign	Total
3. Hosiery & Textiles	20.00	—	—	—	—	20.00
4. Chemical Industries	44.00	—	—	0.60	8.00	52.60
5. Printing & Stationery	90.00	6.00	0.75	1.00	—	97.75
6. Glass Works	2.33	—	—	—	—	2.33
7. Button Factories	2.20	—	1.80	—	5.00	9.00
8. Miscellaneous	40.00	5.00	1.00	—	1.50	47.50
Total	417.09	117.24	12.93	3.60	24.50	629.36

During the last fifty years, many handicrafts had become extinct in Lahore. Among those that had virtually died out were gunsmithy woollen cloth weaving, wax cloth printing, kansi working and glass bangle making. These handicrafts were mostly manned and owned by Muslims. These had been replaced by new cottage industries, among which might be mentioned furniture-making, nickel-plating, silk and cotton dyeing, tinsmithy, cutlery, book binding, iron foundry, tailoring, signboard painting, coach building, etc. Small workshops had been started for the manufacture of toys after the Japanese model. The number of these small workshops and cottage establishments in Lahore well exceeded two thousand. Among the small workshops, the most notable were engineering workshops devoted to repair work. These were mostly owned by Hindus and Sikhs, though the labour mechanic employed therein was Muslim. Other small scale industries like the manufacture of aerated water, fruit canning, flour-milling, oil extraction, hosiery, spinning and weaving, manufacture of hair oil and other toilet goods, furniture making, gold smithy, etc., were practically the monopoly of the non-Muslims. During the war, joint concerns run by Muslims and non-Muslims came into existence, as well as a few exclusively Muslim establishments. But even after allowing for these, the share of the non-Muslims in the ownership of small scale industries did not fall short of 75 per cent.

Lahore was an important banking and commercial centre and the money market there was fairly well developed. The head offices of as many as 26 banks were located in Lahore. A great development of banking had taken place since 1939. Before the Great War of 1914-18, the number of branches of all banks in Lahore hardly exceeded 12. The total number of the bank offices working in Lahore in 1947, however, was ninety. Of the Indian banks and branches in Lahore, only 3 belonged to Muslims.

There were nearly eighty offices of Insurance companies in Lahore. These included the head offices of fifteen Insurance companies. Most of these companies dealt in life-business, but some of the Punjab companies did fire and miscellaneous business also irrelevant. Of Insurance companies and their offices, only two belonged to Muslims.

There were two Stock Exchanges registered as Limited Liability Companies in Lahore. Of the members of both of these, there was only one Muslim, all the rest being Hindus and Sikhs.

Investment Trusts had been formed in Lahore since 1932. Before partition, there were seventeen such trusts operating in Lahore. All these belonged to the non-Muslims.

A noteworthy development that had taken place during the recent years was the formation of associations of almost all types of trades in the province with their headquarters at Lahore. There were five Chambers of Commerce in Lahore. The Indian Chamber of Commerce (Desi Beopar Mandal), Punjab Merchants Chamber, Northern India Chamber of Commerce. Punjab Beopar Mandal and Muslim Chamber of Commerce. The first three Chambers, the membership stood at nearly 635. Of this number, a great majority was non-Muslim. The Muslim Chamber was founded only a few years ago and its membership was very small.

Lahore was an important educational centre of the province and a very great part in its educational development had been played by Hindus, Sikhs, Christians, Brahmo Samaj, Dev Samaj and Arya Samaj. The non-Muslims' share in the promotion and development of educational institutions was stupendous. There were in Lahore as many as 270 educational institutions which were recognised by the Education Department or were affiliated to the Punjab University. Of these, about one hundred institutions were devoted to female education. The number of male students in these institutions was 64,902 and of women students, 23,477. Of the 12 Art and Science Colleges in Lahore, giving education to 10,647 students, only one was run by the Muslims and one by the Government. The other ten were run by the non-Muslims. There were fifteen professional colleges imparting education to 2,020 students. Of this number, excluding three run by the Government, all were run by the non-Muslims. Of the 36 High Schools imparting education to 26,647 students, not more than four were run by the Muslims, one by Government and the remaining 31 by the non-Muslims. The stake of the non-Muslims, who had spent crores of rupees in building up these institutions and devoted the best brains of the community to furthering education, as evidenced by the quoted figures, was very great.

There were a few Hindu and Sikh students studying in Muslim institutions and a few Muslim students studying in Hindu and Sikh institutions. Of the students studying in Government colleges and institutions, half the number may be taken as belonging to the Muslim community. Working on this basis, we find that as many as 89 per cent of students studying in the Lahore educational institutions belonged to the non-Muslim communities. Thus, both from the point of view of the ownership and working and from the point of view of students taught, Lahore educational institutions must be considered as preponderatingly non-Muslim.

There were four important public libraries in Lahore, i.e., The Punjab Public Library, Dyal Singh Library, Dwarka Dass Library and Sir Ganga Ram Library. The first was maintained by the Government, while all the other three were owned and maintained by the non-

Muslims. The Punjab University Library was mainly meant for students and professors while all educational institutions had their own libraries for the use of their own students. It would, thus, be found that no single public library was being run in the city by the Muslims. If Lahore had continued to be within the Hindu and Sikh zone (or the Eastern zone), it would have continued to play a very important part in the educational uplift of East Punjab. It was bound to attract students from all over the East as well as from the West Punjab. As it was placed within Pakistan zone, the loss suffered by the non-Muslim communities in the disruption of their greatest educational centre in North-West India has been irreparable.

Allied with the educational efforts of the Hindus and Sikhs were the newspapers issued from Lahore which served a similarly useful purpose. The number of newspapers issued from the city were as follows:

DAILY NEWSPAPERS:

English	5
Urdu	15
Hindi	2
Gurmukhi	1
Total	**23**
Weekly	129
Fortnightlies	32
Monthlies	170
Quarterlies	24

Lahore was well-supplied with hospitals. The total number of those run on up-to-date modern allopathic lines was 12. In addition, there were four hospitals run on the indigenous methods of medicine. But it should be noted that not a single hospital run on modern allopathic, or even on the indigenous lines, was run by the Muslims, either for males or for females. Apart from a few dispensaries for outdoor patients, the Muslim contribution to medical relief in Lahore was nil. The Hindus, on the other hand, had spent lakhs of rupees and devoted the best medical brains of the community to the running of up-to-date and first-class hospitals, for both men and women. The hospitals at Lahore served the needs of the entire province of the Punjab as well as of the patients from the N.W.F.P., Kashmir and Sindh. The Government help to these institutions was very little and whatever little it was, it has dried up under the Pakistan Government. Private endowments and public charity which mostly came from Hindus and Sikhs also ended. Most of the hospitals have been left high and dry and the public has suffered a great loss.

□

3

The Holocaust

The other day in a cinema in Delhi a picture was being shown which had a few scenes depicting incidents from Lahore. The Punjabi audience in the cinema hall rose to a man and vociferously cheered when they saw the Mall Road, the Neela Gumbad and the Anarkali scenes. There were shouts of "See the Mall Road", "The Anarkali", "Look at my shop there on the Mall, etc." After the tumult, I found tears in the eyes of some people sitting near me. Lahore had become a dreamland to all those people who had been born and bred in Lahore and whose ancestors for generations had born, bred and died in Lahore. The city founded by Rama's son, which had been their own city till the 17th of August, 1917, had now become a far off town almost like Mecca and Madina—to which entry of other than Muslims was prohibited.

Lahore was a peaceful town right up to 1913 when its affairs used to be managed by the elders of the city, Rai Bahadurs and Khan Bahadurs, a few nominated, majority elected under the presidentship of the Deputy Commissioner. The Muncipal Commissioners, whether Hindus, Muslims or Sikhs, used to be men of property and position, singularly free from any tinge of communalism and commanding universal respect from the citizens of Lahore. Awakening of political consciousness and gradually coming into the forefront of the Congress party after the first Great War by and by changed the atmosphere for the worse. Politics began to be imported into civic affairs. Muslims used to be in minority in the Committee. The first occasion on which the non-official president was to be elected by the Committee, the

Muslims and Christians on one side and the Hindus and Sikhs on the other were in balance. Late Ch. Sir Shahab-ud-Din was the Muslim candidate, and with one Hindu vote, his election could be ensured and that one vote of Dr. Hira Lal was secured for him by Lala Devi Dayal, Professor D.A.V. College, Lahore and, thus, he was duly elected President After that, however, no Hindu or Sikh could ever be elected as president. The presidentship became the close preserve of the Muslim community. Ch. Sir Shahab-ud-din showed himself in true colours after his election—that of a Muslim first and Muslim last. The affairs of the town began to be managed now on communal and political lines. Politics was directly imported when a few Congress members, among whom the leading figure was Dr. Gopi Chand, began to press for a resolution of the Committee asking for the removal of Lord Lawrence's statue from the Mall. The opposition to the resolution became very stiff and quicker came the plans of the provincial government to cut the numerical strength of the Hindus in the Committee. In new Lahore were included the suburbs of Mozang, Ichhra, Nawankot, Baghwanpura, Badami Bagh and new settlements of Ramgali, Gowalmandi, Krishna Nagar, New Mozang, Muslim Town, Model Town, Garden Town, Canal Park, Wasanpura, Dharampura, Misri Shah, Ramgarh, etc. But, in spite of this great expansion, the area of Lahore including Lahore Cantt. was only 39.38 square miles up to August 24, 1939. The Hindu-Muslim population was equally balanced with a slight margin in favour of the non-Muslims. But with a view to inflating the Muslim population, several villages around Lahore within a radius of 9 miles were included within the municipal limits by the Unionist Government. Many of these villages were purely agricultural settlements. There were not even roads connecting them with the town and there was no extension of the electricity and municipal water supply to them. The extension of the limits of the Corporation area was made with a view to give Lahore the semblance of a predominantly Muslim town. The area of Lahore which consisted only of 39.38 sq. miles including the area of 13.3 sq. miles of Lahore Cantt. was by a stroke of pen extended to cover 128.75 sq. miles. In other words, the area of Lahore was more than trebled. The new rural area of Lahore had preponderantly Muslim population, their percentage being 86.7%. The Hindus and Sikhs vigorously protested against these efforts to artificially inflate the Muslim population of the town for the purpose of civic control. The Hindus and Sikhs boycotted the new elections. The Congress members for once sided with the Hindus. But when the Coalition Ministry was formed in the Province and Chaudhri Lehri Singh became the Minister on behalf of the Congress party, the Congress people changed their attitude. The Government had turned a deaf ear to the demand of Hindus and Sikhs that either the ration cards be taken as the basis for determining the figures of the population or a new Census of Lahore be carried out. According to the census of 1941, the Hindu population had been shown lesser, though, in actuality, they numbered more than the Muslims. The Muslims were given more representation in the City of Lahore Corporation than they were entitled to. Hindus and Sikhs made strong protests, but all in vain. Even then, owing to the rival ambitions of the Muslim candidates, it was not easy for the Muslim party to have its own way in the election of office-bearers. There was, according to calculations made, only one vote needed to turn the scales. This time Ch. Lehri Singh played the part of Doctor Hira Lal. Amongst the Harijan members nominated by him, he included the name of Mr. Sukh Lal, though it was known that Mr. Sukh Lal was an anti-nationalist Harijan who would vote with the Muslim League. There were protests in the papers, but as the decision was that of a Congress Minister, the Congress, which was the vocal section of the Hindu community, did not protest and the fate of Lahore was sealed. The Muslim League took possession of the Corporation by nominating only their own party-men to various offices and sub-committees.

That is in brief the background against which we have to study the fate of Lahore in the subsequent months. In spite of the riots in Calcutta, Noakhali, Bihar, Bombay and other parts of the country, the Punjab kept its head cool. The situation in Lahore was normal. Hindus, Muslims and Sikhs were freely getting along with one another and there appeared not the remotest possibility of a communal flare-up in the province right up to the end of 1946. It was in this connection that I wrote an Article in the Tribune—'The Punjabi Oxen'—which was widely appreciated by all communities. Extracts from this Article are worth reprinting.

"John Bull is affectionately known as a 'Bull Dog'; the Americans are Yankies and the Punjabis have been given the epithet of 'Oxen' by people other than Punjabis. They have been called oxen because of certain peculiar qualities they possess, e.g., the quality of eating to their full, doing a day's work and then basking in the sun and chewing the cud. The chirping of the sparrows, the cawing of the crows and the barking of the dogs produce no effect on an ox which is resting after day's work and contentedly digesting the day's food. He is like the proverbial East that sees the legions thunder past and goes to sleep again.

This quality of the Punjabis is galling in the extreme to people in other parts of the country. By constant kicking and twisting of the tail and by regular prodding in the ribs, sometimes the Gujaratis, sometimes the Madrasis, sometimes the Bengalis and, at other times, the Maharashtrians and the Biharis try their best to rouse the ox to fury but finding their efforts producing no effect, they all go away raving at the madness of the Punjab, though praising it for its hospitality. The very contented and well-fed appearance of the Punjabi in itself, in these days, is an eyesore to the thin cadaverous-looking, half-starved prodders from the east and south. Why should the ox in the north not starve when the rabbits and the hares and the sheep and the goats in the south are starving? But the greatest disappointment comes to them from the fact that, in spite of their twisting its tail and kicking it in the ribs, the Punjab ox does not become an infuriated bull, attacking the other ox in the field, chasing the cow and breaking loose from its tether.

The geese and the ducks and cranes all fly in formation and have their well-chosen leaders. A flap of the wings and a sudden quacking note turn the whole formation to the east, west, south or north. Perfect discipline is maintained in following the leader. The sheep follow blindly the leader sheep, but has anybody seen the oxen following a particular ox? The oxen do not believe in having a leader of their own. That perhaps is the reason why Punjab has no leader of all-India repute, either among the Hindus or among the Muslims or among the Christians. The leadership goes abegging.

But nature abhors vacuum. That is why, though the Punjabi oxen have no leader of their own; leaders in large numbers come frequently visiting the province from other places, each coming with a view to leading the whole herd away to its own cherished pen. The Punjab oxen do show a momentary enthusiasm for such leaders, but oxen are oxen and as the prodders go away, they resume their usual routine of basking in the sun and chewing the cud, unmindful of the sheep and the cawing of the crows around them.

The Punjabi ox is generous in parting with its food for the sake of other starving animals, but it is reluctant in changing its own habits. For the past forty years, I have seen food going out to feed the people in other provinces, money going out to help the poor and volunteers going out to render first aid to the sufferers in other places. But I have never seen either food or money or volunteers ever coming to the Punjab to help the Punjabi oxen in their troubles. The only thing that comes in is an army of prodders, each bent upon their fellow creatures in far-off fields and pastures.

The latest happenings in the country also follow the same pattern. One section would like the Punjabi oxen on its neighbours to avenge Calcutta and Noakhali; another section would like them to do the same thing, but to avenge Bihar and Bombay. The prodders and the meddlers are busy. As the well-fed appearance of the Punjabi ox was an eyesore to them before, the well-kept peace and order in the province is a greater eyesore to them now. Why should the Punjabi oxen bathe in the morning sun when the other animals in animal fury are bathing in each other's blood? But thanks to the Punjabi ox, it has remained an ox. The herd instinct of the Punjabis and their ingrained habits are standing them well in resisting such pleadings. The name of the province was not tarnished by the occurrence of ghastly events that had disfigured the banners of others. Alas! this was not to be."

The province was being invaded from the east and the south by leaders in search of followers. Every one of them was rousing political passions and painting horrid pictures that if, in the new political set-up, his party was not given cent per cent of what it had asked for. The sturdy Punjabi with his broad common-sense was being assailed from all sides, day in and day out, with the result that he lost his bearing. The Punjabi ox became an infuriated bull. The transformation was sudden and the first victims of its fury were the Hindus and Sikhs of Rawalpindi, then of Amritsar and Lahore, and later on, of other parts of the province.

Thousands of Hindus and Sikhs fleeing in terror from Rawalpindi Division were given shelter in Lahore. Several thousands passed on after a temporary sojourn to Haridwar, Dehradun and Delhi. The work of giving relief to the unfortunate minorities of West Punjab was organised in Lahore by the Hindus in which the leading part was played by the R.S.S. The attack on Hindus and Sikhs had begun on 5th of March, 1947.

The Muslim League which had carried on defiance of he Unionist Ministry for a period of two months had secretly organised itself for an offensive against the minorities though, outwardly, it kept up a façade of neutrality towards all the hostility only to the Muslim ministers of the Unionist Government. The resignation of Sir Khizar Hayat about which he had not consulted beforehand with his Hindu and Sikh colleagues, was the signal for the outbreak of trouble. Master Tara Singh, frank as he was, did one of the most dramatic things that was wilfully misconstrued and misrepresented to the Muslims of Punjab. He drew his sword from the scabbard in front of the assembly hall in which action he was followed by Sardar Swaran Singh and all the other Sikh MLAs. A mammoth gathering of Hindus and Sikhs was addressed by the Congress and Sikh leaders in Kapurthala House in the evening. The meeting continued late at night and its proceedings were interspersed by loud shouts of 'Muslim League Murdabad', 'Coalition Ministry Zindabad', 'Akhand Hindustan Zindabad' and 'Hai, Hai', etc.

Next day the college students of Lahore, who had seen the

Muslim League processions in defiance of law and order not being checked by the police, organised a protest procession of their own in favour of a Coalition Government for the province. The police swooped down on this procession with a hail of lathies and bullets. The first blood was drawn in the capital of the province. The victims were mostly Hindus and Sikhs and the British rulers of the Punjab showed by their action that though they had a soft corner for the Muslim League, they proposed to have no such soft leanings towards the minorities.

The ferocity of the riots in Rawalpindi had shocked everybody. The Deputy Inspector General of Police, Mr. Scott, returning after an extensive tour of riot-affected areas in his range, appeared greatly moved with ghastly scenes of brutal murders, loot and arson. "I could never believe that such barbarous acts as were committed on innocent people in the rural areas of Rawalpindi District could be possible in the Punjab. I have every sympathy with the victims of the worst type of communal frenzy in riot-stricken areas of Rawalpindi Division," said Mr. Scott as reported in the *Civil & Military Gazette of March 26, 1947*.

Though he expressed his grim determination to deal with the situation as sternly as the circumstances demanded, the machinery of law was such that right up to the partition of the Punjab in August 1947, not a single criminal could be brought to book. Meanwhile, the riots had spread to the central district of the Punjab. The biggest disaster was the burning of Amritsar. The Hindus and Sikhs of the Punjab began bleeding at many places and thousands of them lost everything they had. By March 20, 1947, as many as 984 complaints were registered with the police in respect of cases of arson, loot, injuries, murders, etc., only in one town of Amritsar. The reported loss of property was over ₹2,26,00,000 (Two crores twenty-six lakhs of rupees).

The pamphlet 'Rape of Rawalpindi' gives gruesome details of what was done to the minorities in the Rawalpindi Division. No such details have been published for other towns, but the pattern of barbarities committed by the Muslim League goondas was the same everywhere.

The exodus of minorities from the affected areas assumed vast proportions in the month of April 1947. But the Congress leaders of Gujarat and Jhelum were reported to be asking the minorities to stick to their places and appeals were made in a section of the press asking Mahatma Gandhi to visit Punjab. *The Tribune* dated 15-4-1947, discussing this request, said: "Will his visit do any good to the province?" The best answer to this can be got from the Noakhali area. Mahatma Gandhi toured that area. The press talked very highly of it. It was termed as historic tour. But, had this tour impressed the Muslims? Had he been able to restore confidence in the Hindus? Apparently not. What good then his tour of the Punjab will did its people?

The police and the judiciary became demoralised and the former in which there was 85% representation of the Muslim community soon became a tool in the hands of the Muslim League workers. The best of them would take no action in defence of minorities or stay neutral even when ordered by their officers to arrest a member of their own community. This attitude later on changed into active participation in the riots and loot. By June 1947, the Hindus and Sikhs in the West Punjab were being made the victims not of the so-called goondas, but of 'goondaism in uniform'.

The greatest massacre in Punjab, the slaughter of Hindus and Sikhs at Sheikhupura, was carried out by the police and Baloch troops and organised by some persons holding position of power in Punjab. One of the ministers paid a prior visit to Sheikhupura and four days before the slaughter started, all roads leading out of Sheikhupura were picketed by men in police and military uniforms and the fleeing Hindus and Sikhs were turned back to the town. Though no riots had taken place in the town, a curfew was imposed with a view to prevent the exodus of the terror-stricken minorities. The rat was not to be allowed to go out of the trap. The Tiwana Superintendent of Police, whose presence was a source of strength to the minorities, was purposely transferred from Sheikhupura and an Anglo-Indian, known for his partiality towards Muslims and for weakness as an administrator was made the Deputy Commissioner of the district.

What was the Punjab Government doing to control the conflagration and what was the Central Government, now run by the Congress leaders, doing in defence of minorities? Not much as judged from their actions, excepting issuing of reassuring statements as to what they proposed to do. In spite of the best efforts made by the press and deputations of Hindus and Sikhs and urgent memorials and telegrams, no Martial Law was declared, though it was announced on the 26th of May, 1947 that four divisions of troops would be detailed for duty in the province for suppression of riots. It was later on found that there was much exaggeration in the figures announced and under the pressure of the Muslim League representatives in the Indian Cabinet and due to the weakness of Congress representatives, a greater part of this force was stationed in the East Punjab and not in the riot-affected areas of West Punjab. Demonstrations of how quickly the military could reach any disturbed area by 'paradrops' were held in Lahore and elsewhere, but failed to inspire confidence. Thc Governor of Punjab steadfastly refused to acknowledge that the situation had deteriorated to any great extent. Of course, it was natural. No officer would acknowledge his failure by accepting this view. The theory that held the field in official circles at this time in Punjab was that prevention was better than punishment and that instead of trying to control the situation in West Punjab, it was better to prevent the situation from becoming bad in East Punjab. In other words, the Hindus and the Sikhs of West Punjab were given up as already lost and beyond help, while Muslims of East Punjab were to be protected at all costs.

The riots spread to the N.W. Frontier Province in June. On the 3rd of June, the Hindus and Sikhs of D.I. Khan who had been living peacefully were suddenly attacked, 1,200 houses were burnt down, 1,600 were looted, 2,000 Hindus and Sikhs were forcibly converted to Islam and the loss of property amounted to ₹10 crores. As many as 1,200 people were killed. The story was repeated in Bahawalpur State. Posters were put on the city walls asking Hindus to quit or they would be murdered and looted. The actual operations for compelling the Hindus to quit were taken in hand in the first week of June when complete demoralisation set in among them.

The Meo Rebellion

Meanwhile, under the very nose of the Government of India, but in a District of the Punjab, the Gurgaon district, the Meos, a fanatical Muslim clan, that had always joined the army in large numbers, were on the war path against the Hindu Jats. There were stories of the current Communist and Leftist leaders working amongst them secretly for several months past, but nobody thought that there would be a sudden flare up on a vast scale in the group of prosperous villages on the Alwar Road. The ferocity of the communal outbreak was so severe that while reporting in the *Statesman* of May 30, 1947, the special correspondent of the paper said: "In the strip of territory between Gurgaon and the village of Nuh, about 30 miles up the Alwar Road, well over a score of villages have been destroyed in a few days' time." There was evidence of very careful planning and the weapons used were not only knives, lathies and brickbats, but modern arms, many of European make, souvenirs brought home from the war. Many of the defenders also had modern weapons and, although outnumbered, fought back desperately and to such purpose that their enemies had to abandon the siege. According to an official, the attackers used a mortar. The Hindu Jats were taken unaware at first, but retaliation was swift and ruthless in the riots which almost took the shape of a revolt against authority. Village after village was set ablaze, their inhabitants finding shelter in friendly villages or camping along the roadsides. Twenty villages in an area of 400 square miles were burnt in the course of one week. At least 200 people were killed and many injured. The two Punjab M.L.A.s, Rao Bahadur Chaudhary Suraj Mal and Pt. Siri Ram Sharma, who visited the disturbed areas, attributed the trouble to 'mis-handling' of the situation by the Punjab Government who, they said, "took an unwise step in arresting all influential persons belonging to one community including Rao Sahib Mohar Singh, M.L.A., Rao Sahib Chaudhry Jugal Kishore, President of the District Peace Committee,

Rao Gajraj Singh, President of the District Congress Committee and Pandit Harihar Lal Bhargava." The question of the suppression of the riot was made a communal question. A deputation on behalf of the Muslim League of Gurgaon District waited upon Raja Gazanffar Ali Khan, Health Minister, and sought his help. Sardar Patel motored to the disturbed areas and came back with the impression that the situation in the country continued to cause concern.

The disorders had now overtaken the whole of the Frontier Province, Bahawalpur and the West Punjab. Gurgaon district was the only district affected in East Punjab. The despair of the Hindus and Sikhs was mounting. To all intents and purposes, they were being left defenceless and worse than defenceless because a civil war was now waging in West Punjab with a ferocity of which the outsiders could have no conception. There was a disintegration of judiciary and various services; the poison of racial hatred had done its work in the services promptly and stealthily. Millions were doomed to death, and they did not know where to turn for succour. The '*Pratap*' in its issue of 1-6-47 voiced the true feelings of the Punjab Hindus and Sikhs when it wrote: 'Mahatma Gandhi wants the British to quit at once, but has Gandhi ever consulted the man in the street about it? The people feel that if with the British in the country, they have become victims of communal frenzy, who will protect them when the British have actually left? The lesson of the Frontier Province and Punjab is there for Hindus to learn.'

The Punjab Government in the meanwhile was busy in drawing paper plans which were to come into force from 18th June, 1947 when the Province was to be divided into three areas, north, central and eastern, each under the command of a Major General. 'Breaches of any prohibitory order will render the offender liable to be shot with or without warning. Detailed instructions have been given to all Punjab Districts'. This was announced at a conference at Government House when strong measures were calculated to check communal disturbances in Punjab and to ensure peaceful implementation of the procedure of transfer of power were finalised.

That the Governor of Punjab was busy in paper planning

when Punjab was burning is also proved from an announcement made on the 1st of June, 1947 that the Government thinking it futile to attempt to rehabilitate all the refugees in all the villages of Rawalpindi Division had decided to select some centres in each district for their rehabilitation. Gujjar Khan, Kallar, Sukho and Daultala in the Rawalpindi district, Chakwal and Dudial in Jhelum district and Fatehjang, Pindigheb, Talagang and Jand in Attock district were selected for this purpose. Apparently, the Governor of the Punjab had not realised by this time the full force of the revolutionary upheaval that was taking place in the West Punjab, the aim of which was to bodily throw out every Hindu and Sikh from the area and to take possession of their accumulated wealth of centuries in the shape of moveable and immoveable goods. The scheme was disclosed by the Governor to the prominent leaders of the minorities in Punjab, representing the Punjab Relief Committee and the Punjab Riot Sufferers Relief Committee. That it was impossible for Hindus and Sikhs to return to their homes in the Rawalpindi Division was proved by a complaint lodged by Sardar Singh against Mohd. Raban and 46 other Muslims in the court of the District Magistrate Rawalpindi on the 1st of June under Sections 302, 436, 395, 298, 149 and 148 I.P.C. A mob of Muslims had plundered the property of the complainant and his family—the only non-Muslim family in that village—and also burnt their houses. Nine members of his family were murdered or burnt dead or half alive. The only survivors were the complainant and his sister, Miss Jaya Kaur, both of whom were forcibly converted. Such news continued to come from the affected areas. The Governor's scheme was looked down with scorn by the people for whom it was proposed.

Meanwhile, the June 2, 1947 statement had been made and accepted by the leaders of the Congress, Sikhs and Muslims. In the announcement over the radio, one could detect a tone of muffled joy in the voice of Mr. Jinnah. He began and ended his oration by 'Pakistan Zindabad'. The voice of Pt. Jawaharlal Nehru was that of a tired man who was speaking with an uneasy conscience, while S. Baldev Singh, who should have been the most affected of all as his home province was going to be vivisected, did not show any tremors or emotions. The statement greatly narrowed the margin of difference between the Punjab political parties. Whether division or partition was good in itself or wholly undesirable was no longer the issue. The main question to be decided was which town or village would go where. The Rawalpindi, Multan and Ambala division people now had a clear-cut picture before them, while the central districts of the Punjab which were the brain and the heart of the province were now thrown in a ferment. The provisional announcement had given Lahore and Gurdaspur districts to the Muslim League and Amritsar and Jalandhar districts to East Punjab. The real battle for Lahore began now, not only in the councils of political parties and in their statements, but also in every nook and corner of the urban area and in every street of the city. The riots became more widespread and uncontrolled. Now, there was no value attached to human life. The Hindus and Sikhs organised defence in their mohallas (localities). Shahalmi Gate area in the city and Krishan Nagar area in the civil station began to be looked upon as strongholds of the Hindus. Mozang, Mochi, Bhatigate, Taxali Gate, etc., were the strongholds of the Muslims from where they sallied forth in bands armed with daggers in search of preys on various unguarded roads of Lahore. But whenever an attempt was made by a mob to invade the Hindu and Sikh areas in strength, it was always foiled. Man to man, the Hindus and Sikhs proved themselves superior and better fighters than the Muslims. But the stab in the back and hide and seek guerilla attacks of the Muslims could never be parried. Bombs began now to be freely used, but a diabolical brain among the Muslims soon hit upon the idea of taking the offensive against the Hindus against their weakest point. The slogan went forth—"burn the property of Hindus, burn the rat out of its hole". The campaign was very well organised, young urchins were pressed into service for this purpose, and the Municipal Fire squads were assigned their due role in this new Jihad. Cash rewards were given for the nefarious work done. A woman leader of the Muslim League frustrated in love and ambition had turned into a fury. She was said to have openly declared in a meeting of the League that her heart would become full of joy only when she could see Lahore burning from air. The technique employed in this campaign could never be discovered by the Hindus. But building after building in different parts of the city were set on fire without the culprits ever being caught. By this time, a pretty large number of houses were vacant as the owners or the tenants had left Lahore. The task of incendiaries was, therefore, easy and they took full advantage of it. That the fire menace over-shadowed all other dangers is proved by the proclamation of the Deputy Commissioner Lahore, Mr. Eustace. This is what he said: "What people should do?":

1. Remain alert to prevent damage and particularly arson.
2. Report incidents only after you have verified them.
3. Make your report at once to your nearest police station.
4. If there is a case of fire in your own or in a neighbour's house, try to put it out yourself and do not leave everything to the fire-brigade which may be engaged elsewhere.
5. Keep every vessel you can filled with water on all storeys and not only on the ground floor, water thrown on adjoining houses will prevent the fire spreading.
6. When the police and fire-brigade arrive, afford them every facility in getting to the scene of the trouble and in assuming and maintaining control of the whole vicinity.
7. Police and firemen usually have to reach a point of vantage on a high roof both to attack the fire *and to prevent attacks on themselves.* When the police appear on the roof, persons who are not concerned should get off their roof-tops immediately. No one will then run the risk of being injured by mistake.
8. Help the police trace anyone in your neighbourhood who has been throwing stones or incendiary missiles or firing weapons.
9. There is reason to believe that much of the mischief done recently has not been caused by residents of

area involved. Prevent and report gangs entering your neighbourhood. The arrival of any strangers should be immediately reported.

10. Complete evacuation of property allows mischief mongers the opportunity of doing greater damage with less risk. If evacuation of women and children or property takes place, men should remain at the premises to prevent illegal entry and to report attack.

11. Adequate precautions can only be taken by the district authorities if there is full cooperation from the public. This is being given in many areas. Make sure that your neighbourhood is one of them.

The Corporation Engineer also came out with the following instructions:

"The wooden fittings of houses which are abutting on street sides be painted with a fire-proof paint. Such paint can be easily made as under:

1. Carbide wastage 1 part
2. Washing soda 1 part
3. Slacked lime dust 1 part
4. Multani Clay (Gachni) 1 part

The above material may be dissolved in water and a thick paint may be made which should be applied on the wooden fittings in two or three coats.

Every house should have 8 fire buckets full of water and 4 buckets full of sand with other reserve stock of water and sand in all sorts of containers for use at the time of emergency.

All houses should be well and adequately lighted towards streets at night time so that the mischief-mongers have little opportunity to attempt at fires and, in case they do so, they could be easily detected."

Leaders' Assurances

It was all very well for the last English Deputy Commissioner of Lahore to tell what the people of Lahore should do. But the people of Lahore, Hindus and Sikhs in particular, were asking what the Government should do. There were still some people in Lahore who had some faith left in their leaders and, therefore, the common subject of talk among them was what the leaders should do. The leaders, in turn, were busy in issuing re-assuring statements and telling the people of Lahore to stay where they were. The opinion in the Hindu and Sikh circles at this stage was that Lahore was definitely being alloted to the Indian Union and, therefore, they had to endure the trials, troubles and transitional difficulties only for a short while. Everything would be all right by the 15th of August, 1947 and the cowards who were fleeing away from Lahore will only stand to suffer in the long run. That explains why Lahore became empty of various sections of people in the following order: the beggars, mendicants and lepers were the first to leave Lahore, next went the coolies, labourers, domestic servants and the Bhayyas or Purbias who had been earning their honest living in Lahore. The tenants of houses and Kothis followed suit, but a good proportion of owners of the immoveable property stayed behind. Women and children were sent away first and when the police terror of arrests and detentions of the minorities was at its height, all young men were sent away by their parents. Towards the end of July, only old men were left here and there and the once thickly populated Krishan Nagar area was now inhabited only by pensioners, sick and weak people in their dotage. The silent resolve of all who left Lahore was to come back as soon as normal conditions prevailed after the 15th of August. As regards moveable property, at first, there was considerable panic leading to fight of capital and valuables from West Punjab, but the Congress leaders in their great wisdom announced the terms of the Stand-still Agreement that had been entered into with the Muslim League. This Agreement gave an assurance to the people that there would be no restrictions imposed on the movement of men, money and material even after the establishment of Pakistan. There would be no passport system and no limitations on the banks and other institutions to remit money out of Pakistan and *vice versa*. The Stand-still Agreement did more harm to the Hindus and Sikhs than has been done by any other announcement of the Congress leaders. Those of them who could not stand the daily increasing fires, murders and police terror left for a temporary sojourn in the Indian Dominion, leaving almost everything behind, hoping to claim or retrieve these after the establishment of Pakistan.

There was a scare created in Lahore when it came to be known that the East Punjab Provisional Government had been asked to remove their records to Shimla. People interpreted this news to be a sure sign of Lahore going to Pakistan. Many government servants of the Secretariat made haste to leave Lahore. But the people 'en masse' still stuck to their homes heartened by the newspaper report of Sardar Baldev Singh's inteview with a journalist. A journalist asked S. Baldev Singh whether his next visit to Lahore after the 15th of August, 1947 will be to the Capital of the Punjab or to the Capital of Pakistan. Sardar Baldev Singh, replying firmly, said, "So far as we are concerned, I can assure you that Lahore will never go to Pakistan."

Burnings and stabbings, however, continued. There was an insistent demand of the minorities for the imposition of the Martial Law which, in the words of Sardar Baldev Singh, was an extreme course and could not be resorted to unless there was a complete breakdown of civil administration. A complete breakdown of civil administration had taken place so far as protection of life and property was concerned. But living in the cool heights of Shimla, Sardar Baldev Singh could not realise this. Though Pt. Jawaharlal Nehru was the Vice President of the Government of India and the strong man of the Congress, Sardar Patel also being in the cabinet, both failed to persuade the Governor-General to accede to this demand. Deputations saw them, telegrams were sent in hundred letters poured in by thousands, the Chambers of Commerce and representatives of various other institutions sent urgent memoranda, but nothing was done. Rana Jang Bahadur Singh of the Tribune, other than whom there was no more vocal champion of the Lahore Hindus and Sikhs at this time, went to

Delhi and saw personally all the big guns of the Congress there. He urged them to impress upon the authorities the need for the declaration of the 'martial law' which in his view was the only cure. He pleaded passionately, "Come and see things for yourselves." "The great men heard every syllable of what I said with rapt attention. Quite frequently, they interrupted me and asked me questions and explained their position. One of them promised to try to extricate himself from high politics for a while and snatch a visit to Lahore. But, as regards the use of the suggested desperate remedy, no assurance could be given to me." At this time, Sardar Baldev Singh paid a visit to Lahore and paid a tribute to H.E. Sir Evan Jenkins for his utmost vigilance and determination to put down lawlessness. "I am satisfied with the arrangements made to restore peace," declared Sardar Baldev Singh. After giving this certificate of good conduct to the Governor, the Defence Member hastily slipped away to his Shimla abode, lest he should become unpopular. S. Baldev Singh, however, received various deputations of the people who had suffered and were suffering in Lahore. This is what he said after meeting with the deputation of ladies who had been grossly insulted and detained by the Lahore Police under the orders of Mr. Cheema, a Lahore Magistrate who was fast becoming a hero of the Muslim League. "The sad tale, which these ladies narrated to me of what disgrace was offered to them while in detention, is most shocking. Such a thing as that can never be tolerated in any civilised society. Serious allegations have been made by these ladies against a Magistrate. Surely, ladies, to whatever community or section of the community they may belong, deserve much better treatment. Any insulting words used by any officer of any Government against any ladies, belonging to respectable families, can do no credit to anyone." He further added that, "These ladies while talking to me were all in tears, not because of fear, but on account of the alleged treatment which had been accorded to them and which to say the least was disgraceful."

S. Baldev Singh also gave assurances of help to the principal and students of the Sikh National College who had been terrorised by the police during the course of a search of the college premises lasting from 5 a.m. to 6 p.m.

Mahatma Gandhi passed through Amritsar and Lahore on his way to Kashmir via Rawalpindi on the 31st of July, 1947. He was going on the political mission of persuading the Maharaja of Kashmir to accede to the Indian Dominion. The riots at that time had taken a serious turn and the nerves of Hindus and Sikhs were on their edge. The *Statesman* of August 1, 1947 reported that an unsuccessful attempt to blow up the Frontier Mail in which Mahatma Gandhi and party were passengers was made near Phillaur the day before. Undaunted, he continued his journey. Unfortunately, for the Punjabi Hindus and Sikhs, a section of young men went to the railway station at Amritsar and shouted defiance at Mahatmaji, asking him to go back if he could not save them from the fury of the Muslim League terrorists. This was the first shock of life to Mahatma ji who had always been received in the province before with chants of 'Mahatma Gandhi Zindabad'. Mahatma Gandhi was a master of his passions. Though outwardly he ignored this incident, I believe he as well as his Bhakts and Chelas (followers) never forgave the Punjabis for this insult to him. Mahatma Gandhi for all his greatness was known to be a man of long memory. All those who stood against him fell. Dr. Khare was Dr. Khare (genuine) when he was in his good books, but as soon as he defied him, he became Khare (bitter). Mahatma Gandhi's statements and utterances while in the Punjab did not give solace to the minorities. He was still living in a dreamland where every Muslim was a 'Devta' (Saint) and every Hindu and Sikh a false complainant. He became conscious of the fact that he was no *persona grata* with the Punjabi Hindus and Sikhs. But he believed that the fault was entirely of the Hindus and Sikhs and not his. On his return journey, he had to be stealthily smuggled out of Lahore by being de-trained at Shahdara and by being whisked away to Moghalpura. On either side, elaborate arrangements were made for his protection. At the Moghalpura station, in addition to the police and military protection, he had the added protection of the Congress volunteers, armed with lathies.

A few young men of Lahore Cantt., who came to know of Mahatma Gandhi's secret departure from the Moghalpura station, collected and shouted the usual slogans, but were mercilessly beaten by the non-violent Congress volunteers. The only counsel was given by Mahatma Gandhi to the Hindus and Sikhs of Lahore during his brief sojourn. There was a counsel of perfection in the only counsel. "If you think Lahore is dead or is dying, do not run away from it, but die with what you think is the dying Lahore." Little did Mahatma ji know that example was better than precept. Everybody believed that had Mahatma ji chosen Lahore for his stay during troublous days, the tragedy of Lahore would have been averted. Even if Lahore had gone to Pakistan, the people of Lahore would have preferred to stay there. The presence of Mahatmaji in the heart of the Punjab at this juncture would have radically altered the situation and perhaps prevented the partition and post-partition holocaust. But that was not to be as the inner voice of Mahatmaji's conscience and the openly expressed popular voice of the Hindus and Sikhs of Lahore did not coincide. These coincided very well later on in Calcutta and Delhi, but the minorities in both these places happened to be other than Hindus and Sikhs.

Lahore in Flames

Mr. M.G. Cheema, Magistrate First Class of Lahore, at this time was fast acquiring notoriety as the great oppressor of Hindus and Sikhs. He took upon himself to be another Mahmud of Ghazni, out to smash the temple of Somnath of the Lahore minorities. Shahalmi Gate was a stronghold of the Hindus and Sikhs of Lahore. Its narrow streets barred with iron gates afforded protection against Muslim League offensive. The bazaar was narrow and if the worst came to the worst, it could be defended at both the ends by a few determined young men. This was an eye sore to the Muslims and the credit must go to Mr. Cheema of attacking and breaking this last citadel of the Hindu and Sikh minorities in Lahore. On the 21st of June, 1947, the Shahalmi Bazar was raided by Mr. Cheema in the dead of night. Fire was opened at all those who peeped out from the windows of their houses. Those who came out in the streets were shot dead including one public servant, Mr. Ramanand, an engineer of the Electric Supply Co., who was doing his tour of duty. The houses and shops were set on fire. Some persons including women and children were roasted alive in the burning houses. It was Mr. Cheema's night.

The loss of over ₹1 crore was caused by the devastating fire which burnt down a large number of shops in the Shahalmi Gate and almost the whole of Paper Mandi. Persons who came out to extinguish the fire were shot at by the police under Mr. Cheema's orders. The two bazaars, which were the main centres of supply of various kinds of food stuffs and clothes and other requirements of daily life and where transactions worth lakhs of rupees were made daily, were turned into heaps of debris. All this happened overnight. Those who had lakhs and possessed huge properties became paupers. Before the two bazaars were set on fire, this part of the city had been covered under the curfew blanket and police pickets had been posted all around the area. How was it possible without the connivance of the police and the magistracy for miscreants to enter this area? To add to the misery of the people and to terrorise them further, Mr. Cheema took about 150 persons from the locality into custody. These persons, many of whom were the only male members of the families, were made to sit on the road in the sun. The searches of the houses of the persons taken into custody and of other houses in the locality which escaped fire were ordered. Locks were broken open and goods looted by the police search parties.

The fire brigade arrived late and, even after arrival, did not render any effective aid for a couple of hours because water was not available from the corporation tube well which was found to be not working properly on account of some burnt fuse. The Chief Executive Officer, Mr. Mangat Rai, came to the scene of occurence and ultimately succeeded in getting the fuse set right which should have been set right by the Muslim mistry (foreman) under whose charge it was. The two fully equipped private fire engines sent by the Gowalmandi Hindus and Sikhs (Gandhi Square) to help in fighting the fire were prevented from doing so by the Muslim police who took the honourary workers into custody. It was alleged, though no proof could be offered, that the practice of the Corporation fire brigade, which was then entirely manned by non-Hindus was to throw petrol instead of water on the burning fires. The next morning, a wholesale exodus of Hindus and Sikhs from Shahalmi Gate area took place. There was an unending stream of people going out in tongas, carts and on foot carrying with them what little was left of their belongings, giving blackmail at every chowk to any policeman and goonda who stopped them in the name of law or with the flourish of a dagger.

The night of June 20, 1947 will always be remembered by the Lahore Hindus and Sikhs as the tragic night in the history of their beloved town. Eighteen (18) killed, over 55 (fifty-five) injured and as many as 47 cases of arson in one day (official news) was the shocking record of that day. It was followed by the devastating fire of the Shahalmi Gate on the 21st and yet the Punjab Governor, Sir Evan Jenkins did not consider it advisable to enforce Martial Law in Lahore. Everyone else, except the Governor and the Viceroy, with whose permission alone he could declare Martial Law, felt that there was no other remedy left to quell the disturbances. The 'Tribune' vainly urged the people in its issue of 23rd June, 1947, not to get panicky and demoralised and demanded the immediate institution of an impartial and sifting inquiry into the happenings inside Shahalmi Gate and enforcement of Martial Law in Lahore.

Shahalmi Gate fire gave a new interpretation of the curfew. People whose houses were set on fire were prevented from coming out into the open street because of the curfew. Naturally, neighbours also could not come to the help of persons trapped in the burning houses as in doing so, they might have had to cross the open street and, thus, draw upon themselves the police fire directed by Mr. Cheema. A letter by Prof. Sant Ram Sayal to the 'Tribune' very pertinently posed this question, "Will someone guide the unfortunate people of Lahore as to how they should act in the following situation: During curfew hours, when all law-abiding citizens are inside their homes and miscreants come and set fire to a house, what should the inmates do? (a) Allow themselves to be burnt alive?; (b)Try to extinguish the fire without coming into the open?; (c) Or come into the open while extinguishing the fire and be shot at or be taken into custody?; (d) Try to contact the fire brigade when there is no telephone within hearing distance or; (e) How otherwise to save one's life, dependents and property? What should the neighbours do? (a) Come out to help extinguish the fire and be shot at or arrested?; (b) Stay in till their own houses are reduced to ashes along with the inmates?; (c) How otherwise to do their duty as good citizens and render themselves useful and helpful to the neighbours and society?"

The Hindus and Sikhs of Lahore were completely demoralised after this action and the city began to be emptied by tens and thousands of people day and night. Mr. Cheema was a bold man indeed because on another occasion, when he was summoned by the Lahore High Court in connection with the *habeas corpus* application of 70 respectable citizens of Kucha Babian who had been arrested and detained under Mr. Cheema's orders, he straightaway told Mr. Justice Teja Singh, "My Lord, the counsel is trying to browbeat me. I have been intimidated. In fact, some members of the Bar told me that I might be hauled up for contempt of court." This was nothing but contempt of Court. But by taking the bull by the horns, he had actually succeeded in brow beating the court into not taking any action against him.

The political leaders continued to issue statements from safe places outside Punjab, but none thought it prudent to come and stay in Lahore. On that day, there was comparative calm prevailing in the town. In spite of the Punjab Government's censorship order about comments on the situation in the province, Rana Jang Bahadur Singh came out with facts and suggestions for Pt. Jawaharlal Nehru's consideration, in an issue of the 'Tribune' of Lahore. He did some plain talking in it and wanted him to know from the Governor, how it was that the overwhelming majority of those persons who had been killed or injured in their streets or on the roofs of their houses as a result of the police firings on different occasions in different parts of the city belong to two particular communities only. This was a significant fact. Members of these two particular communities alleged that the partisanship of certain sections of the police hindered their defence work and obstructed their fire-fighting activity.

In the matter of searches and arrests, the spirit of partisanship was rampant.

As the 15th of August, 1947 came nearer and nearer, the stay of the Hindus and Sikhs became more and more difficult. Sikhs were an anathema to the Muslims, and they could be easily spotted out. They were invariably attacked when going about unguarded. The Hindu and Muslim educated classes could not be easily distinguished from each other. That alone saved many of them. There were certain areas of Lahore which no Hindu or Sikh could visit even in day time without the risk of losing his limb or life. One of such areas was what was popularly known as the 'Barood Khana' or the Fort area. It was the strong-hold of the well-known Mian family, one of whom was at that time the Mayor of Lahore Corporation. This area became the rendezvous of all the Muslim goondas of the city. There was a free kitchen where hot food was served to all the goondas during all the 24 hours of the day. Cash rewards were said to be offered by a prominent person to all those assassins who killed a Hindu or a Sikh. At first, the amount per head was ₹100. Later on it was reduced to ₹50/-, while for incendiarism the amount was said to be only ₹25/- per building. The police could not or would not enter this area for arresting the well known 'Badmashes' (hooligans) of Lahore who were on their list and were absconding from the other parts of the town. The C.I.D. Hindu and Sikh officers, at a great personal risk to their lives and career as their senior officer was a Muslim (Mr. Razvi), had succeeded in preparing these lists for different localities. Orders were even reluctantly issued for the arrest of some of them, but no one, not even Mr. Jenkins, the D.I.G., C.I.D., who was very popular in the Muslim League circles for his attempt at bringing about rapproachement between Khizar and the

League during the latter's one month's civil disobedience campaign, could offend Mian Amirud-din, who was the undisputed monarch of the 'Barood Khana' area in those days. A 59-hour curfew was imposed in Barood khana area on the 19th of June, 1947. A Sikh had been stabbed while returning after visiting Baoli Sahib Gurdwara and another person who was stabbed was an old man who had been living in this locality for the last 20 years and was known and friendly to all the residents of the locality. Of the residents of the locality, who had to remain under the curfew blanket of 59 hours, was the Mayor of the Corporation himself. The list of the goondas on the police list of 'wanted' persons is reproduced below. I believe many of them must have continued to indulge in their nefarious game even after the establishment of Pakistan. Now that there are no non-Muslims left in Lahore, the Pakistan Government would be well advised to study their old C.I.D. record and take action against these persons in the interest of peace and humanity.

Kucha Shahadat Jat

1. Hafiz
2. Zahura S/o Eliahi Bux
3. Nazir
4. Ch. Ziu-ud-Din
   s/o Umer Din
5. Ghulam Mohd
   s/o Shahaba
6. Kaka s/o Imam Din
   c/o K.K. Washing Factory

Kucha Gul Faroshan

1. Gulam Mohd.
   s/o Hussain Bux
2. Munshi Imam Din
3. Shafi s/o Imam Din
4. Shaida s/o Imam Din
5. Shaunki

Kucha Beri Walla, Opp. Shiwala Amolak Rani

1. Isa Tailor
2. Hamida
3. Butt
4. Hallo
5. Haji Salim

Near Bheron Asthan

1. Ramzan
2. Riaz ali alias Pesho
   s/o Anwra Jogi

Kucha Gogi Tarkhan.

1. Mohd. Sadiq

Chowk Devi Ditta

1. Hassan s/o Kamal Din
2. Kamal Din s/o Mohd. Din
3. Ashak Hussain
   s/o Ghulam Mohd. (No 10)
4. Shida s/o Ghulam Mohd.
5. Labha s/o Abdul Ghani
6. Hamid-ud-Din s/o Siraj Din
7. Mohd. Ishaq s/o M. Katha
8. Mohd. Yasin
   s/o Ghulam Abas

Bazar Sathan, near Masjid Hassan Din

1. Mohd. Ramzan
   s/o Allah Ditia
2. Idda s/o Miran Bux
3. Ghulam Farid s/o Miran Bux
4. Mohd. Said s/o Idda
5. Miraj Din s/o Fazal Din
6. Mohd. Shafi Guddi Farosh
7. Jewopa s/o Mana Lohar (Jogi)
8. Mohd. Amin alias Mian Baswala
9. Miraj Din s/o Feroze Din

Kucha Jowahar Singh

1. Sain s/o Mehtab Din.
2. Mana s/o Mehtab Din
3. Sher Mohd alias Sheri
(Surkah Baz)

Kucha Wan Watta

1. Mohd. Aslam s/o Allah Ditta
2. Mohd. Rubani
3. Mohd. Yakub

Kucha Mashkian

1. Hara s/o Wazir Mohd.

Phalla Nanak

1. Manzur Ahmad s/o Farid
2. Miraj Din s/o Shamas Din
3. Kumar Din s/o Shamas Din
4. Ahmad Din. Arain
5. Abdur Rashid
   s/o Hakim Din
6. Umer Din s/o Siraj Din
7. Mohd. Shah Dhobi

Sheesh Mahal

1. Sadiq Arain
2. Hazura

Outside Wadha Wehra

1. Iman Din
2. Bassa
3. Mohd. Ali
4. Fazal Ellahi
5. Mohd. Din
6. Imam Bux
7. Mohd. Shafi
8. Ismail
9. Ghulam Mohy-ud-Din
   s/o Ellahi Bux

Kucha Hira Devi

1. Imam Din
2. Ibrahim
3. Mina s/o Imam Din

Lahore became the most disputed area in the division of the Punjab. Hindus claimed it as their old city founded by Lord Rama's son 'Lav'. They contributed to 80 per cent of the taxes and land revenue, controlled 70 per cent of the trade and owned 85 per cent of the landed property. The Muslim claim was based on the 1941 Census figures according to which they were 52 per cent of the population while the Hindus and Sikhs were only 48 per cent. But the Hindus pleaded that these figures were based on faulty figures.

According to ration cards, the Muslims were 50.8 per cent while the non-Muslims were 49.2 per cent. It was at that time believed that it was quite likely that one portion of Lahore may go to the Muslims and the other to the Non-Muslims, river Ravi or the Bari Doab canal might be the dividing line. According to a news report from London, considerations of property were not to be completely ruled out in the division. It was even given out that the Muslim League had already started planning the Capital of Pakistan somewhere between Rawalpindi and Murree. Such news coming from an English source and the reassuring statements of the Congress leaders who even at this stage were not tired of asking the people to stick to their homes were responsible for a good many of the propertied classes among Hindus and Sikhs sticking to Lahore and undergoing all the torture of incessant attacks on person and property of the helpless minorities. In the heart of their hearts, they just thought that by Lahore coming to them, they would get equal with their oppressors. That day, however, was not to dawn.

Pt. Jawaharlal Nehru at this time was busy in making announcements in the Inter-Asian Conference about building up One World where freedom was universal and there was equality of opportunity between races and people. The people of Lahore, inspite of the tragedy surrounding them on all sides, could not help laughing in their sleeves at the utterances of the great dreamer who could not ensure for a small corner of his own country the freedom and equality of opportunity which he wanted to establish in the whole universe.

Curfews for long hours—50 to 60 hours—now became the order of the day. There was in the later period another notable change visible in the tactics of the Muslim League. Instead of quantity, quality murder became popular. Eminent Hindus and Sikhs began to be singled out for murderous attacks. It is not known who supplied them the information about their movements or whereabouts, the Muslim section of the C.I.D. or their own net of espionage, but it is a fact that doctors, lawyers, journalists and others began to be singled out. There are too many names to mention all here, but in the tragic list stand out the names of a few prominent Lahore citizens. Mr. Wir Bhan, Assistant Director of Industries, was living on the Jail Road. He had hired two trucks and loaded them with his belongings. His own driver, a Muslim, had arranged this transport, but in the guise of bringing coolies for loading the luggage, he had brought goondas from Mozang. When everything was loaded, Mr. Wir Bhan was attacked and killed at the spot and the loaded trucks taken to an unknown place. It was with great difficulty that his two unmarried daughters escaped from the backdoor of the Kothi (bunglow) into the Mozang cemetery and made good their way to Krishan Nagar. There was one Mr. Arjan Dev, the Editor of 'Karam Vir' and 'Sunday Times', who was stabbed in front of his own house near the Bradlaugh Hall. Dr. Shyam Sunder Thakur was stabbed in the garden outside Mochi Gate and by Muslims who knew him very well as he was himself the resident of that locality. Mr. Arjan Dev Bagai, a successful advocate of the Lahore High Court, was stabbed outside Mochi Gate while taking his goods in a tonga to the railway station. Mr. Ranbir of the 'Daily Milap' narrowly escaped a similar fate in the same place where he had gone to fetch some paper. Dr. Bhagat Ram, who could be spotted out from a mile as a Hindu owing to the heavy Khaddar turban he used to wear, was stabbed on the Nisbet Road, though not fatally.

Prof. Brij Narain was a friend of the Muslims. His writings were always acceptable to the opponents of the Congress. This had emboldened him to believe that no harm would come to him from the Muslims of Lahore. When a mob attacked his house, in spite of the remonstrances of Principal Bhupal Singh, he went out to meet it and dissuade it from attacking him and his property. He was speared to death in front of his house and his valuable library was looted and burnt. Principal Bhupal Singh had a narrow escape from the back-door of his house. Mr. Dev Chander of the well-known Hindi Bhawan Pustakalaya, Lahore was stabbed on the Dhani Ram Road. There were numerous others who laid down their lives in accordance with the openly expressed advice of Mahatma Gandhi. Mr. Badri Nath Bali, a well-known landlord of Cooper Road who was always in the forefront of social service in the locality was stabbed in front of his house having been earlier pointed out to the goondas by his own Muslim tenants. S.B. Chiranjeet Singh, great patron of sports, who had opted for Pakistan, was killed in his bungalow. The press was gagged at this time and names of Hindus and Sikhs who were murdered were never published unless they were very well known to the journalists. The communal frenzy of the Muslim League was at its height in the beginning of August 1917, but as the examples given above show, there was a method now in this madness. A policeman stationed at the electric sub-station at Sanda Road, at a stone's throw from my bungalow, went berserk. He would now and then open fire on passers-by Hindus and Sikhs. He aimed a few shots in the direction of even Seth Rattan Lal's Bungalow, who had, for the past several weeks, been supplying to the Police Chowki free milk and rations. These muskets were nothing as compared to the high-velocity rifles with which I could return their fire. But now the town being controlled by the Muslim police and pro-Muslim English officers, it was dangerous to pay them back in their own coins. It would have been given the label of a fight of an individual with the Government established by Law, though, in reality, it was now a government established by the awe of goonda's knife. The 11th of August was the worst day in Lahore. The Hindu and Sikh staff of various Government Departments and private and public firms and institutions had been leaving Lahore or moving out to safer areas which were fast diminishing in numbers. On the 11th and during the three succeeding days, there was a veritable terror let loose on the railway station and in all parts of the town. A whole train-load of Hindus and Sikhs coming from Rawalpindi side (Sindh Express) was purposely taken to a siding between the Badami Bagh and Lahore stations by its Muslim driver and halted there for no apparent reason. The reason, however, soon became apparent when the train was surrounded from all sides by a furious mob. On a given signal, all the Hindu and Sikh passengers, including women and children, were butchered in cold blood and their belongings looted. Another train, which is known as 'Babu' train, which used to leave for the C.M.A.'s Office in the Lahore Cantt., had met with a similar fate near the outer signal of the main railway station. Earlier, on July 23, 1947, a train of workshop labourers was attacked by its Muslim workers and all the Hindu and Sikh labourers were killed or wounded. As many as 90 were admitted to hospital, but how many of them returned alive from there is not known to anybody. The routes leading to railway station were all littered with the dead and dying Hindus and Sikhs. No count could be kept of the corpses brought to the morgue in the Mayo Hospital and the stench of the dead bodies was fouling the air up to Nila Gumbad mosque on one side and the Anarkali end of Dhani Ram Street on the other. Dead and dying were all heaped together. The injured Hindus and Sikhs brought to Mayo Hospital were given short shrift. Being sent to Mayo Hospital was equal to being sent to the other world. All the Hindu and Sikh medical students and staff had already left. There could be no worse example of a man's inhumanity to a man than that provided by the votaries of what is known as the noblest profession of the Mayo Hospital of Lahore in those dark days. Many Muslim tongawalas became Chhurawalas (stabbers) in disguise. It became dangerous to move out on foot or in a tonga. The buses moving with military convoys were the only means left for safe escape towards Moghulpura railway station or Amritsar. Black market fares for such conveyances became the order of the day. Krishan Nagar, the last strong-hold of the Hindus and Sikhs, soon began to empty out. Young men had already been sent out along with women and children. Even the old people now began to leave. The most pitiable was the state of the cattle let loose by the owners at the time of their departure. They could not persuade any Muslim to purchase a cow or a buffalo worth several hundred rupees even for a song so to say. Of course, the slaughter-house was near and most of the stray cattle ultimately found their way there. The 14th of August (1947) was a day of jubilation for the rest of India, but it was a day of death and destruction for the Hindus and Sikhs of Lahore and the rest of West Punjab.

Prof. R.R. Sethi, Mr. Madan Lal, myself and my sons were the only persons left in our Sanda Road area. Krishan Nagar on our left and Rajgarh on our right had been denuded of their Hindu and Sikh inhabitants. I penned down the reactions of the 14th of August and the ghastly night that followed in my diary—the extracts from which, though these look disjointed in a book, would give as nothing else can give a pen picture of Lahore on the eve of India's freedom.

□

4

The First Independence Day in Lahore

It was the fifteenth of August, 1947—the fateful date fixed by the magnanimous British for handing over power to the impatient Indian leaders. The British intention of leaving India at the earliest moment and staying behind for some more time only if the Congress and Muslim leaders unanimously requested them to do so had come as a surprise to the leaders. That such an offer could come from a 'satanic' Government was a little perplexing to the 'angels'. But as the 'angels' realised the full implications of the offer, their mouths watered. Here was the prospect of enjoying to their hearts' content the feast of Kubla Khan. The vista of unlimited number of appetising dishes—of position, power, pelf and patronage being offered on a golden platter—was too alluring to postpone the Banquet day. A unanimous request was made to the British by the leaders of both the parties to expedite rather than to postpone their date of departure.

Will 15th of August, 1947 do? "Fifteen months hence?" "Oh No," was the reply. "All right, will 31st of December, 1947 do? It will enable us to successfully perform the Partition Operation and the patient will have recovered from convalescence." "The convalescence operation be blowed. Have we no home doctors and nurses to look after the patient?" was the indignant reply.

The die was cast. In lesser time than it takes to partition a small family property among real brothers, the partition of two big provinces of India and of the assets and liabilities of such a big continent as India was attempted to be done.

The fateful day arrived. Delhi and other provincial capitals were agog with excitement and enthusiasm. In obedience to the orders of the High Command, the Congress rulers of East Punjab also issued an order for illuminations, flag hoisting and feasting while the Punjab was profusely bleeding and furiously burning. But no sooner was the order given than it was counter-manded. The East Punjab Government—Dr. Gopi Chand and S. Swaran Singh—realised the enormity of the crime they would be committing against their own people by adhering to this programme.

I was in Lahore during August 1947. The orgy of blood, loot and arson was let loose on the town. But, whereas, formerly victims belonged to both the communities, now the victims were only the Hindus and Sikhs. It was now a one-way traffic in loot, murder and arson. A well-known Muslim Corporation member had organised the mass killing of the Hindus and Sikhs and a still better-known Muslim League woman had taken control of squads of hooligans feverishly engaged in arson. A woman turned 'fury' is a terrible thing, and this woman frustrated in love and ambition was now the supreme commander of the faithful 'fire' men.

The evening was drawing to a close. I turned the radio to Delhi. The babble of tongues, the excitement of the vast assembled crowd near the Red Fort could be clearly heard. The announcer was giving a running commentary on the whole show; the Independence of India was being inaugurated. The surging crowd had broken the bounds fixed for them, discipline had given way to enthusiasm, the Viceroy's bodyguard was separated from the body of the Viceroy, the stage from the leaders where they could make a good show for the camera and it was with great difficulty that path could be made for the carriage of Pandit Jawaharlal Nehru and Lord Mountbatten. And, suddenly, the announcer in his dulcet voice said, "Look, the sky has become overcast with clouds—it appears it is going to rain—yes it is drizzling. It is raining. What a good augury for Independence Day? Oh, now it has stopped raining." And after a few minutes, with a triumphant note in his voice, he announced. "Look, there is a rainbow in the sky—what a grand rainbow? And how auspicious it is?" Just then a bullet was fired in the Sanda Road Chowk, hardly fifty yards from my bungalow. A constable of the Additional Police guarding the electric sub-station had shot at an innocent non-Muslim wayfarer. A thick cloud of soot and smoke rose towards the sky on Lohari Gate side. It turned into a vast red tongue shooting upwards. A little to the left towards Gurudutta Bhavan was visible another huge sheet of fire. The two fires between them formed a 'Firebow' in the sky. A word was soon brought that the holiest of the holies of the Hindus of Lahore—the Sheetla Mandir—was ablaze. In his dulcet voice, the announcer was still cooing: "How auspicious, how beautiful the rainbow in the sky?" The voice no longer sounded sweet. It sounded harsh. It seemed to be mocking at us and all others who from the tops of their houses were looking at the 'Firebow' in the sky. "Azadi", "Azadi" was on the lips of the Delhi crowds. "Barbadi", "Barbadi" was the anguished cry of every Lahore Hindu and Sikh.

The night following Independence Day celebration was truly a terrible one for Lahore minorities. At about ten o'clock, shouts of "Allah, O Akbar" in an increasing crescendo were heard from corner in Mozang. After about half an hour, bursts of rifle fire were heard. The firing continued intermittently for another hour. Then there was lull broken now and then by mighty shouts of "Allah O Akbar", "Pakistan Zindabad", "Hindustan Murdabad" and the shouts were coming too uncomfortably nearer towards Krishan Nagar. We manned the morchas of our houses, resolved to self, our lives dearly. Suddenly, the shouts became less and less audible and now they appeared to come from the northern corner of Mozang.

It was a hell of a night to go through. It was not a night; it was a nightmare. How narrow had been our escape was confirmed the next day by a Muslim friend from Mozang. The Gurdwara 'Chhevin Padshahi' Mozang sacred to the memory of the Sixth Guru, had been silently surrounded by a mob and all the inmates—eleven Sevadars and one woman—butchered in cold blood. When the butchery was over, the police had begun to fire in the air—not a single casualty had occurred as a result of their firing. The crowd then had reached the Sanatan Dharam College Chauk when somebody suggested the looting of Hindu Kothis (house) on the Begum Road. That explained our deliverance. But how many Hindus and Sikhs lost their all in Mozang area that night will perhaps never be known.

Of course, the Delhiwalas (Delhiites) must have had a gala night. Stuffing themselves with fruits, sweets and drinks, soft or strong, they must have gone to sleep dreaming of pleasant dreams. Some of them had been planning even in their sleep as to how next day or next week or next month they would distribute their newly acquired patronage among their friends, relatives, caste-fellows, retainers and comrades! Of course, a few of them had seen but many of them had only heard that there was 'some trouble' in the Punjab. But what was Punjab's trouble as compared to the Azadi of the other parts of the country? Was not U.P. safe and free as also Bihar and Orissa, Assam, Madras, C.P., Bombay and Gujarat, Rajputana, Delhi, Ajmer and Marwar? Only three per cent of the total population of India was involved in difficulty, ninety-seven per cent was jubilant and free. And the leaders had now come into the absolute control of an empire which was bigger than the empires ruled over by Chandra Gupta Morya, Ashoka, Akbar or Aurangzeb. The mere Punjabis, Bengalis, Sindhis and Sarhadies could not be permitted to stand in the way of India's freedom!

Two Independence Days have come around since then and the ruling class on both the occasions ordered 'Azadi' celebrations all over the country. But the Punjabis who have lost their all can only beat their breast and shout "Pit o jatta gai Vaisakhi". Fellow beat your breast. 'You have lost your days of happiness for all times'.

□

5

Critical Days of August and September 1947

Even on the fifteenth of August, there was still a flickering hope that the award of the Boundary Commission might yet be founded on truth and justice of the minorities' case. The previous night the well-known Gurdwara of Mozang had been burnt and the worshippers butchered there. The Boundary Force Commander, General Rees, next day put a company of Gurkhas to patrol the Mewa Mandi, Islamia College and Mozang areas and a company of Balochies in the Hindu areas of the town. All sorts of rumours about the fate of Lahore were at work, but the decision when announced two days later frustrated all hopes. It was now a stark reality that the most cherished town of the Hindus and Sikhs of Punjab to the building of which they had contributed so much had been amputated from the Indian Dominion. Those of them who would prefer to live here now would have to become full-fledged citizens of Pakistan. I can say that many of the house owners wanted to become so. The feeling in their sub-conscious mind, which they sometimes openly expressed, was that beyond discriminatory taxation of the Jazia type or some minor Acts of legislation against the minorities, there would be nothing more serious done against them. The minorities at this time put great faith in the announcements of Mr. Jinnah holding out promises of protection to all loyal citizens. Unlike some Congress leaders who were and are still in the habit of issuing statements with every breath of their life, Mr. Jinnah was a leader who knew the virtue of silence. He had made very few public announcements and the experience of the people was that on occasions when he spoke, he generally meant what he said. All those Hindus and Sikhs, therefore, who found themselves on the wrong side of the Ravi river after the Boundary Award took heart from his assurances. And, truly speaking, all stabbings and burnings, etc., stopped on the morning of the 15th of August in Lahore. The leaders of the Muslim League had mysteriously close connections with the underworld. A word went around and all the Mullahs in various mosques preached tolerance the next day and the rank and file obeyed. But a new source of trouble now appeared. Streams of Muslim refugees from Amritsar began to pour into Lahore. On the 17th of August, a band of Muslim policemen who were deserters from Amritsar with arms and ammunition arrived in Lahore and spread all sorts of nefarious tales about the Hindu and Sikh attacks on Muslims there. The news of riots and disturbances in the East Punjab began to pour in. The first batch of refugees that arrived in Lahore was received with open arms by the Muslim residents, but soon it became clear that it was not a question of a few batches of Muslim refugees arriving from Amritsar, but that of the whole Muslim population migrating en masse from East Punjab. What had been a one-way traffic so far now became a two-way traffic.

The news about the tragic happenings in West Punjab was completely blacked out from the Lahore newspapers. The refugees arriving in Lahore, particularly the policemen from Amritsar, were the first to start disturbances once in Lahore. The Muslim Leaguers do not believe in the pseudo non-violence of a few people of Hindustan. They believe in retaliation and react quickly to any real or supposed affront to their religion and community. The sight of their brethren in distress enraged them and putting Mr. Jinnah's injunctions to the wind, they again launched upon a blood bath in which the victims were to be the remaining Hindus and Sikhs of West Pakistan. I firmly believe that Mr. Jinnah was honest when he gave the assurance of protection to the minorities and that Pakistan authorities had no idea then of turning out the Hindus and Sikhs from their homelands. The events elsewhere, however, forced them to take retaliatory action. The slaughter at Sheikhupura and mass massacres in Buddomalli, Kanjroor Duttan and the adjoining areas in the Shakkar Garh Tehsil were planned from Lahore. A minister flew by air to Karachi with the proposals and plans and after his return to Lahore, another Minister flew to Sheikhupura, Lyallpur, Narowal, etc. The writings and speeches of Gandhiji at this moment from which only disjointed extracts were published in Pakistan did much to incite the Muslims to take revenge on Hindus and Sikhs. One fine morning, large-sized posters were found pasted on the walls of Lahore—"What Mahatma Gandhi says?", "Mahatma Gandhiji ka Farman" and this proved a signal for a fresh and very serious outbreak of rioting in Lahore. Mahatma Gandhi had exhorted the Hindus and Sikhs not to kill the Muslims or throw them out of trains, etc., alleged incidents which had been reported to him.

Slaughter of Sheikhupura

The slaughter of Sheikhupura was a well-planned affair. The Superintendent of Police, a cousin of Khizar Hayat Khan Tiwana was in charge of the district during the troublous days preceding the partition. He had not allowed any lawlessness to break out anywhere in his district. He would personally visit any and every part of the district from where he received reports of Hindu-Muslim tension and very often before he left, the Hindus, Muslims and Sikhs would be busy treating one another with sweets. The relations between various communities remained cordial. The first step, therefore, was to get such a man out of the way, even though he was a Muslim. Diwan Sukhanand, the Hindu Deputy Commissioner had given over charge to his A.D.M. Mr. C.H. Disney—an Anglo Indian—who was reputed to be a cat's paw in the hands of Sheikh Karamat Ali of Sheikhupura who was now the Minister of Education in West Punjab. The Hindus and Sikhs of Sheikhupura town who had been living in a state of bewilderness since partition did not know what to do. They had, however, reconciled themselves to live in Pakistan, though some of them wanted to leave for a while for the Indian Dominion, hoping to return to their homes when the communal situation in the province had become normal. On the advice of the new Superintendent of Police, Mirza Mohd. Baker, the Deputy Commissioner imposed Section 144 on the town of Sheikhupura and it was announced by the beat of drums on the 22nd of August, 1947 that nobody could leave Sheikhupura town without the District Magistrate's permit. This order was proclaimed only for the Sheikhupura town, but in actual practice, people were turned back from the Chichoki-Malian Canal bridge and were not allowed to proceed to Lahore even though they had not come from Sheikhupura town. The town was, thus, turned into a sort of mouse-trap for the Hindus. The Baloch military during these four days had a free run of the town. They would go about in military trucks, pick up any Hindu or Sikh woman from her doorsteps and enter the houses of respectable people and stay at the top storeys of houses for the night against the protests of the house-owners.

On the morning of the 25th of August, 1947, a few shops of the Hindus and Sikhs were looted and set on fire by the goondas and all those Hindus and Sikhs who ran to help extinguish the fire were fired upon by the Baloch military and killed. Among the first victims to fall was Sardar Lachman Singh Pansari. Curfew for 72 hours was thereafter imposed and the Baloch military with a detachment of police under Sub-Inspector Sajawal Khan entered the Ram Garha area of Sheikhupura Sikhs. Every one of Hindus and Sikhs in that area was killed. The same day, at 6 p.m., Mohalla Khandpuria was invaded and houses thereof set on fire. Hardly ten people escaped alive from this Mohalla. Thereafter, the massacre became general. The Baloch military accompanied by the police and followed by a huge mob of blood-thirsty goondas armed with all sorts of deadly weapons descended upon the Hindu and Sikh localities of the town. The military and the police would first open fire through doors, windows, ventilators and from the roofs of the houses. The mob would, thereafter, enter and kill the wounded, kidnap and rape the women who were still alive and behead or spear to death the menfolk. Some of the Hindus and Sikhs were able to hide themselves here and there. They all began to collect together on the 3rd day in the factory compound of S. Atma Singh. They were hungry and thirsty for the last three days and as they were drinking water at the factory tap, the factory was surrounded again by the military and the police. They were asked to surrender to them every valuable that they possessed and all arms. After looting and disarming them, the Balochies began to kill in cold blood, all the people assembled there. The women were kidnapped and raped. Similar acts of barbarism were committed in a part of the Civil Line of Sheikhupura town. The New Mohalla between the old and the new city became a scene of carnage, S. Chandraman Singh, a retired H.V.C. of Sheikhupura who during his whole life had never offended anybody and was held in great esteem was murdered along with his mother, son, grandson and daughter-in-law. Lala Chuni Shah of Dhaban Singh Mandi, who had sought shelter in the house of Zulfikar Ali Khan, the registrar's clerk, in spite of the latter's pleading, was not spared. Gosain Maya Ram, the well-known criminal lawyer of Sheikhupura, was killed in his house. Dr. Saleemi was a popular figure of Sheikhupura. He was a Pucca Muslim, but had very good relations with the Hindus and Sikhs. I have known him and his sons intimately and I could never believe when I was told that they played a leading part in the kidnapping of Hindu and Sikh girls of respectable families of the civil station. What a change had the Muslim League's hymn of hatred wrought among the educated and cultured people of Pakistan? The Muslim mob was shouting, "We will avenge Patiala. Pakistan is ours. We are free to do what we like, Qaid-e-Azam Zindabad."

Swami Nand Singh, Rais and Municipal Commissioner, who was an active member of the Peace Commitee of Sheikhupura, was wounded, but not killed by police firing. A Muslim League worker cut down his head with his sword and stuck in the head the Muslim League Flag and shouted "Muslim League Zindabad". The head with the flag sticking out was then paraded in streets.

The total Hindu and Sikh population of Sheikhupura was estimated at twenty thousand. Hardly four or five thousand of it succeeded in coming out of Sheikhupura to the Indian Dominion. But for the heavy rains on the 28th, 29th and 30th of August, which made communications difficult, more Hindus and Sikhs would have been killed as they would have been followed in the villages and the fields surrounding Sheikhupura to which they had run for safety. From the total number of the Hindus and Sikhs killed and the diabolical cunningness with which the whole thing was planned, one comes to the conclusion that it was planned with the connivance or advice of some of the ministers of the Pakistan Government. For the brutal manner in which the massacre of a whole town was carried out, the Sheikhupura slaughter will stand out as the darkest page in the history of Pakistan. The few people who escaped death on that day were saved owing to the incidental appearance of an aeroplane in the sky which was flying low over S. Atam Singh's factory. The 'brave' Balochies thought it to be an Indian Union's aeroplane and ran away to their posts. It was later on discovered that it was a Muslim League leader of Lahore who had flown out to Sheikhupura to see the results of his handiwork.

Pt. Jawaharlal Nehru paid a flying visit to Sheikhupura and Chuharkana (present-day Farrooqabad), accompanied by his Muslim League friends. It was reported that when told the full story of Sheikhupura slaughter, his eyes were dimmed with moisture. These were, however, tears of helplessness. Any other man in his position would have then and there taken a vow of smashing the clique that was responsible for such cold-blooded murder of a whole townful of innocent people who were none else but Nehru's own kith and kin before partition.

All the people who were left in Lahore now had to seek shelter in the D.A.V. College Refugee Camp. For Hindus and Sikhs, the vast city of Lahore now shrunk to the size of a college hostel.

No Hindu or Sikh outside the refugee camp was safe now and no place, howsoever sacred it was in the eyes of a particular community, was safe either. From June 15, 1947, when a bomb was thrown within the premises of the Arya Samaj Anarkali when the congregation was just about to disperse, it had become a planned routine of the Muslim League to attack all mandirs, gurdwaras in the city. It may be noted that the refugees coming from the Frontier and Rawalpindi side used to find temporary shelter in these places. These now became absolutely deserted. The process of combing out Hindus and Sikhs from every nook and corner of Lahore was seriously taken in hand by the local Muslims aided by the Jathas of incoming refugees. The assassins would be lurking in the corner of every street and sometime it also happened that a group of Muslims playing cards or smoking *hukka* on the footpath of the Lower Mall and the Upper Mall would suddenly pounce upon an unsuspecting Hindu pedestrian and stab him to death and then quietly continue to play or smoke *hukka*. Whenever they were searched, not a trace of weapons could be found. A Muslim friend of mine warned me to be careful while going about on the streets of Lahore and particularly to beware of such group of people who would seem to be busy in playing cards or talking to each other. According to him, these were trained *goondas* and their *modus operandi* was to approach the pedestrian for a cigarette or a matchbox and to quickly find out whether the intended victim was a Hindu or a Muslim. He also told me that the weapons—knives and daggers—would be buried under a few inches of soil near the place where these men would be sitting. They could never be found on their person and after murdering a person, they would put these back underground near about. He also told me that while moving from one place to the other, they would tie these daggers on the inside of their thighs with the far end of their *langot* (underwear). Thus, even when the policemen would search their turban, their shirt pockets or trousers by passing their hand over their body, the dagger tied in this way to the inside of the thigh could never be discovered. He also told me that in spite of strict police searches of pedestrians for fire weapons, the *goondas* were going about with pistols on their persons. He mentioned the name of a particular resident of Mozang who had passed through three such searching stations carrying a pistol without being discovered. He used to carry it inside his *langot*.

During this period, there were cases on record when the Hindus and Sikhs arrested by the police for inquiry would be huddled together in a compound and bombs would be thrown on them under the very nose of the police officers.

Right up to the first week of August 1947, people staying in Lahore, mostly house owners or owners of prosperous shops of the Mall Road and Anarkali, were determined to stay on in Lahore, whether Pakistan or no Pakistan. Even the employees of various offices were staying in Lahore, hoping for quick return of peace after the 15th of August. The people staying back used to make fun of the weak-minded, cowards who were fleeing away from Lahore. Inwardly, they took pride for staying behind. They considered themselves as heroes, while the fleeing masses were considered as chicken-hearted fools. Imbibing the spirit of Mahatma Gandhi, several officers of government departments went so far as to threaten dismissal from service of all those members of the staff who would desert their jobs. They exhorted them to be brave and quoted Shakespeare: "Cowards die many times before their death, the valiants never taste of death but once." A few days later, they themselves had precipitately fled from Lahore, taking along their friends and personal belongings in trucks supplied by the Government without rescinding their orders to unhappy staff. Similar things were happening in private offices. Leaving a skeleton staff behind, the proprietors or managers of all firms, private or public, had left Lahore. Even the skeleton staff left behind now found shelter only in the refugee camp. Lala Amar Nath Chopra, Secretary of the Punjab National Bank and a Congressman of the old school started a sort of refugee camp for the bank employees in the Punjab National Bank, Mall Road office. Employees of all other banks including those of the Imperia, the Reserve and the English banks found food and shelter and warm welcome there. There was some safety in the cantonment if you knew an officer there. Excepting these three islands of refugees, all other places in Lahore were submerged in a sea of blood. I stayed in my own Sanda Road Kothi up to the end of August by which time Krishan Nagar area, though deserted, had not been invaded by the Muslim refugees. Col. Prof. Mohd. Aslam, who was now Commanding Officer of the Lahore

Battalion of U.O.T.C., was going to Batala with an armed escort. He offered to take me to Amritsar, though a good deal of luggage had to be left behind. A few days later, Col. Mohd. Aslam dropped in at the Amritsar Sugar Mills to see me and told me that he had come there with the luggage of Mr. Madan Gopal Singh, Registrar, Punjab University, on the request of the Vice Chancellor. He told me that Madan Gopal Singh would be coming the day after and would stay temporarily with me in Amritsar. The day after, however, the U.O.T.C. lorry came to my place bringing the remaining luggage of Mr. Madan Gopal Singh and his wife who looked haggard and utterly grief-stricken. Our tears burst out when we heard the tragic tale. The news of Mr. Madan Gopal Singh's death could not be kept secret but the details of how he met with death were sedulously suppressed. His residence was opposite to his office and he had just walked to his office after his breakfast when he was pounced upon by four ruffians on the front steps of office. He was taken inside and laid on the floor. The assassin then saying 'Takbir' or 'Kalma' actually slaughtered him as he would slaughter a goat, while his associates kept Mr. Madan Gopal Singh pinned to the ground. As in halal slaughter, his jugular vein was only half cut and he was left there to writhe in agony. The assassins then left. He was rushed to the hospital, but died on the way due to loss of blood. Such a fiendish and diabolical murder of a human being had never been planned or executed even in the worst days of Muslim tyranny in the history of India.

The murder of a University Officer of such a high standing could not go unnoticed by the Punjab Government. I believe protests were made and an inquiry was promised. The police first gave out that it was a case of private revenge and, later on, actually challaned a man who has now been acquitted (Dec. 1948) without being tried on the unheard plea in legal history of refusal of the prosecution witnesses to attend the court.

It was only on coming out from Lahore that I came to know for the first time about the Sheikhupura slaughter and gruesome happenings in the Shakkargarh Tehsil and also about the massacre of train loads of Hindus and Sikhs coming from western districts at various railway stations *en route*. I had come out on a 15-day, leave but it was now clear that it was going to be a compulsory exile from home and hearth not for 15 days but for several 15 months. I then believed and even now believe that Hindus and Sikhs will go back some day to their own places in West Punjab. All events point towards this and there is not a single Hindu and Sikh heart which is not yearning for such a culmination. I believe that with the exception of those Muslims who were destitute here, but who have come into the possession of vast properties and palatial buildings after their migration from India, all other Muslim evacuees of Delhi and East Punjab are also yearning to come back. But the issue will be decided not by peace parleys, but by war. The pacifists and defeatists are the sole stumbling block in the way of the only logical settlement of the issues between the two artificially created dominions. No party is going to be in power for all times. India is now a democratic state and no one person can have the dictatorial powers that he may be exercising now in the transition period. The Congress party may be thrown out during elections in a few years' time. The Hindus of India other than refugees resent what they call the invasion of refugees of their close preserves of trade, employment and industry in the Indian Dominion. The refugees themselves hate their present environment and would not like to stay for a day longer than is absolutely necessary, among people whom, with a few exceptions, they have now found out to be devoid of all sentiments except that of making money. The Muslims of India fully realise the great change that has taken place in their political status during the last two years. Submerged in an ocean of Hindudom and deprived of real political power, their present status is that of a weak and poor relation who must always fawn upon his seniors and protectors. Like the Hindus in Pakistan, even the tallest among them cannot be tall enough to walk with an erect head. The state is secular and must in law remain so, but, in practice, the fact cannot be altered that 3.5 crores of Muslims are living in the midst of 35.5 crores of Hindus, only a handful of who understand the fine implications of a secular state. Only in a re-united secular India, when there are no Liaqat Ali Khans to incite them, could they breathe as free as before. Britain had administered the country for more than a century in a way that had brought to India's enormous and most tangled community real order and stability. Their rule had kept the age-old hatreds of Hindus, Muslims and Sikhs on the level of mutual forbearance. One terrible outburst after the other, however, had shown the interim government to be incompetent in meeting and controlling the situation. Maulana Alama Mashriqi, the Khaksar boss, admitted that longing for the continuation of the British Rule was there all over Northern India as a result of the disturbances that never gave peace to the people. The Indian Interim Government had shown herself to India and the world as a complete failure, and, as a direct result of this, terrible religious hatred had been given a new lease of life with a scope and intensity unparalleled in the last 200 years.

The communal riots and disturbances had become the order of the day from one end of the country to the other. Unlike Britain, in the 4th century, India had a very well-equipped army, a well-organised police and a civil service trained to do its job. India's Army, after the defeat of Japan, was the best in Asia barring Soviet Russia's, and its strength was sufficient for the suppression of the riots, if only the largest party in the government, the Congress, had shown a firm determination to do so. Military aid was now being requisitioned by the civil authorities in many provinces of India including Assam, but the aid sent was not sufficient and the troops were nowhere entrusted with direct responsibility of maintaining peace and order. The criminal neglect not to declare martial law in any of the centres of disturbances showed that either the Government of India did not know how to deal with the ugly situation that had arisen in the country or they were prevented from doing so by the Governor-General or it may be that their own ideological faith in non-violence prevented the Congress members to propose any such measures. If the opposition to taking strong action was coming from the Governor-General, the straight course for Pt. Jawaharlal Nehru would have been to say it publicly and resign from the government. The blame in that case, for the weak-kneed policy being pursued during those critical months of India's history, would have rested on shoulders other than his. It is true that Pt. Jawaharlal Nehru showed commendable speed and strength in suppressing the Bihar riots where Muslim Minority was the victim. But why did he not show the same strength and speed in tackling the aggressors in Calcutta, Rawalpindi and Multan?

Except for the sad events in Bihar, which were directly the result of retaliation on the part of a very large number of Durbans, Chowkidars, and labourers who had suffered grievously and had been forced out of Calcutta by the Muslim attack in August 1946, the responsibility for initiating all communal riots in all other parts of the country must be laid on the shoulders of the Muslim League. It was alleged by people, though no direct proof was available, that the League had the secret sympathy and even the encouragement of some of the British civilians and officials in her nefarious activities at least in West Punjab. It was a pity that the British who had ruled over India for 150 years with such integrity should have now behaved in a manner that brought discredit to their country. In contrast to the 'Great Englishmen' at home and to the Labour Party running their government which had nothing but sympathy for Indian independence, these 'little Englishmen' in India—the civilians and the police— had a lurking spite against the Hindus and Sikhs, who they thought had forced the British to quit. These 'little Englishmen' gave every support and encouragement to the League. Even clandestine supply of arms to certain secret organisations was facilitated by them. Rawalpindi in the Punjab had become the headquarters for the supply of such arms and many a times, a retiring military officer was running the racket.

For full one month before Sir Khizar resigned, there was total defiance of the government by the followers of the League. They used the tactics of the military without any action having been taken against them. When the riots had actually broken out in Punjab, there were instances of groups of people of the minority conmunities who had defended themselves against heavy odds, being led into traps by the so-called friendly intermediaries and brutally butchered. There were instances of the beleaguered villages being fired upon by uniformed gangs whom the minorities at first sight mistook for the military and to whom they looked for help and protection. In these cold-blooded massacres, some officers played a conniving role. Even when urgent appeals for help were made to them, they moved not a finger and in case something was done, it was belated and done as a make-belief. In several cases, helpless people in peril were punished instead of being protected. Is it not strange that in all the districts, where there were Indian Deputy Commissioners, peace was maintained or the outbreak of communal frenzy suppressed in no time, while in all those districts where Englishmen were in charge, the communal riots were aggravated everyday and could not be suppressed? The last British administrators of Punjab, with a few exceptions, proved to be the worst specimen of their noble race.

As soon as the British government and the Congress had conceded the Pakistan demand, Mr. Jinnah's followers became busy with the partition work. Up to that date, the Muslim League had felt that it was in its interest to create an atmosphere of conflict and strife; henceforth, it was obviously in its interest to create order and see to the peaceful implementation of partition. The Muslim team taking part in departmental discussions relating to partition was much stronger than their Congress opposites. This was because the key posts and posts of trust had been freely given to Muslims in preference to the Hindus by the British and because Muslim officers had been working in close alliance with the League members of the interim government for some months. Their plans were ready as Muslim officers had free access and contact with League leaders. On the other hand, the non-Congress and non-League members had been virtually isolated for various reasons from Congress leaders who had always been busy with 'Big affairs' and had not taken keen or sustained interest in 'small things' like posts or administration. The majority of Muslim officers were trusted men of the League high command and had experience and enthusiasm while their

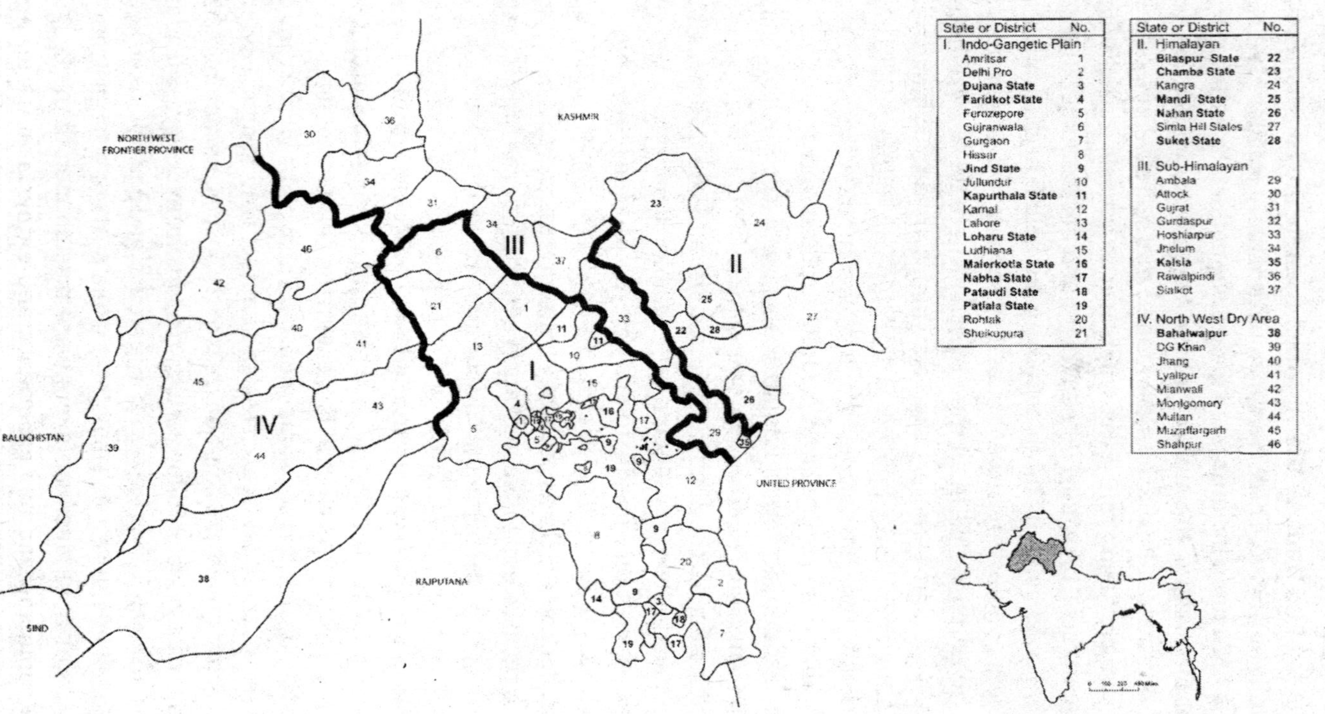

State or District	No.
I. Indo-Gangetic Plain	
Amritsar	1
Delhi Pro	2
Dujana State	**3**
Faridkot State	**4**
Ferozepore	5
Gujranwala	6
Gurgaon	7
Hissar	8
Jind State	**9**
Jullundur	10
Kapurthala State	**11**
Karnal	12
Lahore	13
Loharu State	**14**
Ludhiana	15
Malerkotla State	**16**
Nabha State	**17**
Pataudi State	**18**
Patiala State	**19**
Rohtak	20
Sheikupura	21

State or District	No.
II. Himalayan	
Bilaspur State	**22**
Chamba State	**23**
Kangra	24
Mandi State	**25**
Nahan State	**26**
Simla Hill States	27
Suket State	**28**
III. Sub-Himalayan	
Ambala	29
Attock	30
Gujrat	31
Gurdaspur	32
Hoshiarpur	33
Jhelum	34
Kalsia	**35**
Rawalpindi	36
Sialkot	37
IV. North West Dry Area	
Bahalwalpur	**38**
DG Khan	39
Jhang	40
Lyallpur	41
Mianwali	42
Montgomery	43
Multan	44
Muzaffargarh	45
Shahpur	46

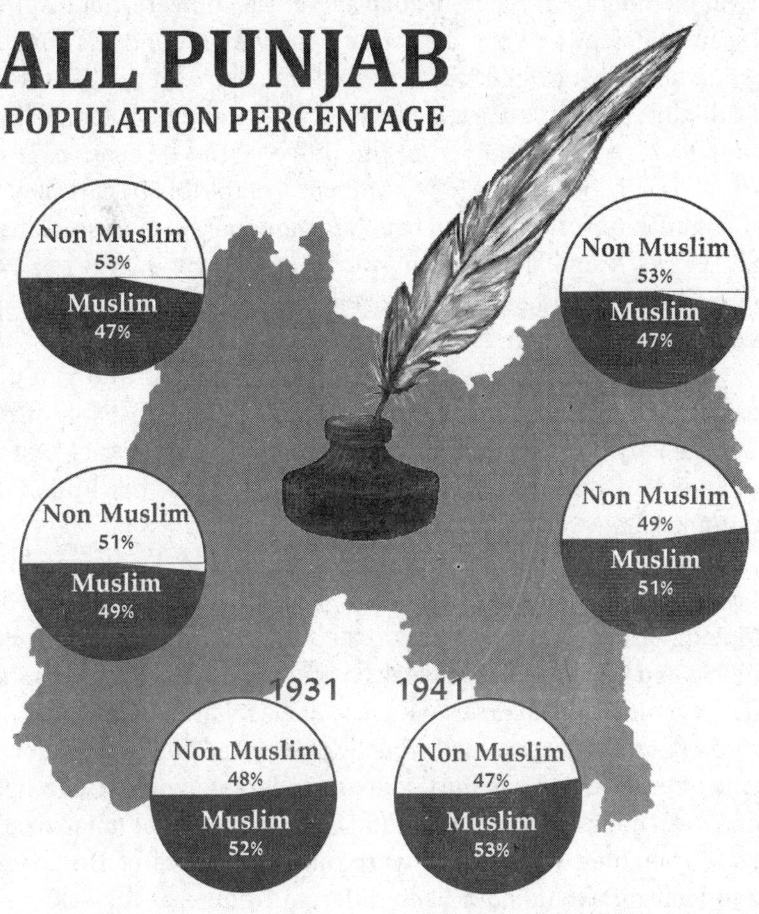

NON-MUSLIM PROVINCE

Converted by the

ENUMERATOR'S PEN

into

MUSLIM PROVINCE

rival members were merely good secretariat officers, not inspired by any ideology and not always trusted by their Congress bosses.

The story of Delhi was repeated in Lahore. In the 'Partap' of 26th June, 1947, it was reported that a large number of important files had been removed from the office of the Director of Land Records in Lahore. For a long number of years, this Department of the Punjab Government had been the monopoly of Muslim officers and clerks. A similar complaint was being heard about the removal of records from other Punjab Government offices. All these things were being done with the connivance of the British officers.

The decision of the Punjab University Senate to divide the assets of the University was superceded by the decision of the Central Partition Council to leave these assets to whoever, Muslims or non-Muslims, inherited Lahore as a result of the Boundary Commission Award.

The tragic story of the doings of the Muslim League and the Congress unfolded above show how practical and hard-headed the Muslims are, if once they make up their mind to achieve a particular object and how supine and weak has been the Congress leadership in the hands of visionaries who lost the last battle of India's unity to their opponents so ingloriously. Even after their surrender in conceding Pakistan had the Congress leaders shown some strength and determination, the Hindus and Sikhs in the West Punjab would have remained where they were and the stories of Hindustan and Pakistan would have been different from what they are now. Mr. Jinnah on 8.8.47 was reported to have said: "The past must be buried and let us start afresh as two independent sovereign states of Hindustan and Pakistan. I wish Hindustan prosperity and peace." But, unfortunately, that was not to be.

□

6

The Background in Retrospect

It is not the place to go into the question of how the Congress and the Muslim League won the 1946 elections. The skilful way in which the Congress made use of the I.N.A. agitation and the Muslim League of the now thoroughly roused religious passions of the Muslims is known to all. One thing, however, was clear. The Muslim League had the whole-hearted support of the entire Muslim community in India. The nationalist Muslims had been utterly routed. The Congress had the fullest support of the Hindu community and Hindu Mahasabha and other parties were nowhere in the picture. The British government naturally interpreted the results of the elections as showing that in their political talks about the future of India, they had now in the Congress and the Muslim League, the accredited representatives of the Hindus and the Muslims respectively and that the claim to speak on behalf of these communities of any other person or party was not based on facts. The Akali Dal Party alone in Punjab had succeeded in winning the majority of Sikh seats. Hence, when the time came for the new set-up of affairs, invitations were issued only to the Congress, the Muslim League and the undisputed leader of the Sikh party, Master Tara Singh; the Hindu Mahasabha was entirely ignored. The arena for the wrestling bout was now set on the stage of India with Britain acting as a refree. All the three parties had made definite election pledges and committed themselves irretrievably, one to an Akhand Hindustan (undivided Hindustan), the second to an independent Pakistan resulting from the division of the country and the third to a home land (Khalistan) for the Sikhs extending from the river

Chenab on the west to river Jamuna in the east. Of course, these demands were mutually contradictory and the vast majority of electors, Hindus, Muslims and Sikhs were very anxious to know how these apparently irreconcilable views would be reconciled by the British and how the leaders would wriggle out of their plighted word to them. Little did the electors know about the capacity of the politicians in turning every situation to their own credit.

The dramatic offer of Pt. Jawaharlal Nehru to Britain to bring India into the Empire after the formation of an independent Indian government right away with himself as the leader, reported in newspapers on March 30, 1947, was expected to smooth out matters for the transfer of power to a united India, but having come late by two years, misfired. Who knows what counter-offer had been made by Mr. Jinnah to Mr. Attlee? It was soon clear that though the British government might quit India, they were not prepared to hand over the reins of government to the Hindus as represented by the Congress without either the Congress coming to terms with Mr. Jinnah or agreeing to hand over a part of India to him. The Congress, under the leadership of Mahatma Gandhi and Rajagopalachari, had, however, by this time, been frustrated in its efforts to appease the Muslims by giving them concessions after concessions; these had only whetted the latter's appetite. There was a glorious occasion later on of accepting the Cabinet Mission's proposals about grouping of the provinces with a centre in charge of Defence and Communications. In the light of what has happened after the partition, it is now clear that this proposal would have been far better than the June 2, 1947 proposals to which the Congress leaders agreed in haste. The Cabinet Mission proposals had been accepted by both, the League and the Congress and to be fair to Mr. Jinnah, it may be conceded that it was Mahatma Gandhi and the other Congress leaders who later on wriggled out of their earlier acceptance and not Mr. Jinnah.

The Muslim League after going into the wilderness temporarily out of sheer pique had now joined the Government of India. Mr. Jinnah very astutely chose as his cabinet ministers, persons whose nuisance value in the government would be the maximum. Mr. Ghazanfar Ali Khan (Raja by caste and not by status) from Punjab was an open-mouthed speaker who could never keep his mouth shut in the Punjab Legislature. Abdur Rab Nishtar was literally a 'Nishtar' or a lance in the side of the Congress ministers of the government. Mr. Chundrigar had a worse reputation in Bombay than Mr. Ghazanfar Ali had in Punjab. Mr. Liaqat Ali Khan was chosen because he and his begum had good relations with Pt. Jawaharlal Nehru. He was gifted with the sweetest of tongues and sharpest of claws. As a counterblast against the inclusion of Maulana Azad in the government, Mr. Jinnah had chosen Mr. Mandal from East Bengal. Thus, the two wings of the government were fully matched in the political tug of war with the Christian and the Parsi members expected to remain neutral. The Muslim League team, in fact, was more than a match for the Hindu Congress ministers. The League had joined the government and their leaders had not made a secret of it, whatever Mr. Jinnah may have conveyed to Lord Wavell in private, not to work it but to wreck it from inside, and wreck indeed they did from inside because on all and every occasion, however trivial the matter that was being discussed, they opposed whatever was proposed by the Congress members. They made a nuisance of themselves from the point of view of the Congress ministers who had expected a smooth sailing in their new *Gaddies* (seats of power). The Congress had all along been wedded in theory, at least, to the attainment of Swaraj by non-violent methods. The Hindu Mahasabha leaders and other political opponents knew to their cost what amount of non-violence was there in their method during the past 25 years in their slogans, speeches and 'Siapas' organised to browbeat them. But the Muslim League from the date they made the achievement of Pakistan their goal had never shunned the use of any or all methods for the attainment of their objective. What they were doing all over the country through communal killings and disturbances, they began to do in the meetings of the cabinet and in the departments under their control, but, of course, in the shape of orders and decisions aimed at violently upsetting the civil service regulations, the structure of trade and industry and the framework of administration. The shaking of fists in the faces of their Congress colleagues and the use of invectives in colloquial Punjabi and Pushto became the order of the day in the cabinet meetings. Pt. Jawaharlal Nehru and even that strong man of the Congress, Sardar Patel, soon became disgusted with the whole show. They were not used to such receptions of their proposals and plans. I believe the psychological transformation of their minds took place in these crucial days in India's history. They now wanted nothing more than to get rid of this daily nuisance. The Muslim League had also succeeded by the orgy of communal riots organised in different parts of the country with a diabolical cunningness in instilling a fear into their hearts that unless and until the demand for Pakistan was conceded, there would be no peace in the country. In retrospect, when one thinks of the courage and bravery of the Hindus and the Sikhs of what is now known as the Western Pakistan, who had stood the almost unbearable tyranny of the Muslim League since March 1947, one cannot but admire them. Their fortitude stands in splendid contrast to the pussilanimous attitude of the Congress leaders who, when confronted only with the verbal opposition in the cabinet meetings, soon quailed before it. Forgetting their solemn pledges on which they had won the elections, the top leaders of the Congress soon reconciled themselves to the vivisection of their motherland. Among themselves, they decided to have Swaraj at whatever cost. But in the hearts of their heart, they must have had a feeling that whatever shape ultimately Pakistan took, their real cradle of power, e.g., Bombay, Gujarat, Madras, C.P., Bihar, U.P., Orissa and Rajasthan would still be within the Indian dominion. The Punjab and Bengal had always been problem provinces for them. The former in particular was always hated by not a few of them for having provided the British with manpower to win the war and for not having taken an active part in 1942 Quit India movement.

If we correctly understand the psychological background of the Congress leaders' approach to the problem as detailed above, we should not hold them to blame for agreeing to vivisect their motherland. It is true that by accepting the partition plan and agreeing to enter into parleys with Mr. Jinnah, the Congress had accepted the two-nation theory and gone back on all that it had been saying since the day of its birth. But I believe they did so with a mental reservation that this would not be repeated on another occasion. "Let us accept the two-nation theory so far as the creation of Pakistan is concerned, but as soon as we come into independent possession of the rest of India, we must go back to our old one-nation theory of the secular state." This must have been the tacit understanding amongst them. The masses, however, go by the open declarations and not by secret confabulations and the Hindu and Sikh masses in this case had reconciled themselves, though half-heartedly, to the idea of Pakistan in the belief that, as a result of it, there would emerge a strong Hindu and Sikh India as a counter-blast to the strong Muslim India. Their disillusionment on the establishment of the secular state must have been great indeed.

The question of partition began no longer to be tackled from the point of view of its feasibility or its economic repercussions. Tempers ran too high for such an objective approach. Not whether partition was desirable, but how much of the Punjab and the West Bengal could be saved from Pakistan now became the subject of common discussion among the Hindus and Sikhs. Wires began to be pulled from behind the curtains. The demand for the partition of Punjab and Bengal began to be made by their own elected representatives giving it the shape of a popular demand. No referendum or plebiscite was held and the 'Punjabi oxen' once again in their history were led astray to voting their own destruction for the sake of the rest of India. They must die so that India may live.

In Punjab, the fight was triangular. After consideration by some leaders of the Panth, their resolution, "We have come to the conclusion that the Sikhs cannot protect their culture, religion and honour without having some power somewhere" was conveyed to the rulers of the Sikh states of Patiala, Nabha, Jind, Faridkot, Kalsia and Kapurthala. S. Pritam Singh Gujran, President, Shiromani Riasti Akali Dal acted as the mouth-piece of Sikh leaders of the Punjab states who had met in Sangrur. Master Tara Singh in an interview on April 7, 1947 made it clear that the Hindu-Sikh province extended from Chenab to Jamuna. The Sikh M.L.A.s' unequivocal demand at this time was that Punjab must be divided. In a convention of the Hindu-Sikh M.L.A.s of Punjab held on May 2, 1947 in New Delhi under the chairmanship of Ch. Lahri Singh, the following resolution regarding the partition of the province was unanimously passed.

"In view of repeated insistence of the Muslim League upon a division of India and in view of the recent brutal happenings which have caused unheard of sufferings to the Hindus and Sikhs of Punjab at the hands of those who believe in the creed of the Muslim League, robbing the minorities of any sense of security and assurance that their rights, lives and property are capable of protection at the hands of the majority community in Punjab:

'This convention of the Hindu and Sikh legislators of Punjab, members of the central legislature and the constituent assembly has come to the conclusion that the only solution of the political problem in Punjab lies in a just and equitable division of the province assuring the non-Muslim population of the province:

(a) Such territories and assets as they are entitled to according to their numbers and stake in the province;

(b) Such a total area by drawing a line along the River Chenab, including the districts of the three divisions of Ambala, Jalundhar and Lahore and one of the contiguous colony districts of Lyallpur (present-day Faisalabad) or of Montgomery, an area wherein the non-Muslims are in a substantial majority: and

(c) Providing for the preservation of the integrity and homogeneity of the Sikh community, the great bulk of whose population is concentrated in this very area.'

"The division of Punjab on the lines suggested by the convention also assures an equitable and just distribution of the irrigation system and of state lands and other provincial assets created out of the common resources of the province."

"This convention declares that no interim arrangement for the administration of Punjab on a zonal basis should be made which ignores the fundamentals set out above, since any such arrangement would affect prejudicially the rights of the non-Muslims in Punjab."

Explaining the resolution, Diwan said: "From official information gathered by the members of the convention, it appears that a scheme is now before the viceroy providing for a temporary zonal division of Punjab. The scheme, it is stated, contemplates that there should be two such zones, one comprising 12 districts and the other 17 districts. It is also possible that there will be neutral area for the interim period. This scheme is totally unacceptable to the legislators who have assembled in the convention here.

It is well known that since the census figures are inflated and inaccurate, they do not give a correct picture of the numerical strength of the minorities in Punjab, which until the separate electorates were created, were even according to the census figures, actually in majority. Census officers have commented on these figures repeatedly and said that the figures do not show the correct position.

Further, even taking the figures at their face value, the scheme suggested by the convention will assure:

"Firstly, that the minorities in the province would be distributed in the proportion due to them, of the area as well as the assets of the province."

"Secondly, the scheme assures that in the area contemplated by it, minorities will definitely be so substantial that the question of adversely affecting the Muslim population does not arise."

"Thirdly, the Sikh community has no other home except in Punjab and it is obvious that the Sikh community will never agree to a division of the province which would wreck their unity and break it into two, whereas under the scheme suggested by the convention, 90 per cent of the Sikh community will preserve its unity as well as 50 per cent of the Hindu community, without doing any injustice to the Muslims of Punjab."

"Fourthly, the scheme contemplates handing over to them of what might be described as the Hindu and Sikh areas of Punjab and at least one colony system, without which life of Punjab, which is almost entirely agricultural, would come to a standstill."

The Arya Samaj was perturbed. In the practical field of social and educational life, Arya Samajis had built up a new era of splendour and hard-won achievement. From Fort Sandeman (present-day Zhob in Pakistan) and Peshawar to the remotest corners of Punjab, they had established and were maintaining many Arya Samaj temples, and educational, social and philanthropic institutions. The Arya Samajis owned landed property, temples, big college and school buildings, ashrams and various charitable institutions. Offices and buildings of their two central bodies: Arya Pradeshak Pratinidhi Sabha and Arya Pratinidhi Sabha, worth crores of rupees were also situated in West Punjab, but not being a compact or separate community, they could not call any part of Punjab as their own, except perhaps Lahore.

With the Muslim League claiming for Pakistan the area from Khyber and Durand Line to River Sutlej, the problem of partition seemed insoluble. The population figures were the strong point of their case, as the 1941 census figures were to be taken as final for this purpose. The protests of the Hindus and Sikhs that the 1941 census figures were cooked figures were not believed. The percentage variations in the population of the British Punjab from 1900-1941, when the four censuses were taken were 1.8, 5.6, 13.9 and 20.5, respectively, would have convinced any intelligent and critical observer that the 1941 Census was a bogus one. The Punjabis' procreative activities in the decade 1931-1941 could not be so extensive and intensive that the population variation figures could shoot up to 20.5 from 1.8 in 1900-11. The astonishing increase of 58 lakhs in the Punjab population indicated in the 1941 Census was the creation of the dishonest enumerators' manipulating pen.

That a similar phenomenal increase in Muslim population should have been recorded in 1941 census for Bengal and Assam, another Muslim area, showed that the whole thing was planned by some mastermind. From population point of view, it was strange that both the swarming areas of population should be found in the

Muslim zones. Anyhow, it was no longer a question of arguments and the 1941 Census became the arbiter of the destiny of millions of Hindus and Muslims living in the two areas.

Efforts were made by Mr. Jinnah as the result of a suggestion by the viceroy in the middle of May 1947 to bring about a Muslim-Sikh rapprochement. Mr. Jinnah met the Maharaja of Patiala. They explored the possibility of a Muslim-Sikh compromise which would simplify the Punjab problem and avoid any necessity of partitioning the province. The separation of 12 or 13 districts, the Leaguers argued, would mean the splitting of Sikhs into two more or less equal parts. What talk took place between the two is not known to the public, but it is surmised that the Maharaja of Patiala wanted the Pakistan Army to be commanded by a Sikh Commander-in-Chief and the percentage of Sikh strength in the army and civil appointments to be fixed on the basis of a special weightage for the community. The outward reason given out on the breakdown of the negotiations was that the Maharaja felt that his community members had been greatly agitated recently owing to communal disturbances and, therefore, they felt that they were not safe in the hands of the majority community.

The Muslims constituted 56 per cent of the Punjab population, according to 1941 Census, on which the division was to be made. Even if this were to be conceded as the basis for division, Mr. Jinnah could have his pound of flesh, i.e., 56 per cent land of the five rivers and yet leave enough for the Hindus and Sikhs to have their own homeland without suffering a grievous injury. A writer in the *Tribune said*: "The total area of this province is 95,089 square miles and its total population is 2,84,18,819. The total population of the Muslims is 1,62,17,242. They cannot obviously claim to have more than 56,546 square miles. Punjab has five divisions, two, namely the Ambala and Jalundhar divisions are Hindu and Sikh swarming areas and two, namely the Rawalpindi and Multan divisions are Muslim-swarming areas. The Rawalpindi division is 21,381 square miles and the Multan division is 31,763 square miles. The total comes to 53,144 square miles. If this is deducted from 56,546 square miles, which is all that the Muslims can claim to have according to Mr. Jinnah's political arithmetic, we arrive at the figure of 3,402 square miles which is all that the League can claim to possess in the Lahore division. The remaining area of this division should go to the non-Muslims, not only because it includes some non-Muslim-majority districts, but also because it embraces several districts which contain their Meccas and Madinas and whose educational, cultural, artistic, social, industrial and commercial life is built by the talent and industry of the Hindus and Sikhs and is dependent for its existence and growth upon their continued planning and activity. Let us make a fuller analysis of the situation and cast a glance at the whole of Punjab (including the states). The area of the entire province is 1,37,235 square miles and its total population is 3,43,09,851, out of which the Muslims are 1,82,89,744. On the population basis, the League cannot claim to get more than 73,036 square miles. As we have already pointed out, the Rawalpindi and Multan divisions bring them 53,144 square miles. Add to them 14,494 square miles of the Muslim-majority state of Bahawalpur and the total will come to 70,638 square miles. According to these calculations, the Muslim League can claim to possess only 2,398 square miles—(73,036 minus 70,638 is equal to 2,398)—outside the Rawalpindi and Multan divisions and the Bhawalpur State. That is in the Lahore division of the six districts of Lahore, Amritsar, Gurdaspur, Gujranwala, Sheikhupura and Sialkot, the Muslims can claim to possess only one district not exceeding 2,398 square miles in area. We accept Mr. Jinnah's political logic and arithmetic with realistic fervour. Now let us divide Punjab on their basis with strict honesty."

The case for the Sikhs could never be judged by mere population figures. In his letter to Master Tara Singh, Lord Pethick Lawrence, the then Secretary of State for India, had recognised that the Sikhs occupied a special position in Punjab. "The estimate of the importance of your community," he wrote, "would never depend on the number of seats that you hold in the constituent assembly." The Sikhs had been the rulers of the province from Sutlej to Khyber and from Karakoram to Sukkur before the British annexed Punjab to their dominion on an unjust pretext. As the guardians of the young Maharaja Dalip Singh, they had no legal and moral excuse to deprive him of his kingdom because a section of Sikhs had risen in revolt against his authority and had been suppressed with the help of the British troops. Anyhow, the question confronting the Sikhs now was that whereas the Hindus and the Muslims would have some areas in the country, which they could call exclusively their own, the Sikhs would have none if the province were divided at river Ravi. They had their state only in this province which was the cradle of their faith and had been hallowed by the blood of their martyrs. The British Cabinet, in its statement of May 16, 1947, did recognise the necessity of preserving the solidarity of Khalsa, though they did not say how it could be done. The Sikh percentage in Punjab was 13.22, but their actual percentage in Gurdaspur district was 19.18, Montgomery 13.17, Sialkot 11.71 and Gujranwala 10.87. The area covered by these districts was from the religious point of view as sacred to the Sikhs as Mecca or Madina to the Muslims. The most important Sikh religious shrines and mausoleum of Maharaja Ranjit Singh and other places sacred to the memory of the Panth (community) were situated in these central districts of Punjab. The land lying between the Beas and the Chenab was the Sikh home because, in this 'Ilaqua' (area), the Sikh history was made. Those on whom rested the responsibility of dividing the province should have carefully considered these points and seen to it that the division itself did not sow the seeds of discontent and discord and jeopardise the cause of peace and happiness of the people for all times.

It was in the context of these facts that the people of the Punjab began to look forward with great anxiety to what Lord Mountbatten and the Congress and Muslim League leaders were going to do to partition the province. The June 2, 1947 announcement was received with mixed feelings all over the country. It confirmed the worst fears of the Hindus and Sikhs of Punjab. Lord Mountbatten had said ditto to whatever the Muslim League had demanded, giving 17 districts to Pakistan and only 12 to East Punjab. The entire Lahore division with the exception of the district of Amritsar was given to West Punjab. Of course, it was said that the division was provisional and that the Boundary Commission would finally decide the line of demarcation between the two Punjabs and that factors other than population would be given their due weight in the final award. That amounted to keeping the people on tenterhooks. They did not know to the very last day where some of the hotly contested areas would go, and in this contested area was the heart of the Punjab—the capital city of Lahore. The same injustice was done with regard to West Bengal, but the inclusion of Calcutta in West Bengal gave genuine satisfaction to the Punjabis. The Punjabis always think more about other people than about themselves. Every educated Hindu or Sikh you met those days in Lahore was jubilant over Calcutta's inclusion in Hindustan. Little did they realise then that the inclusion of Calcutta in Hindustan meant the exclusion of Lahore from East Punjab. A Muslim friend of mine who was fairly influential in Muslim League circles in those days was also jubilant over this decision. He told me that I should no longer live in a fool's paradise by believing that Lahore would come to the Hindus and Sikhs. He talked about some understanding of the Governor-General with Mr. M.A. Jinnah about this barter, to which, unfortunately, I did not pay any heed.

□

7

The Greatest Farce in History

Can anybody cite any other example from history of a more cruel and gigantic fraud perpetrated on credulous people than that of the Punjab Boundary Commission? In the first place, it was not a commission at all. It was in reality a one man's show and that one man did not even once visit the boundary or hear the arguments of the parties personally. To repeat a phrase that was popular in the days of Rowlatt agitation, the arbitrator gave his award without hearing any Vakil, Daleel or Appeal (no lawyers, no arguments, and no appeal). The announcement of the appointment of the commission set people busy in preparing their cases. Bakshi Sir Tek Chand's house at Fane Road (Lahore) became the centre for such work. The Hindus, the Congress and the Sikhs pooled their efforts and helped Bakshiji in preparing a formidable case for the commission. Thousands of rupees were collected; Lala Yodhraj, Chairman of the Punjab National Bank Ltd., alone donated a sum of ₹25,000/-. Sub-committees were set up, research scholars were engaged, records were ransacked and every statement made in the case was carefully verified before inclusion. Lala Yodhraj was given the task of preparing the case for the inclusion of Lahore in the Indian Dominion. An advance copy of this case was sent to Pt. Jawaharlal Nehru, who, it was said by his personal assistant, had liked it and suggested a few changes here and there. Lala Yodhraj had arranged to engage one of the top-most advocates of the United States of America, the Hon'ble Francis Biddle, ex-Attorney General of the U.S.A. for the brief. An eminent lawyer of Bombay was engaged on a heavy fee (which he refunded later on) and came to Lahore to help prepare the case. As the preparation of the case progressed, the authors became more and more convinced of the justice of their cause. I believe they fell victims to their own arguments. Their optimism was contagious and the upper middle class of the Hindus and Sikhs all became convinced that Lahore would remain in East Punjab. That explains why very few of them cared to remove their goods from Lahore. Bakshi Sir Tek Chand had the finest library of law books in Asia. He did not remove a single book from it then. The Hon'ble Justice Mehr Chand Mahajan on his return from the Boundary Commission's labours in Shimla left Lahore the same evening without removing his household goods and personal belongings from which I could safely conclude that Lahore was certain of being included in East Punjab. I had the time, the means and the resources to remove every single article of my movable goods to Amritsar, but I thought it an unnecessary botheration and trouble. So convinced I was about the soundness and justice of the case prepared for the inclusion of Lahore in East Punjab. I have since then regretted nothing more than the loss of my diaries, note-books and manuscripts on economics which I had taken 30 years to complete. All my efforts to retrieve these have since failed. The retired Jemadar (junior officer) of the army with a pension of ₹50/- per month who has been given the possession of my bungalow, the rental value of which was about ₹100/- p.m., naively remarked, "I used these for my hubble bubble!" The Muslims on the other hand did not take much pains to prepare their case. But they engaged the best lawyer in Muslimdom, Sir Zafarullah Khan, to plead their cause. As the days approached nearer and nearer for the hearing of the case, disquieting news began to percolate to the framers of the Hindu case about the procedure to be employed for the hearing of the case. As it finally turned out to be Hindus, Sikhs and Muslims were left to fight it out or argue it out among themselves, without the bridegroom joining the marriage party. In this way, the British Government very cleverly chose another platform for advertising the differences among the Hindus, Sikhs and Muslims of India. The idea of importing an advocate of international repute for arguing the case before the Boundary Commission was given up and, in fact, the whole Boundary Commission procedure soon degenerated into a farce.

The Congress leaders had grievously erred in the first place by agreeing to one Boundary Commission for Bengal and Punjab, secondly, accepting a one-man commission instead of a three-men Commission, and thirdly, accepting a particularly obscure person, namely Sir Cyril Radcliffe who was neither known for his legal eminence nor for his political impartiality and nor for any special contribution to the public life of England. When the name was proposed, Pt. Jawaharlal Nehru never made any inquiries about his antecedents. That Mr. Jinnah had readily agreed to the name should have caused some suspicion in the mind of Pt. Nehru. But, probably, it was too trivial a matter to engage his serious attention. A letter published in a daily paper of Delhi alleged that years ago, he had worked as a junior counsel to Mr. Jinnah when he had set up his practice in London. This news was never contradicted. Their fourth blunder was in agreeing to waive the right of appeal against the arbitrator's award to the British Government.

Nobody accepting Sir Cyril Radcliffe and Lord Mountbatten know what exactly transpired among themselves when Sir C. Radcliffe handed over his award to the latter, but the gist of the talk Sir C. Radcliffe had with the Hindu, Muslim and Sikh judges associated with him as assessors is now pretty well known. Judged from all reports, Sir C. Radcliffe was a clever man indeed, and an expert in making all the three communities' representatives believe that what he proposed to do was just the best in their interests. Up to the last moment, these representatives believed that the decision would be in their favour.

According to June 2 plan, in the 17 districts which were to comprise the West Punjab, the Muslims were 73 per cent of the population as against 14 per cent of Hindus, 10 per cent of Sikhs and 3 per cent of Indian Christians and others. They had, thus, an absolute majority over all others combined. Such, however, was not the case in the 12 districts of East Punjab. The Hindus here formed 48 per cent, Muslims 32 per cent, Sikhs 18 per cent, Indian Christians and others 2 per cent. Thus, no single community could be in absolute majority here. The Sikhs were almost equally divided under the scheme in East Punjab. While 20 lakhs of them went to the East Punjab where they formed 18 per cent of the population, about 17 lakhs of them remained in the West Punjab constituting 10 per cent of the population. In other words, the national division had practically ensured that the whole of Punjab should remain under Muslim influence.

Economically, the province was indivisible. The only part which could be looped off was the Ambala division whose economic structure could not be affected by the partition. This area depended mainly on the Jamuna system of irrigation and had nothing to do with the Punjab's five rivers. The proposed partition according to the notional plan was going to render both parts poorer, but East Punjab particularly so. The latter could not have sufficient food supplies. Every second or third year, it suffered from famine. In some parts, it had little water even for drinking purposes. There men and buffaloes had to take water and bathe in the same village pond. The province was expected to remain a charge upon the Hindustan Government for decades. On the other hand, West Punjab contained within itself the richest canal colonies in Asia which between them constituted the granary of India. It was for this reason that the Boundary Commission was approached by the Hindus and Sikhs to so alter the notional division as to give to East Punjab not only Lahore and Gurdaspur districts, but also one of the canal colonies. Great concern had been expressed by the British Government to make Pakistan a viable State. The same concern should have been shown for East Punjab—a province which had been the backbone of their stay in India for almost a century.

In a meeting of the Panthik Assembly Party and the Working Committee of the Shiromani Akali Dal and Panthik Pratinidhi Board held to discuss the partition of Punjab on June 13, 1947 in New Delhi, an opinion was expressed that the Boundary Commission should be given an express directive to make recommendations for the transfer of Hindu and Sikh population and property from the western parts of Punjab to the eastern parts after the partition had been effectuated on an equitable basis. The conference apprehended that in the absence of a provision of transfer of population and property, the very purpose of partition would be defeated. The Sikh leaders were, however, too late in making this demand now. Almost two years before, when Mr. M. A. Jinnah had made such a proposal about the transfer of population and property from Pakistan to Hindustan and vice versa, there was a chorus of indignant disapproval from almost all parties. From Mahatma Gandhi down to the man in the street, everybody opposed it. Without exception, the entire Congress and the Sikh press in the country attacked Mr. Jinnah for what was called his fantastic suggestion. Mr. Jinnah kept quiet. But it shows the greatness of the man that he could visualise the coming events correctly as no one else could do. With a planned exchange of population and property between the two Punjabs and two Bengals, the independence of India would have been true independence for all.

The notional plan had allotted 35,314 square miles of land to East Punjab as against 63,775 square miles allotted to the Muslims. Shimla, had an area of 81 square miles only. For all practical purposes, therefore, the non-Muslims had been given 11 districts against 17 districts given to the Muslims. Even of these 11 districts, several were no bigger than the tehsils in certain districts constituting the Muslim zone.

Punjab was being divided admittedly for the Sikhs. It is they whose demand had been accepted in this respect. The division, therefore, should have been such as to satisfy their genuine claims. Mere division they had never wanted, but they now discovered that they had been tricked into accepting the proposal that was going to ruin them most. They had striven hard for the prosperity of Lyallpur, Sargodha, Sheikhupura, Multan and Montgomery. The district of Lyallpur alone paid more revenue than was paid by Jalandhar and Ambala divisions combined. The Hindus and Sikhs had invested all their capital in the colony districts but the June 2 announcement neither gave any of these areas to them nor held out any hope that the Boundary Commission would even consider the case for their inclusion in East Punjab.

The basic principle of division of the assets and liabilities of the Government of India had not been agreed upon, but signs were not wanted that these would be divided on the basis of population in the two dominions. The same uncertainty was left to hang over the terms of reference of the Boundary Commission. The June 2, 1947 announcement had only mentioned population and 'other factors'. But the 'other factors' were not precisely defined. However, hope had not been given up that the British would do justice after all to the Punjabi Hindus and Sikhs who had been their valiant allies for over a century. This hope, however faint it was, was kindled into a bright one by the announcement of Mr. Alexander Butler, the deputy leader of the Conservative Party, published in the papers of July 17, 1947, which said, "In the partition of Punjab, we have left the Sikh community almost exactly divided between one side of the frontier and the other. It is to be hoped that the Boundary Commission will be able to arrange the boundary so that the shrines and properties and other things held so dear by the Sikhs may be amassed as far as possible within one frontier." Similarly, Mr. Arthur Henderson's elucidation of 'other factors' including the location of Sikh shrines in the Punjab came as a tonic to the weakening nerves of the Punjab minorities. These remarks again misled the minorities into believing that the districts of Lahore and Sheikhupura at least would be included in East Punjab. Judging from what happened later on, it was the cruelest joke ever played upon the minorities by these two gentlemen. The 'Dawn' in its issue of July 19, 1947 from New Delhi, under the caption 'Double Crossed Again' threw out the challenge to the government that the League would defy the award of the Boundary Commission if extraneous factors were taken into consideration, regardless of consequences. Mr. Jinnah and Liaqat Ali Khan forwarded strong protests to Lord Mountbatten and the British Government. Lord Mountbatten decided to visit Lahore to meet the Boundary Commission after Mr. Jinnah's protest was lodged. The League leadership was manoeuvering to back out of the commitment that 'other factors' be taken into consideration while demarcating provincial boundaries by abusing the British statesmen who expressed views on the meaning of 'other factors' and succeed they did in the end.

During his visit to Lahore (Sunday, 21st of July, 1947), Lord Mountbatten gave a bit of his mind to the members of the Punjab Partition Committee during his conference with them for their failure to stop the veritable war of statements, whereby spokesmen of the contending parties had been threatening to 'resist' the award of the Boundary Commission should this fall short of their expectations. Lahore being a disputed district, he asked both sides to keep ready to move up or down by August 10, 1947.

So far as the Hindus and Sikhs were concerned, it was not a question of their resisting the boundary award, but of protesting to their own Congress leaders and the British Government that they should not deviate from their original plan of June 2, 1947. The British Plan did not make it clear as to what the status of the Boundary Commission would be and whether its award would be final. What it stated was that the Boundary Commission will be appointed in consultation with various parties who will also be consulted in the matter of fixing the terms of reference. For reasons best known to them, the British Government declared in parliament that the award given by the chairman of the Commission would be final. This was nothing short of amending its plan in a material aspect. It was moreover humanly and physically impossible for the chairman of the Boundary Commission to sift the huge mass of 251 memoranda which had been presented to the Boundary Commission and give his award and yet he was to be the final authority in this matter of life and death of the minorities!

The Hindus and Sikhs prepared their case with consummate skill and took their stand on the terms of reference of the Boundary Commission which was instructed to demarcate the boundaries of the two parts of Punjab on the basis of ascertaining the contiguous majority areas of Muslims and non-Muslims. In doing so, it had to take into account 'other factors'. Among 'other factors', which the Hindus and Sikhs stressed for consideration, the position of Sikhs had a place of pride.

'Out of a total of 4,150,000 in the whole of the British India, they number 3,750,000 in the Punjab. They have their homeland and holy places in Punjab. They are rooted in the soil. The province owes its prosperity very largely to their initiative and courage.'

'In Lyallpur, the Sikhs, along with other non-Muslims, form a majority in a large tract of the district. If this tract could be included in East Punjab along with Sheikhupura and Montgomery, the solidarity of the Sikhs can, in the main, be preserved.'

'An important consideration urged is the location of the Sikh shrines. The greatest of these is the Nankana Sahib, the birthplace of the founder of the Sikh faith. It is situated in the Sheikhupura district.'

'Considerations of strategy justify that one of the big rivers should serve as a boundary. The Chenab is suggested as that river.'

'Not the least important among 'other factors' is the necessity of conferring economic security on both parts of the province. The wheat produced in eastern Punjab of notional division is 29 per cent of the total production as against 71 per cent in the western part. The quantity of wheat available per capita is 15.7 lb against 26.3 Ib in the western part.'

'The figures of rice production show greater disparity. The percentage of rice production in the eastern part is 14.4 per cent as against 85.6 per cent in the western part and the quantities per capita are 1.6 lb and 6.5 lb, respectively.'

'As regards cotton, the out-turn of American cotton in the eastern part is only about 40,000 bales as against 6,99,000 bales in the western part.'

'The disparity in the production of the two parts is accentuated by the density of population in the eastern zone. It is 327 persons per square mile as against 264 persons per square mile in the western part.'

'On the basis of the notional division, the population of eastern

Punjab is 40.6 per cent of the total population while the area allocated to it is 35.6 per cent and the canal-irrigated area is only 18 per cent. Eastern Punjab, is, therefore, entitled to a further area in order to make it economically stable and to provide room for the expansion of its population.'

'Industry and commerce also flourish, largely due to non-Muslim enterprise. In Lahore district, there are 186 power-driven factories. Of these, only 78 are owned by Muslims. In the Montgomery and Lyallpur districts, out of a total of 27 and 57 factories, only 8 and 15 factories, respectively are owned by Muslims.'

'In Lahore alone, there are 97 banks. Of these, only seven are run by Muslims. These banking offices have a working capital of ₹100 crores. Muslim capital is only half a crore. Lahore has 18 insurance offices. No more than two are managed by Muslims. Trade and commerce of the city is mainly in the hands of non-Muslims. Last year, non-Muslims paid ₹5,19,000 as sales tax. Muslims paid ₹66,300.'

After expounding these general considerations, the Hindu and Sikh memorandum proceeded to prove their claim regarding each division and district asked for. "The inclusion of Ambala and Jalandhar divisions, predominantly non-Muslim in composition, was justified on the ground of population and contiguity as well as 'other factors'. Land in these divisions is owned mainly by non-Muslims who have a large stake in the economic structure.

'Amritsar district of Lahore division has a majority of non-Muslims, who form 53.48 per cent of the population. Out of the total land revenue of ₹16 lakhs, Muslims pay ₹3 lakhs. The ownership of urban immovable property is indicated by the figures of the urban immovable property tax, which show that Muslim assessees numbering 1,500 pay about ₹71,800, while non-Muslims, numbering 6,292, pay ₹38,33,754. The figures of sales tax are even more significant. Muslims pay ₹27,500 compared with the non-Muslim share of ₹10,30,648. The Muslim proportion comes to about 3 per cent.

'Gurdaspur district, which has an excess of 26,435 Muslims

over the non-Muslim population, is also claimed. The excess of Muslims over non-Muslims appeared for the first time in 1931. The census figures of 1931 (when the Congress Hindus had boycotted the census under the direction of Mahatma Gandhi) and 1941 are held to be unreliable and 'other factors' weigh heavily in favour of non-Muslims. They have a much larger share in the ownership of agricultural land than Muslims. The only railway and road communication linking Kangra, Kullu, Lahaul, and the States of Chamba, Mandi and Suket with Amritsar and the rest of the Punjab passes through Gurdaspur. If Gurdaspur falls in West Punjab, the whole system of communication would be disrupted.

'The headworks of the Upper Bari Doab Canal are situated at Madhopur in the Pathankot Tehsil of Gurdaspur. This canal is the lifeline of the major portion of Gurdaspur, Amritsar and Lahore districts. It is, therefore, essential that the district where the head-works of the canal are situated should form part of East Punjab.

'The district is closely associated with Sikh history and tradition. Guru Nanak, founder of the Sikh religion, was married at Pakhoki, now called Dera Baba Nanak, and died in Kartarpur in Shakargarh Tehsil.

'In regard to Lahore district, it is urged that the Muslim majority is not as large as shown in the census figures of 1941. According to the census, Muslims number 10,27,772 and non-Muslims 6,67,603.

'Land revenue figures show that out of a total number of 1,81,710 landowners, 98,813 are non-Muslims and 82,897 are Muslims. This gives a percentage of 54.4 to the non-Muslims and 45.6 to the Muslims. Out of a total of ₹17,46,440 paid as land revenue, non-Muslims' share forms 68 per cent.'

Thus says Sir George Abell: 'About 66.7 per cent of the cultivated land in Lahore district is in the hands of the Jats, a great majority of whom are Sikhs....the communal majority in the district belongs to the Muslims, but a great many of them are town-dwellers, menials, landless tenants and very small peasant farmers, and the typical zamindar of the district is the Sikh Jat.'

'For almost identical reasons, Hindus and Sikhs demand the

inclusion of Sialkot, Gujranwala and Sheikhupura in East Punjab.'

The memoranda did not evoke the response which they merited. Sir Stafford Cripps, the Chancellor of Exchequer's assurance that though it was not possible to give each community the complete and undiluted self-government which had been given to the two major communities, Britain's sense of care and interest for the welfare of Sikhs and Pathans would remain undiminished was honoured more in the breach than in the observance.

Sir Cyril Radcliffe did not preside over any of the ten sittings of the commission. Arrangements had to be made to provide him with verbatim reports of the daily hearings. Members of the commission were to report only in an advisory capacity; the last word rested with the chairman.

Meanwhile, the Punjab Partition Committee had been carrying on its work about the division of personnel between the East and West Secretariat. By August 6, 1947, all appointments had been made. Between that date and August 10, the two parallel secretariats began to function in different wings of the Civil Secretariat. On August 10, both secretariats were to close down, to re-open nobody knew where for, this depended on the award of the Boundary Commission. Everybody now, therefore, began to look up anxiously to the award that Sir Cyril Radcliffe was to give. The fate of Lahore hung in the balance. During the anxious and long days of waiting, the few Hindus and Sikhs left in Lahore would be found discussing among themselves each and every detail of the historic June 2 statement and the interpretation put on it by Mr. Henderson, Mr. Butler and by Lord Mountbatten himself in the press conference which he held after the June 2, 1947 announcement. Every para, phrase and even every sentence used to be analysed and interpreted by them till many of them knew by heart, almost the entire relevant portions in various announcements. The arguments used to be interminable. Lord Mountbatten's two sentences in particular used to be discussed threadbare, the one where he had said that the Sikh themselves, through the Congress asked for a division of Punjab. For his part, he had been amazed when he looked at a map of Punjab to find that Sikhs' own demand would mean their division into almost two equal parts. And, by way of condolence over this 'suicide' on their part, he had added that he had real sympathy and admiration for them. Another remark made by him, which was believed to be only witty on that occasion, was that the Labour Government was unlikely to agree to a division based on property. From what transpired later, it is now clear that Lord Mountbatten was terribly honest and frank and not at all witty when he had made that remark. His condolences conveyed to the Sikhs in advance on this occasion were definitely pointing out that they were going to be deprived of their sacred shrines and their cherished homeland. What a pity that the masses did not take his words on their face value and what a greater pity that the Congress and some Sikh leaders continued to mislead the Central Punjab's Hindus and Sikhs in general and the people of Lahore in particular into the belief that river Ravi, if not river Chenab, was going to be the boundary line of East Punjab. Had the people taken Lord Mountbatten's words as just simple words not concealing anything and had the top leaders straightaway told the masses that the notional division was not likely to be changed in any material respect, there was enough time for Hindus and Sikhs of West Punjab to organise a planned exodus from the dangerous areas of West Punjab or definitely to make up their minds to settle permanently in Pakistan as loyal subjects. In the latter case, they would have ceased to look to Delhi for guidance and help and would have entered into some sort of pact with the Muslim League about minority safeguards. All bloodshed and massacres would have been avoided.

There was a sudden announcement late in the second week of August that the Boundary Commission Award had been postponed beyond the I5th of August, 1947. The fatal award made public two days later on the 17th of August, 1947—a day which will remain for all times the blackest of black days in the lives of the Punjab Hindus and Sikhs. The award was really an example of a mountain in labour giving birth to a mouse. No other consideration except that of population of 1941 census was given weight in the final award. The line was arbitrarily drawn here and there, and almost the entire Lahore district was given over to Pakistan. There was no natural boundary line over a considerable part of the territory. Even the predominantly Hindu and Sikh tract of Shakargarh Tehsil along the river Ravi near Darbar Sahib was not included in East Punjab.

There was a deep gloom among the Hindus and Sikhs and a visible joy on the faces of Muslims. To come into possession of Lahore which had been built to its present position by others was a resounding victory indeed for them in their battle of wits with the Congress leaders. The division of India was now an accomplished fact—thanks to the grit of their leaders. It had been proposed in June 1947 and completed on the I7th of August, 1947. Though freedom had been celebrated in Delhi and other centres in India through illuminations and unfurling of national flags and distribution of sweets, no amount of phrase building or linguistic acrobatics on the part of the Congress leaders could conceal the fact that the cutting up of the whole of India through peaceful methods into two and the bisecting of the two provinces was the worst disaster that had ever overtaken the country in all its history.

Why was the award not announced on the given date? Was it because the Congress and the League leaders and Lord Mountbatten did not want to mar the joy of freedom celebrations or was there any change made in the award by the governor-general after consultation with the British Cabinet at the last moment? Or was the tentative award discussed in confidence with the governor-general by Sir C. Radcliffe and changes made in it on the suggestion of the governor-general? Who were the people behind the Purdah (curtains) who pulled the wires during the last crucial days of the formulation of the award? Was the delay in announcement really due to the delay in printing or was it merely a camouflage intended to cover the last-minute changes made in it by the governor-general or Sir C. Radcliffe? These questions can only be correctly answered by Lord Mountbatten or Sir C. Radcliffe. Probably, these will remain unanswered till their deaths. By admitting that changes were made at the last minute,

Sir C. Radcliffe would be confessing to his partiality or weakness, and Lord Mountbatten would be adjudged guilty of interference in a matter which was not his concern. Whether Mr. Jinnah or Pandit Jawaharlal Nehru knew anything or had anything to do with the final shape in which the award was announced also remains an unsolved mystery. There are, however, several stories current in Delhi circles. All in the absence of a confession, by one of the principal actors in the tragic drama have to be taken as false; some of these even may be the result of wish being father to thought.

According to one version, Sir C. Radcliffe was prepared to give the district of Lahore, including the city of Lahore, to East Punjab, provided the entire district of Gurdaspur was given to Pakistan. In doing so, the chief consideration with him was the consideration which every Englishman had in his heart, that of surrounding the State of Kashmir almost on all sides with Pakistan. There are three routes to Kashmir. The two had already been engulfed in Pakistan. The third remaining route was the Pathankot-Kathua-Jammu Road, which, though not very well developed, was capable of being developed into a first-class route from the Indian dominion to Kashmir. If this remaining lifeline of supply to Kashmir were handed over to Pakistan, there would have been no choice left to the Maharaja of Jammu and Kashmir except to accede to Pakistan or be devoured by it. India would also have recognised in that case the futility of any help it could render to Kashmir in fighting against invasion or accession to Pakistan. It is said that Pt. Jawaharlal Nehru was not prepared to give up this last remaining route from India to Kashmir. That fact also explains why Sir Bakshi Tek Chand, who was in charge of preparing the case for the Boundary Commission, was asked to take special pains to collect data regarding the inclusion of Gurdaspur district in East Punjab. This story, if true, shows how shortsighted was our choice. With Lahore in the hands of Hindus and Sikhs, the dislocation and disruption of the Punjabi Hindus' and Sikhs' social, economic, educational and cultural life would not have taken place on a scale on which it had taken place now. The flocking of refugees to Delhi would have been avoided. The gruesome happenings in Punjab like the slaughter of Sheikhupura and the massacre of Baddomalhi, etc., would not have taken place. In a trial of strength in the emergency that arose owing to the invasion of Kashmir by Pakistan, India would have taken the straight course to meet it—by marching its troops through Pakistan to Kashmir.

According to the second story current in Delhi, Sir Cyril Radcliffe had drawn his boundary line along the river Ravi in its northern sector and then along the Bari Doab canal running straight through Moghulpura Canal Park and on to canal fall on the river Ravi near Niaz Beg. The entire territory east of Bari Doab Canal, the Model Town and Lahore Cantt., and a considerable part of the district of Lahore would have gone to the Indian dominion. It is said that this was agreed to by Lord Mountbatten, but was finally rejected owing to the last-minute intervention of Mr. Abell, private secretary to the viceroy. Mr. Abell was a Punjab civilian and very much pro-Muslim in his sympathies. He, it is further said, had also sought the help of Mr. Ismay who had come from England as adviser to the viceroy.

The Muslim League circles believe and one of their ministers gave public expression to it in a speech in London that the original award had made river Sutlej as the boundary line and had given the districts of Jalandhar and Amritsar to Pakistan.

Of all the three versions given above as to what happened when the Award was made, the last appears to be the least credible of all.

The Hindus and Sikhs of the Punjab are 'oxen' indeed because ever since India chose Lord Mountbatten to be its first Governor-General and Pakistan chose Mr. M.A. Jinnah in preference to the former, it was believed by them that the Boundary Commission Award would be more favourable to them than to Pakistan. Lord Mountbatten would, it was said, exercise his influence with Sir Cyril Radcliffe to get justice done to the Hindus and Sikhs of Punjab. Little did they know the character of an Englishman. Placed as he was, the correct reading of the situation would have been that he would rather go out of his way to help the other party to place his impartiality beyond even the merest doubt. Be as it may, this idea had sustained the morale of thousands of Lahories and lakhs of Punjabis, both Hindus and Sikhs, for several weeks.

Sir Cyril Radcliffe had merely drawn a blue pencil across the map and said that the west of the line belonged to Pakistan and east of the line to Hindustan. By doing so, he thought he had solved the problem. Actually, he created more problems than could be solved both for Pakistan and Hindustan. While he gave a well-defended North-West frontier to Pakistan, to India, he merely gave a thin line across fields and pastures to be later on delineated on the ground by mutual concord or quarrel. That such quarrels are a daily occurrence is proved by stories of border raids, both along India's eastern and western frontiers. There are disclosures of Pakistan's infiltration into Indian Union territory on the Assam-East Bengal border in violation of the mutually agreed boundary line in terms of the award. In this connection, the disclosures made by a Calcutta editor in a memorandum submitted to the West Bengal government are startling indeed. One of the disclosures made was that the Survey Department misled Sir C. Radcliffe by supplying him with imaginary and false maps which did not fit in with geographical facts. It is also alleged that the map which was relied upon by Sir C. Radcliffe was a different one from those given to the Hindu members of the commission and these in their turn materially differed from the maps supplied to the Muslim members. If true, this just revives the memories of what Lord Clive did in his dealings with Raja Uma Chand. The history has repeated itself, but at what a terrible cost to the Hindus of Bengal.

In a note for the consideration of the Boundary Commission, an advance copy of which had been sent to Pt. Jawaharlal Nehru for his perusal by Lala Yodh Raj, reasons had been adduced for the creation of a 'tenable' frontier for Hindustan. The Boundary Commission paid not the least heed to it. An extract from this note reproduced below will be read with great interest because some of the fears expressed therein have unfortunately come out to be true. Afghanistan is not acquiescing in the conquest of Pathan territory within the Indus and Durand line made by the British or earlier by

Lala Yodh Raj, who put little faith in the statements that everything will 'stand still', took steps in time to safeguard the economic interests of his people. He planned wisely and executed boldly the measures to retrieve as much as was possible from a hopeless situation and, succeeding admirably in this task, prevented what would otherwise have been a colossal crash and an utter ruination of unfortunate people.

the Sikhs. They are aspiring to the recovery of Peshawar and the entire tract to the west of the river Indus. Secondly, the Muslim League rulers of Pakistan in their Pan-Islamic zeal actually called in to their aid the Pathans as foretold in the note for the invasion of Kashmir. They have also recruited the highland Muslims in large numbers to defend the Muslim lowlanders of the Pakistan zone and, finally, Pakistan has now begun to hob-nob with Soviet Russia, apparently to the detriment of Indian, U.S.A. and British interests. All these things were correctly forecast in the note the relevant extract from which is given below:

'One of the attributes of a sovereign state is to have frontiers. But when a new state is formed, the task of defining its frontiers and of seeking new agreements with its neighbours is not at all easy. In such a case, it is not a question of changing or drawing a boundary line, but of making one where none exists. The new sovereign state of Pakistan to be created in the North-West of India will, however, start with an advantage.'

'It has a well-defended frontier in the north-west and its frontier to the north with the Kashmir state is fixed by specific treaties and defined by traditional usage with boundary posts and customs barriers, excepting in wild and inaccessible regions of no economic or strategic importance in the hills. The frontier along the tribal areas of the N.W.F. and Balochistan has been evolved by the British through a long series of experiments and adjustments. The 'frontier' or India's boundary under this system is not so much a line as a zone, with the tribes and principalities forming buffers between British India and Afghanistan. Hundreds of crores of rupees have gone into establishing this frontier. Costly wars have been waged. A system of the grants of annual subsidies to the Maliks and of utilising the local tribes as Khasadars for the protection of roads running through their territory has done much to keep the peace. The pickets and posts along the frontier are stringed about at every bend and corner of the road, and at all the vantage points. These are manned day and night by India's best trained troops and are in wireless communication with the headquarters.

'Considerable attention has been paid to the defence in depth. While Peshawar, Kohat, Bannu, Razmak and Quetta may be considered as the main points on the semi-circle of defence, the pivot goes back far behind to important supply centres in Punjab and Sindh. The whole of the administered areas of the Frontier Province may be really considered as the rear of the defence line which runs through, or is on the fringe of the tribal territory. The Afghan frontier is, thus, at a respectable distance from the administered area. The defences all face towards the North-West and may be compared to the fingers of an outstretched hand. The striking arm and elbow behind is the vast military and economic potential of rest of the British India. The purpose of the troops stationed in the frontier is to absorb the first shock of an attack. Their role is the role of covering troops, which, by holding the first attack, give time to the rest of the Army in India to mobilise and move forward in its support. This is the reason why all the important towns along the railway line and main roads in the Punjab are lined by cantonments. The portion of the Army stationed in United Provinces or Central India may act as the 'Army in Reserve'.

'From the point of view of the defence of British India, as at present, the whole of the N.W.F.P., Balochistan, Sindh and Punjab must be considered as one deeply integrated area, or one unit. All questions, therefore, about cutting a portion of this area to form part of north-western Pakistan zone must be considered from the point of view of the rest of Hindustan. If Punjab is to be artificially divided into two zones, not only the defence requirements of the two zones, but those of the rest of India, must be carefully kept in view.'

'The second main consideration that should weigh with the boundary commissioners is the possibility that with the lapse of 'paramountcy' of the British King, the treaties and agreements of the states and tribal areas with the Government of India may also lapse, unless tribal chiefs voluntarily conclude similar treaties with the new Pakistan government. The question of the defence of north-western boundary of Pakistan may be thrown into the melting pot once again. The work of a century may be undone in a few months.

Will Afghanistan continue to acquiesce in the conquest of Pathan territory made by the British or earlier by the Sikhs? Will they not aspire to the recovery of Peshawar, which is the minimum Afghan aspiration?'

"Then there is another consideration. The Muslim League rulers of Pakistan, in their Pan-Islamic zeal, may not choose to fight against their own co-religionists. They may even call them in to their aid in order to suppress the recalcitrant minorities in their midst. Or the highland Muslims may be recruited in large numbers to defend the Muslim low-landers of the Pakistan zone, in their new frontier along the eastern Punjab and western Bengal. In the case of such an eventuality, western Punjab zone may be considered as having fallen a prey to the Pathans of the frontier and Afghanistan. This will prepare the way for an eventual Afghan-Pathan penetration into India.'

'The fourth main consideration is the possibility, at not a very remote stage, of a flare up in Central Asia between the ever-expanding Soviet Russia and the western Powers like the U.S.A. and Britain in which Hindustan sides with the latter. The North-West zone, in that case, will look like the fist of the hand with the arm cut off. There would be no defence in depth possible for a territory in western Punjab, which, at the greatest depth, is not more than 250 miles. With a friendly Pakistan, several divisions of army could cross the frontier defences and land in Jhelum, where the hills debouch into plains, and where vast deployment of troops for the invasion of the country becomes easy.'

'I have briefly touched these points, but this brief-narration should be sufficient to convince the Boundary Commission about the needs for demarcating a boundary between the eastern and western Punjab in a zone where not the defence of East Punjab, but the defence of the whole of Hindustan zone can be planned and made invulnerable.'

'Boundary pillars and posts across the village lands can never serve a satisfactory purpose. Some natural line must be chosen, such as a river, and a zone must be selected, the inhabitants of which, like the inhabitants of the tribal area between Afghanistan and the administered districts of present Hindustan, can form a buffer between the Hindustan zone and the Pakistan zone. Stationing of troops along the frontier posts at strategic points does serve a useful purpose, but the inhabitants of the zone in which these troops are spread must also be well trained to take up arms in support of the troops.'

'In the Punjab of today, both these conditions are fully satisfied if river Chenab inclusive is made the boundary line of the Hindustan zone. In that case, the tract between the river Chenab and the river Sutlej will comprise within itself a vast bulk of the Sikh population of Punjab, among whom are found India's best trained soldiers. This new tract would be a sort of North-West Frontier Province of Hindustan with the only difference that, in the place of war-like Pathans, it would have members of the war-like Sikh tribes with a much higher standard of education, culture, training and wealth. Even river Ravi as a boundary line between the two zones would be better than a line drawn across fields and pastures between the districts of Lahore and Amritsar.'

'But if Ravi is to be chosen as the boundary line, the whole of Montgomery and part of Multan should be given to the eastern zone, and exchange of the land-holdings of the Sikh peasantry must be arranged to bring them from the scattered districts of Pakistan to thc frontier districts of IIindustan.'

'The provisional division of Punjab into 12 and 17 districts, as announced at present, is highly unsatisfactory from the point of view of defence of the Hindustan zone. The Amritsar district cuts the Bari-Doab tract into two portions. Amritsar district is like a head projected forward, which, by a pincer movement from the north-west and south-west corners of Gurdaspur and Lahore jointly, can be cut off in no time. The Pakistan frontier as at present, delineated obtrudes into Chamba state and districts of Kangra, Hoshiarpur, Jalandhar and Ferozepore, while it surrounds on three sides the district of Amritsar. This is the most untenable frontier to be held by the Hindustan zone.'

'The boundary line should run along river Ravi (and inclusive of it) up to the point where it leaves the Montgomery district. It should then turn south-east to include the Montgomery district in the Hindustan zone. This arrangement would leave only a short length of land demarcated boundary in the south-west of Montgomery district, but for a length of 50 miles, the boundary will run along the natural landmark of a river. Defence in depth could be arranged by continuing Ferozepore, Jalandhar, Ambala as the supply centres in the rear, with other interior towns in Delhi and United Provinces behind, as maintaining basis.'

'The question of delineating a boundary between the two portions of Punjab is not a merely local question which the Punjabis may be left to decide among themselves. On this decision depends the ultimate defence plans of the rest of India. It must, therefore, be viewed from the larger point of safety and defence of the vast subcontinent of Hindustan. The problem before the commission is not that of rectifying the boundary line between the two Punjab zones by the inclusion or exclusion of a few zilas or tehsils here and there, but of creating a new North-West Frontier Province of India in place of the old one. The tract between the Chenab and the Sutlej is the ideal tract to be selected for this purpose. The irreducible minimum would be the tract between the Ravi and the Sutlej. In no other way could a spearhead of defence be created for the safety and security of Hindustan.'

□

8

The League and the Congress Leadership

The Congress held a historic session on the banks of the river Ravi in 1929 under the presidentship of Pt. Jawaharlal Nehru and declared independence or 'Purna Swaraj' to be the goal of India. On the 26th of January, an Independence Pledge drafted by the working committee of the Congress was read and broadcast. Twenty-sixth of January became the Independence Day for India ever after that year. Eleven years later, in April 1940, the Muslim League also met at Minto Park on the banks of Chhota Ravi in Lahore and declared independent Pakistan as Indian Muslims' goal and everyday after that date, agitation for Pakistan became stronger and stronger. Mr. Jinnah's demand for Pakistan at first was considered by the Congress, the Hindu Mahasabha, and the Sikhs as 'fantastic non-sense' as was the Congress Committee's own demand for independence regarded by the British rulers earlier. Fifteenth of August, 1947 saw the fulfilment of the aspirations of both the Congress and the Muslim League—the former got a dominion about the name of which its followers were not able to come to an agreement with the result that their offspring remained unbaptised for a long time and the latter got Pakistan which was called by its critics 'truncated and moth-eaten'. The Congress had lost the historic bank of river Ravi from where its leaders had proclaimed India to be free. None of them is now 'free' to go there without danger. The 'moth-eaten and truncated' Pakistan in the course of two years has made an astonishing recovery. She has a favourable balance of trade with hard currency areas and with India to the tune of crores of rupees. The prices of necessaries of life are lower there and the cost of living of the workers has gone down. The centuries-long accumulated wealth of the Hindus and the Sikhs, they have been able to secure just by the way. In Punjab, every time a youngster purchases a commodity from a shopkeeper, he is given a small additional quantity known as 'Jhunga'. Pakistan has got the palatial buildings of the Hindus and the Sikhs and their vast and fertile lands and commercial and industrial properties as a 'jhunga' along with freedom. But with this difference that whereas the 'jhunga' usually is only a very small part of the total quantity purchased, this 'jhunga' in the shape of moveable and immoveable properties of the Hindus and the Sikhs exceeds the total value of Pakistan by several times over. The jugular vein of India's two principal industries, cotton and jute, is held in the pincer grip of Pakistanis. They can throttle these at any time they like and though, in the process of doing so, they are likely to receive a grievous wound—their wound is not going to be fatal as in the case of India. Their state is a closely knit empire in the east, cemented by the religious fervour of Islam. It is a religious State or a Muslim state governed in accordance with the ideology of Mohd.—the Prophet. The rulers of Pakistan are hard-boiled practical men, who know their own mind very well, and who also know in their dealings with Hindustan as to which side of the bread is buttered. Their chief spokesmen, at present, Nawabzada Liaqat Ali Khan and Sir M. Zafarullah Khan, are known for their astuteness, sharp-wit and keen intelligence. Sir M. Zafarullah Khan, as an advocate and experienced administrator with many long years of experience in representing the government at various international conferences, is one of the cleverest men in Pakistan. The way in which he turns a hopelessly bad case into a good one and the manner in which he gets the ear of the world to whatever grievance he is ventilating at the time is simply marvellous. India's representatives are able and sincere, no doubt, but, without meaning any disrespect to them, it must be confessed that they look like pygmies before a giant when pitted against him.

India as the elder brother started with all the advantages that the elder brother has at the time of division of family property, but the elder is now diminishing rapidly. There has been considerable deterioration in her economic and social conditions and if politically the Nehru Government has succeeded in establishing peace in the country, that has been established through curtailment of the civil liberties of the people in the name of 'security of the State'. The government has made it absolutely insecure for individuals, groups and parties opposed to it, to openly write, speak or agitate for the ventilation of their complaints and redress of their grievances. It has, in the short period of two years, lost the confidence of trade, industry and investors. For new resources, her own credit in the loans-market is at zero, while the cash balances have dwindled at an alarming rate.

The present rulers of India do not know their own mind, and in spite of professions to the contrary, they are not prepared to learn and profit from other peoples' experiences. Pt. Nehru is the Prince of Denmark in the government who is not sure even up to this time about 'to be or not to be', of many a crucial problem. One thing is, however, certain and clear and on this, Pandit Nehru knows his mind very well. It is to give way before Pakistan on any issue on which they become obdurate. Take the case of dispute over canal water in Punjab. According to the Boundary Commission Award, all the natural resources available in each of the two parts of the province were to belong for exploitation to the province where these were situated. The East Punjab government, on account of this decision, made up their mind to utilise the water of the canals going through their own territory for irrigation of the parched land of Amritsar district, where quite a large number of refugees have been settled. They took appropriate action to warn the Pakistan government in time to arrange for alternative sources of irrigation for the small area which would be, thus deprived of canal water. Pakistan raised hell and ran straight to the Government of India. The Government of India, paying little heed to the reasons which had prompted the East Punjab government to take this action, at once, took the matter in their own hands. The Punjab government was ordered to defer action in the matter and to justify this uncalled for interference, Pt. Jawaharlal Nehru entered into a sort of agreement with Pakistan, which her representatives have now completely repudiated. The compliment paid to Pandit Jawaharlal Nehru by Pakistan at that time was a good pointer of what they thought of him. "The great Brahmin in his great mercy came to the rescue of Pakistan." In other words, they considered him not to be a good administrator or leader of his people, but only a charitably disposed 'Brahmin'. What a compliment! The same tale was repeated on the question of the payment of ₹50 crores in cash to Pakistan which had by then invaded a part of India and, thus, was at war with her. It is true that Pt. Jawaharlal Nehru *countermanded* his first orders on the intervention of Mahatma Gandhi, but constitutionally speaking, was there the least ground for doing so?

It is now known to the general public that on the Kashmir issue, the Government of India, in full consultation with the Diwan and the Maharaja of Kashmir, had decided to march their armies to Lahore in order to strike at the concentration points in West Punjab from where the Kashmir offensive was being mounted by the so-called Azad Kashmir forces. All preparations had been made. The units of the army had moved to their proper places. A national militia was organised and even the date was fixed. The British personnel in West Pakistan was advised by their government to move to secure places from the threatened area. When all preparations had been made and even the zero hour fixed, Pt. Nehru changed his mind. Perhaps Lord Mountbatten and the English Commander-in-Chief had some hand in changing his plans. It is said that Pt. Jawaharlal Nehru hastily called another conference of the parties concerned and *countermanded* his previous orders. "Where will you stop?" "What would be the outcome?" He fired this and other such questions in quick succession on his military advisers. "Where will the petrol come from, the petrol I say," and before waiting for a reply, he gave out his final orders to cancel operations.

It is now crystal clear that the long delay caused in tackling the Hyderabad issue was directly due to Pt. Jawaharlal Nehru's own vacillation. It is true again that Lord Mountbatten and the English Commander-in-Chief had much to do in creating the spirit of hesitancy on the part of Pt. Jawaharlal Nehru. But that he should be always ignoring the advice of his own deputy prime minister and listening to what the foreigners said does not show him in a very good light as the first Prime Minister of India. What cost in men, money, material and misery would have been avoided had Pakistan been smashed on the very first occasion when she had by her wanton act of aggression put herself beyond the pale of civilisation. I do not know how far the story is correct, but it is being openly told that even on the night of 13th September, 1948, when all preparations for police action against Hyderabad had been made and orders given to the troops to march at the appointed time, Pt. Jawaharlal Nehru's mind once again changed. It is said that General Bucher, the Commander-in-Chief, saw Pt. Jawaharlal Nehru at midnight and told him that according to the news in his possession, Delhi was going to be bombarded by Hyderabad planes and that there would be fire and devastation in all the important cities of India and that the armies of Pakistan might also march in. Pt. Jawaharlal Nehru, at once, rang up the defence minister and asked him to postpone operations. The defence minister is credited for once as having shown pluck and courage by telling Pt. Jawaharlal Nehru that the zero hour had passed and that the Hakimpet air field had already been bombed by our planes. Pt. Jawaharlal Nehru threw down the receiver in great chagrin. The story may or may not be true, but all Indians felt happy when the Government of India decided not to renew the term of Lord Mountbatten as Governor-General for a further period or to allow to the English Commander-in-Chief to continue in his seat of authority.

In the matter of the return of refugees to their own dominion, the policy of the Government of India up to July 1948 was just as harmful to India's interests as her bungling in the matter of Kashmir. No efforts were spared in preventing the exodus of Muslims from India and particularly from Delhi and in giving full latitude to the

Muslim evacuees to return to India and to take possession of their properties. What happened in Dehradun, Haridwar, Saharanpur and Meerut also happened, though on a larger scale in Delhi. In Delhi, according to an announcement, more than lakhs of people returned to India in a few months' time. Meanwhile, thousands of houses belonging to them were kept sealed awaiting their return. Lakhs of Hindu and Sikh refugees, men, women and children, who were pouring into Delhi at that time were forced to live on the roads or in hastily improvised camps in great misery. Pt. Rameshwar Dayal, the present Deputy Commissioner of Delhi, was the Deputy Commissioner of Saharanpur during those critical days. To him goes the credit of persuading the butchers of Saharanpur and Jwalapur to once again return to their homes and hearths and settle on the sacred banks of the Ganges. In Dehradun, the refugees were maltreated by the U.P. authorities and on one occasion, a few of them were even shot at when trying to occupy the evacuee's property. Thus, for eleven months after the creation of Pakistan, the Government of India had not taken any action, whatsoever, to prevent the flow back of those Muslims who had gone to Pakistan looking upon that country as their sacred land. Lakhs of Hindus and Sikhs had come out of Pakistan and more were being driven out everyday, but the Government of India did not take any action to stop this forcible eviction of their own kith and kin from the other dominion.

The Indian government's policy, with regard to the Hindu and Sikh evacuee property left in Pakistan, is as difficult to understand as her policy with regard to the bringing in of refugees and dumping them helter skelter, anywhere and everywhere in India. I was in Lahore when it was announced that the proprietorship of evacuees' property, movable or immovable, would remain inviolate. It was at that time announced that even if a caretaker was left in charge of vacant property, that property would not be considered as evacuee property and the owner could come back to it when he felt secure. Putting faith in this announcement, I left my own bungalow at Lahore and my village land in charge of duly accredited men. In fact, there were three persons living in my bungalow situated on Sandha Road when I came out on a 15-day leave to Amritsar, but the Pakistan authorities later on changed their mind and turning out my men, gave possession of the bungalow to a Muslim, whose monthly pension was only ₹50/-, but who possessed the great qualification of having given his daughter in marriage to a Muslim M.L.A. of Hoshiarpur. I will not go into the question of evacuees' property here. This is discussed in a separate chapter. But what is intended to be pointed out here is that whereas the Pakistan government has gone forward step by step to confiscate the Hindus' and Sikhs' property amounting to ₹4 thousand crores, according to an incomplete estimate, the Government of India has not still finalised its plans with regard to the property of those Muslims who have permanently gone to Pakistan. "Heads I win and tails you lose" is the motto of action for Pakistan which our government has timely accepted.

Preparations for Pakistan

Mr. Suhrawardy is one of those Muslim League leaders on whom fell the choice of inaugurating the first battle of Pakistan in Calcutta. His 'Direct Action Programme Day' on the 16th of August, 1946 unfolded for the first time the pattern of the war which the Muslim League wanted to wage against Hindus and Sikhs for the attainment of her objective. It was organised with a diabolical cunningness. Several days before, all the 'Bastis' (colonies) around Calcutta and Howrah were seen full of up-country dangerous-looking men moving hither and thither suspiciously. The great Calcutta-killing set a new standard in barbarities, excelling even the barbarities committed by the pagan kings, Changez Khan and Halaqu Khan against the Muslims in Asia Minor.

Mr. Suhrawardy, with a view to overawe the Cabinet Mission, referring to the Congress demand for a united India, said: "This I call insanity induced by the lust for power. The Cabinet Mission is not so blind as to entrust the destinies of India to this gang." Mr. Suhrawardy also maintained that there was no Muslim today whether he was a renegade from Sindh or Punjab, who was against Pakistan. He also held out a threat to the Hindus and Sikhs by adding: "There is no room today for anyone in this country who does not believe in Pakistan."

There is always more vine and vinegar when Muslims fight the election issue. This is what Nawabzada Khurshid Ali Khan wrote about Sir Feroze Khan Noon on 21.11.45: "Sir Feroze Khan Noon seems to be daily excelling himself in the use of indecent language. This kind of language is in consonance with the expression he has used in his book on India called 'The Scented Dust'. I wish the local leaders of the Muslim League would realise how the dignity of their organisation is being lowered by this new convert to their creed. Sir Feroze Khan Noon's obvious anxiety is to prove the genuineness of his conversion."

The zeal shown by the use of abusive language, both towards his Muslim opponents and towards Hindus and Sikhs, however, did not help Sir Feroze Khan Noon to the 'Throne of Premiership' in the Punjab, even though he did succeed in winning the elections. After the result of the election was announced, Mr. M.A. Jinnah told an Associated Press of India's correspondent on 10-12-45: "I remain convinced that Pakistan is the only hope for a fair and lasting settlement of the Indian problem. The deadlock in this country is not so much between India and the British. It is between the Hindi Congress and the Muslim League."

The Muslim League having won the Central Assembly election prepared itself to win the provincial elections in 1946 again by the use of bold invectives. Speaking of the Indian National Congress, one of their leaders said in a statement published on 18th January, 1946 in the Tribune of Lahore: "They are not going to give us an honest and straight fight on the paramount issue of Pakistan, but their cowardly policy of remaining as the hidden hand behind some non-descript Muslims, pushing them up and financing them under the false label of nationalist Muslims will be repeated." Speaking of the Ahrars, the Khaksars and other parties, he remarked, "Mushroom gangs with false labels are nothing but the henchmen of our enemies."

Mr. Jinnah was in a defiant mood after cent percent success of the Muslim League in the central elections. "The Congress had run away," he said, "in the first round of the battle, when they did not put up a single Congressite Muslim against the Muslim League, but instead supported the so-called 'Nationalist Muslims' and gave them lakhs of rupees of the black market meant for black purposes. We secured cent percent success in the elections and, what is more, the bulk of our opponents lost their securities. Some of them also saved some money that the Congress gave them. We won the first round of the battle."

Mr. Jinnah had won the first round of the battle and he soon won the second round with an even more resounding success. After the issue had become clear as to who could authoritatively speak for the Muslims, it was only a question of persisting in his demand to win Pakistan. The Sindh Hindus realising the danger of being left alone, owing to the weakness of their leaders in their fight with the Muslim League, raised their feeble voice in favour of being allowed to have 'Sind Hindustan' comprising Karachi, Hyderabad and Thar and Parkar districts in which they had the clearest majority. The voice of Shamdas P. Gidwani was, however, drowned in the chorus of disapproval raised by the Congress Hindus themselves.

The Muslim League was now becoming aggressive all over the country and on all occasions whenever there was an opportunity of making itself felt. As early as on 28th January, 1946, the Muslim students of D.A.V. School, Allahabad hoisted the Pakistan Flag on the school building and in a free fight with the Hindu students and teachers inflicted injuries on the headmaster and scores of Hindu students. The Muslim girls seeking admission in the Punjab University had begun adding Pakistan to their addresses.

The Muslim League had become the single largest party in the Punjab Assembly. Had the Governor of the Punjab called upon the leader of the party to help him in the formation of a stable ministry, the League leader would have called upon the Congress, the Akalis and the scheduled caste members to cooperate with him on the basis of an agreed programme for the administration of the province. Preliminary parleys were held but there could be no compromise between the Sikhs and the Muslims and, unfortunately (in the light of events that happened afterwards), the governor entrusted the formation of the ministry to the Congress-Unionist Coalition. Perhaps the history of Punjab would have been a little different if the Muslim League majority had been appeased by being entrusted with the running of the government. The Congress leaders who had always followed the policy of appeasement towards Muslims, however, felt shy of doing so on this occasion.

Even the Sikhs were not satisfied with the new set-up of things brought about by the intervention of Maulana Azad. The Nawab of Mamdot, referring to the League-Congress and League-Akali talks for forming an all-community government, said, "For days on end, the Muslim League party leader carried on negotiation with the Congress and Akali parties. He offered to the Congress, to nominate its members and likewise proposed to the Akali Party to nominate its members from amongst the Sikhs. What better method could be adopted by the League to establish a government which could command the confidence of all the communities? But the Congress rejected the League offer." The rejection of the League offer by the Congress was called by him as 'cheating the Muslims of their due rights'.

On the other corner of India, in Assam also, similar things were happening. The Muslim League advised immigrants from East Bengal to spread out in Assam, and to cultivate all the wasteland available there. Mr. Abdul Matin Chowdhury, ex-Minister, speaking of this threat in March 1946, called this a Satyagraha or civil disobedience against the Congress ministry of Assam. From the figures given out in the Indian assembly, it appears that the League pretty well succeeded in its efforts. As many as 3 lakhs of Muslims from East Bengal squatted in Assam and took possession of the Assamese lands, their homes and hearths in numerous villages and even of their women-folk.

Mr. Attlee's speech, as reported in the *Civil and Military Gazette* of 22.3.46, created a grave alarm among the Muslims who for the first time realised that the British government had already been shaken and might be stampeded by the Congress into leaving the country. Speaking about this, Mr. Jinnah said, "We are prepared for the very worst and no amount of maneuvering, threatening, coercion or bullying is going to make us swerve by a hair's breadth from our resolve and demand of Pakistan". He held out dire threats and said, "If the British government fails to assess and appraise the situation properly and play into the hands of the Congress, it will be a tragedy of which there has been no precedent in the history of India." Even the Muslim states were not lagging behind in creating a reign of terror for the Hindus and Sikhs. Highway men began to enjoy state protection in Hyderabad. Arabs—an important element in the state—armed to the teeth with guns and daggers, began roaming all over the state and even at the slightest provocation from the Hindus outcame their daggers from the scabbards or bullets from their guns.

By May 1946, the Muslim League had perfected its propaganda machine and chalked out a secret plan of action. At the time of Shimla Conference, League volunteers coined a new slogan emitting fire and violence and it soon became their most popular slogan all over the country. "Kaise Loge Pakistan?", "Jaise Liya Tha Hindustan".

Conferences, processions, demonstrations, violent speeches and a spate of statements now became the order of the day in the country. The more the Congress, the Hindu Mahasabha and the Sikh leaders spoke against Pakistan, the more violent became the demand of the Muslims. The atmosphere in the whole country was surcharged with dangerous elements. The law and order was balanced most precariously on the edge of an abyss. The lead in these demonstrations was given by the people in towns who were ready to 'demonstrate' against someone or something on every occasion. The goonda element was soon coming to look upon these as golden opportunities for arson and loot. But instead of launching upon a campaign of repression of these outbreaks of communal frenzy, the new Government of India childishly put their faith in the hope that the gathering clouds will be miraculously swept out of the sky by constitutional changes. "Only the British had to leave and everything will be all right" was the slogan of the Congress leaders. As against this, Nawabzada Liaqat Ali Khan was of the opinion that "If Pt. Jawaharlal Nehru thinks that he can free India by the slogan 'Delhi Chalo', then he is sadly mistaken. India can only attain freedom through Pakistan." Subsequent events showed that Congress leaders were wrong and Nawabzada Liaqat Ali Khan was right. A call for 'truce' on the basis of Pakistan, elimination of British in India and India for Indians was made by Mr. Jinnah while speaking at a reception given in his honour by the Memon Chamber of Commerce in Bombay on March 27, 1947. "Pakistan is coming nearer and nearer. Therefore, let us now call for a truce and let us agree on Pakistan. It is better to divide and flourish than to be united and destroy everything. There is no other alternative. United India will only result in destruction."

Mr. Jinnah, by calling for a 'Truce' for the first time, officially admitted that his followers were waging a war against the Hindus and Sikhs in India.

Viewed in this light, the historical perspective of the past few months became quite clear. The League first gave an ultimatum in Delhi when blood-curdling threats were held out to the Hindus and minorities living in predominantly Muslim areas. Visions of the blood orgies of Halaqu Khan and Chengez Khan were conjured up. This was the first stage in the declaration of war, i.e., the ultimatum. The second stage was the open declaration of War on August 16, 1946 through 'Direct Action Day'. 'The Great Calcutta Killing' which followed was the first battle of the war.

The war declared on that day was still raging. In eight months of this war, the League had seen many ups and downs, but their general staff was always well prepared to meet any situation. After all, you cannot win all the battles in a war. In the latest battle in the North and South-West Punjab, they had a sweeping victory, mainly through the surprise and swiftness of action with which the battle was planned and launched.

The ultimate object of all warfare is not the destruction of life and property or even the destruction of the armed forces of the enemy but the *overcoming of the will of the opponent.* Losses are inevitable and the general staff coldly calculate in advance the losses in material and manpower that their people will have to bear before they can overcome the will of the opponent and smash his morale. The general staff is never sentimental about it and is never carried away by emotion. They rarely visit fields of battle. If they did so, their judgement would be warped or influenced by local conditions.

The third stage of war is for one party to call for a truce. Usually, it is the stronger party that offers truce, the weaker party sues peace conditionally or unconditionally.

Mr. Jinnah had shown expert leadership. The quality of the staff work put in was of the highest order. He did not even once visit the 'battlefields' of Calcutta, Bihar, Noakhali, Mukteshwar, Rawalpindi and Multan. By keeping himself aloof from the din and turnmoil of 'battles', he was coolly and calmly planning to win the 'war' and overcome the will of his opponents. The Hindu leaders, on the other hand, committed blunders. In the first place, they refused to take the ultimatum seriously and wishfully looked upon it as a mere camouflage. In the second place, even when the war was declared, they refused to see in it anything but a 'phoney' war that could be won by mere statements and fasts. Even when the war was raging with full fury, they refused to see behind it, a master plan and a military direction. They were busy organising ambulance work and missions of mercy for the victims of battle, but they still refused to believe that battles were being fought and that these were a part of a planned war that was raging in the country. The offer of a truce should have opened eyes to the grim realities, but alas, it was not to be!

Mr. Jinnah was succeeding to all intents and purposes. He had won the first round. The will of his opponents was weakening. By successive stages, they had accepted his one condition after the other. But these were the days of unconditional surrender and signs were not wanting that this would also be forthcoming not before long unless, in the meantime, a miracle happened and practical-minded Hindus and Sikhs took the place of visionaries and idealists who lived more in all-Asia, all-world plane than in an India of warring factions.

But that was not to be. The visionaries continued to be the leaders of the Hindus and the Sikhs and there was every sign that in their keen desire to control India's destinies in the shortest period of time, they would even make an unconditional surrender to Mr. Jinnah.

Mr. Jinnah had threatened utter destruction unless his demand for Pakistan was conceded. This utter destruction was now taking place in the peaceful Punjab. The idea that the British were planning to leave India spread from one corner of the country to the other and the struggle of the peaceful masses against the 'onslaughts' of the political parties, each bent upon carving out an empire of its own began. The North-West and South-West corners of Punjab were in turmoil. History began to repeat itself. The 4th Century had witnessed the downfall of the Roman Empire in Britain. Life and property then became insecure and here and there, villages were burnt or deserted. The Romanised Britons found themselves left to their own devices and had to fend for themselves against heavy odds. The British themselves were now planning to leave India and the peaceful masses found themselves exactly in the same position as the Britons had found themselves when the Romans had left.

Under the British, if there was no liberty, there was peace and so real had been the 'Pax Britannica' that in a population of 40 crores, the only people trained to fight were the soldiers of the regular army. This was one reason why the civilised Britonised Hindus were falling so easy a prey to the invaders of their homes and hearths. They had taken the continuation of the protection of the British legions for granted. They infringed no law and kept not the simplest weapons for their defence, much less firearms which their invaders had in large quantities. Whole villages were levelled to the ground and their innocent Hindu and Sikh inhabitants kidnapped, converted or slaughtered. The priests and the people alike were put to the sword; the flames were crackling all around their places of worship. Public and private war became the rule rather than the exception.

The change of Raj, as the history of the world shows, has always been accompanied or preceded by bloodshed and anarchy. We were witnessing another spectacle of the same type again in the twentieth century. It was hoped that one hundred years of British rule in Punjab had made the people civilised and democratic. But alas, it was hoping against hope! Barbarity, hooliganism and mobocracy still ruled the day. "Religion in danger", the old war cry of the reactionaries still struck a sympathetic chord in the hearts of the fanatics, and nobody, except the politicians, felt safe. The masses of all castes and creeds wanted peace and one could hear their murmur that if Swaraj was to be obtained at the sacrifice of their hearths and homes and the honour of their womenfolk, that Swaraj was not worth having as it was no better than the "Suar Raj"—or the rule of the swine. But there was no one strong enough in the country to so canalise this low murmuring of the multitudes as to make it swell into a mighty roar. Already, the Hindus of Calcutta and Noakhali were openly saying that British Raj was better than the Muslim Raj; the Mohammedans of Bihar were saying that the British Raj was better than the Hindu Raj. The Sikh sufferers of Sindh were decrying both the Hindu and the Muslim Raj. A camel was asked what it preferred: going uphill or coming downhill. "Har do lanat" (accursed be both) was its reply. The Indian camel, docile as he is and can be led by the nose, was beginning to say, "You ask me for a choice between the Hindu and the Muslim Raj? Accursed be both, say I."

Not more than three weeks had elapsed since Khizar was compelled to resign by his compatriots of the Muslim League, and already the saner elements of all the three communities, Hindus, Muslims and Sikhs were saying that Khizar Raj was better than the Raj of the Chengiz Khans of Sargodha, Rawalpindi and Multan. "For forms of Government, let the fools contest; whatever is the best administered is the best." Was the poet not right when he wrote these lines? This was the question which every Punjabi put to the other in those crucial days. In a country of warring factions, the government that could protect person and property and the honour of the womenfolk was far superior to a government that could propose and plan a paradise on earth, but could not protect the people and their possessions. "Had the leaders of India and Pakistan got guts strong enough to successfully shoulder the responsibility that was going to be passed on to them in less than a year and a half's time?" was another question they used to discuss. The portents were that they would stagger under the weight—the Pax Britannica had made them so weak.

The highest leaders and the biggest parties were now waging a ceaseless battle at Delhi in the shape of bans and budgets that kept the whole country on tenterhooks. The constituent assembly had met in Delhi. It had up to that time only constituted itself and there was no sign that it would constitute anything else. The bungling on the one side and the wrangling on the other were producing bickerings all over the country. Even the intelligentsia, like the masses in Bengal, Bihar and Punjab, began to say that the rule of the old Lord Wavells was better than the rule of the new Lord Waverers who did not know their own mind.

□

9

Professions and Practice

The 'Quit India' movement of the Congressmen launched in the year 1942 had resulted in their quitting their homes for the jails. The worst period of the war was, thus, spent by them behind the bars. When they came out, they were thinking as to what should be their line of action in their political field. Mahatma Gandhi's inner voice was not yet so strong as to be audible. The British had overthrown the mighty Germany of Hitler and Macado's Empire lay sprawling under their feet. They had survived the most serious war in their history, but had been severely mauled in the course of this fight with the Swastika and the Sun. Britain was yet licking her wounds. There was a silent respect for the qualities of British character that had made British victory possible against seemingly heavy odds, but there were doubts as to their farsightedness in killing the 'Eagle' in the west and in eclipsing the 'Sun' in the east for the sake of the 'Bear' that was now raising its ugly head and sharp claws. In no uncertain manner, she was now claiming the entire land mass in Europe and Asia as her special domain.

India had made a magnificent effort to help Britain win the War. Her industrial production reached its peak and her army was the best to the east of Suez Canal. Nearly two million people had joined it. This time it was not only a question of helping the Allies to win the war, but a question of repelling a direct attack on India. India paid a heavy price for her defence of the Allies and for her own defence from the enemy. The Bengal famine was a direct result of it. The great inflation of currency was also directly connected with the war. The urban people had borne heavy strain due to high cost of living and deprivation of many amenities that make life worth living.

The British having prostrated their mortal foe, there appeared to be no chance of another power to compel her to give up her possessions in the east. India was the most valuable diadem in the crown of His Majesty, the King Emperor and it seemed the most remote chance that the British would give up India without a fight. There was, thus, a sense of frustration that had taken hold of the Indian leaders. It was in this atmosphere that when the question of elections was first mooted, the 'Council of Provincial Congress Committee' of the United Provinces expressed a vague opinion that the Congress should not contest elections. Among those present in the meeting of the council held on September 6, 1945 at Allahabad were Pt. Jawaharlal Nehru, Mr. Narender Deo, Mr. Sri Prakash, Mr. Sampurana Nand, Mr. Rafi Ahmed Kidwai, Dr. Katju and Babu Purshottam Das Tandon.

Mr. Sham Dass P. Gidwani on the same date interviewed Mahatma Gandhi and Sardar Vallabhbhai Patel and tried to impress upon them the desirability of the Congress not opposing the candidates of the Hindu Independent Party and the Hindu Mahasabha. What a difference it would have made in the destinies of India if Mahatma Gandhi had listened to the advice of Mr. S.P. Gidwani! Mr. Jinnah was on the war path and his two-nation theory was finding credence not only with the Muslim masses, but also with the British government. If the Hindu Mahasabha had been left to contest elections on the Hindu tickets, it could have in the later negotiations played a much more useful role than the Congress did, handicapped as the latter was because of its professions to speak for the whole of India including the Muslims. The Congress President, in an interview, reported in the Lahore papers of 9th September, 1945, expressed the determination of the Congress to make no more overtures to the Muslim League. This was just timely. There was the need now in Indian politics of what is known as the 'Tilak tradition of realism', which was evidently something utterly different from the woolly idealism of Pandit Jawaharlal Nehru and the tragic pessimism of Mahatma Gandhi. On account of its weak and indecisive attitude on the communal issue, the Congress Party in the legislature could neither protect the just interests of the Hindu community nor prevent the threatened partition of the country.

It was in the same vein that Mr. Hardayal Devgun, honorary Organiser of the All India Hindu Mahasabha, pressed upon the Congress leaders the necessity of making a common cause with the Hindu Mahasabha on the question of the country's freedom. "Mr. Gandhi, Mr. Bholabhai Desai and Mr. Rajagopalachari go to any length in appeasing Mr. Jinnah and other Muslim League leaders and are never tired of playing the sycophant to them, why should they not take the Hindu Mahasabha into confidence on a matter which is as dear to the Sabha as to the Congress?"

The Congress Working Committee, however, decided later on to contest the elections and formed an election board. This board did not have any representative of Punjab, North-West Frontier Province, Sindh, Assam and Bengal on it, though there were two representatives of Madras. The Hindu Mahasabha also began to move in the matter. An election board for the Punjab including the writer was formed by Dr. Syama Prasad Mukherjee, the then president of the All-India Hindu Mahasabha. The rank and file of the Congress Working Committee were beginning to despair of the prospect of attaining the Congress ideal of free India. The 'realists' in the Congress's inner cabinet were already endeavouring to convert their colleagues to the idea of accepting Mr. Jinnah's demand. The outward facade of an absolute hostility to a divided India was scrupulously maintained only to mislead the Hindu masses. When Mr. Jinnah insulted the Congress President, Maulana Abul Kalam Azad, by styling him as a 'show boy' of the Congress, there was a moment of repentance among the Congress leaders at their too much sychophancy of Mr. Jinnah. This is what one of them was reported to have said: "We did our utmost to appease the League. Our most esteemed leader went to their leader repeatedly, but in vain. How can we forget the insulting language employed by the League leader against our president. Until a full-fledged apology comes forth from the person who employed those disgraceful words, the Congress would keep itself away at a distance of 10 thousand miles from such an organisation whose leader can employ those words... with Muslims he would deal, he said, but with the Muslim League, never." No sooner were the words spoken than they were forgotten. Not only did the League not apologise for its president's insult to Maulana Azad as a 'show boy' of the Congress, but it continued to heap further insults on him and other Congress Muslims. The words were forgotten as soon as these were uttered and the Congress leaders not only continued to deal with the League leaders, but also took special care to come as near to them on the conference table as was possible. Ten thousand miles became hardly ten inches in actual practice.

It is not my purpose to go into the details of how the election was fought and with what results. The Congress had come out triumphant under the skilful generalship of Pt. Jawaharlal Nehru who made the most of the I.N.A. cause for winning over the electorates, nor is it the place to discuss the instructions issued to Congress volunteers on October 13 at Ellore by Dr. P. Sitaramayya telling them that they should carry lathies to defend themselves if occasion arose and that nonviolence was a weapon designed to be used only against the British to wrest the country's freedom. Among the Congress candidates seeking the elections most in favour were those who had been to jails. Intellectuals and persons of constructive ideas who had made their mark in trade, industry and banking were given the go-by.

Mr. C. Rajagopalachari this time was not exactly a favourite with the Congress masses. Among the charges levelled against him as that he had increased the strength of the Muslim League.

He was finding it difficult to address public meetings. At one such meeting held in Bombay, rotten eggs and tomatoes were thrown at him. He was, however, very strong in his defence. As reported in the papers of October 15, 1945, he had said that the whole argument that he gave strength to the Muslim League was wrong. Had not Gandhiji accepted his proposal and also declared that he stood by them? Did not Gandhiji discuss the matter with Mr. Jinnah? How could a thing become wrong if done by him and right when done by Mahatma Gandhi? What he did was the right thing and independently also he had the support of Gandhiji. The public memory is always short and it was not for Mr. C. Rajagopalachari to remind them that it was he himself who had brought about a transformation in the views of Mahatma Gandhi on the question of Pakistan.

The Muslim League was the only opponent of the Congress left in the field, but the Congress did not accept its challenge and did not put up Congress Muslims to contest the Muslim seats.

The League leaders, sure of their success, were at this time busy, indulging in cheap jibes at the expense of the Congress leaders, a sample of which taken from the papers of the 7th of October, 1945 is reproduced below:

"We are accused of having made no sacrifice for our goal. I am afraid we cannot contribute that sort of sacrifice to which the Congress seems accustomed.

Thanks to obtain leadership, to sit like a goat under the police lathi charge, then to go to jail, then to complain loss of weight and then to manage release. (Loud laughter).

"I do not believe in that sort of struggle, but, when the time for suffering comes, I will be the first to get bullet shots in my chest.

"We are also accused of being tools of the British government, but the Shimla conference should open the eyes of those who have listened to such accusation against us.

"May I know from the Congress, where is its 'Quit India' resolution? Why did Congress leaders stoop to a position of humiliation in Shimla? Telling Lord Wavell: "Sir, you are our leader," (laughter) "We will run your executive council."

"The main object was to get the League ignored and to bring some trouble on me and Lord Wavell. They were licking his feet to install them in the 'Gaddi' (throne). This was the state of affairs then.

"Where is the 'Quit India' resolution? The main object of the Congress is to grab power by getting the 'gaddi' and then to crush the Muslims with British bayonets.

"However, our demand for Pakistan is clear. The areas in

which Muslims are numerically in a majority, should be grouped to constitute an independent state."

Mr. William Cove, M.P. in an election-eve message to India said on October 29, 1945, "I am sure that no British government, much less a Labour government, would agree to the partition of India on a communal basis. Everyone knows that this is politically and economically impossible."

"In the face of Indian realities, a vote for Pakistan is a vote against independence. Independence is the major issue and one of the problems facing India can be solved unless India is free."

But Mr. William Cove had addressed this appeal to the congressmen and not to the Muslims who, as it later on transpired and was clear even on the eve of elections, had all been won over to the idea of Pakistan.

Mian Iftikhar-ud-Din, the much fawned-upon president of the Punjab Provincial Congress Committee, in a statement had declared: "After being in the Congress for two or three years, I was convinced that there was no place for the Muslims in that organisation". He regarded Pakistan and the country's freedom as inter-dependent as one could not be secured without the other and vice versa.

Mr. Abdul Sattar Sahib, a member of the All-India Congress Committee and of the Tamilnad Provincial Congress Committee, was another Muslim Congress leader who denounced the Congress and joined the Muslim League.

Chaudhry Mohd. Hassan, M.L.A., who was officiating as leader of the 'Punjab Assembly Congress Party' and had sometimes acted as the opposition leader in the assembly, also left the Congress and joined the Muslim League (November 20, 1945).

In order to allay the fears of the Hindu electorate Dr. Gopichand Bhargava, Maulana Dawood Ghaznavi and Dewan Chaman Lal gave a signed statement to Dr. Gokal Chand Narang when requesting him to withdraw from the assembly contest in favour of the Congress candidate, in which they said, "We do not subscribe to Pakistan. Not only do we not subscribe to it, we are vehemently opposed to it. In view of what we have stated above, it is incumbent upon us to oppose, and we are bound to oppose, both of these proposals wherever and whenever they are brought up."

With this assurance given, the path for the Congress steamroller was made clear and all opposition vanished in thin air. In fact, there was no election contest so far as the Hindu seats were concerned. The Congress candidates were returned unopposed. A rout had taken place in the Hindu Mahasabha ranks. It was the proud boast of Congress workers that they could have a lamp post or a dog elected by giving him the ticket.

Of course, the statement was a two-edged sword. It showed how utterly demoralised had the Hindu voters become, hypnotised as they were by the Congress leaders. They had given up thinking on their own account, but it was also a slur on all those people who had been given the Congress ticket for the elections.

Bombay had been the stronghold of the Congress and money had flown like water into the Congress coffers from there ever since Gujaratis became the leaders of the Congress. But in order to coerce them further into giving votes and more money on the eve of election, dire threats were being held out by Congress leaders. Mr. Morarji Desai, former revenue minister in the then Congress government in Bombay and, at present, the home minister of Bombay, speaking at a reception given by the president of the Surat Chamber of Commerce said on January 21, 1946, "If businessmen thought that the national government will not impose taxes on them or will not do anything against them, they are wrong. Even a people's government will have to do many things which are contrary to their interests. More taxes may be in the offing for them on the national government assuming charge."

Between mantras, maulanas, memorials and ministries, the tempo of public life in the United Provinces was also going up. But there was considerable dissatisfaction with the arbitrary manner in which the Provincial Congress Parliamentary Board had selected candidates for the provincial assembly. Twenty-six political prisoners headed by Prof. Shibbanlal Saxena threatened to go on a hunger strike as a protest against this (January 26, 1946). The 'rebels' won with flying colours after a two-day heated debate in a meeting of the board. As many as 12 changes were made in the list of the Congress nominees drawn up by the election board and among the day's rejections was Mr. Feroze Gandhi, son-in-law of Pt. Jawaharlal Nehru (February 2, 1946).

After the elections were over, a hunt in full cry for ministerial jobs was soon in progress and it promised to become a scramble in blatant defiance of sporting (or should one say) political ideals of the Congress. In Punjab, Diwan Chaman Lal secured 33 votes of the Congress Assembly Party to support his candidature for the leadership of the party and his party members met Maulana Abul Kalam Azad, the then Congress president and told him that he should be elected as leader of the party because he had the support of the majority. But the mandate of the Congress president that the Assembly Party should accept Lala Bhim Sen Sachar as their leader was finally accepted. Punjab was made the special charge of Maulana Azad. He was a scholar as well as a politician. His 'letters' were just published in time. Enquiries made by the-United Press revealed that Maulana Saheb had received a sum of ₹75,000 by way of royalties for one year for the publication of these 'letters'. It is presumed that with the exception of Mahatma Gandhi, no other Indian writer had obtained such royalties for one publication.

The greatest sales took place in the days of elections and every candidate for a Congress ticket in those days would place orders for a very large number of copies of the book and pay in cash. Whether the books were actually distributed or read is not the point. The main thing for such people was to woo Maulana Azad by telling him that for his book, there was a very great demand all over the country. It is doubtful whether after the elections, the book ever sold in such large numbers.

Maulana Azad's intervention in Sindh affairs after the elections was most unhappy. It resulted in the weakening of the Hindus of the Congress Party and in the strengthening of the Muslim League. The efforts of Mr. G.M. Syed and Mr. Gazdar for a coalition with the Congress proved abortive mainly because of Maulana Abul Kalam

Azad's refusal to agree to this. Mr. Gazdar met M. Abul Kalam Azad and Mr. Asaf Ali who showed anxiety to help him in re-establishing Muslim unity in Sindh.

In the struggle for political power after the elections, the Punjab Hindus in general and Sikhs in particular were very much perturbed about their future. In spite of the election campaign of the Congress, the intelligentsia among the Hindus and Sikhs had a lurking fear that the Congress would betray them. A silver-lining in the clouds, however, was the openly expressed pledge of Mahatma Gandhi that the British would divide India only over his dead body. People had great faith in what Mahatma Gandhi said and they thought that being the sincerest man in India, he had literally meant what he said. Mahatma Gandhi's silence during these crucial days was a little disquieting. Sikhs under the leadership of Master Tara Singh began to contact Mr. Jinnah and other Muslim League leaders of Punjab with a view to explore avenues of a compromise on the question of Pakistan. Pandit Jawaharlal Nehru, on this, issued a statement attacking him and accusing him of "sitting at one and the same time on about fifteen stools." Master Tara Singh's reply to this was:

"Suppose I am what Pt. Jawaharlal describes me to be, how does this clear the position of the Congress, which it took in the Poona Resolution, and which gives the right of secession to units, conceding thereby virtually the right of secession to the Muslims in Punjab or, in at least, the greater part of Punjab?"

"Then what about the famous Gandhi-Rajaji offer to Mr. Jinnah and the subsequent talks with him? Pandit Jawaharlal's present statement also confirms what I had said. It is reported that Pandit Nehru reiterated that particular areas which wanted to part company would not be compelled to remain. This is the position which vitally affects the position of the Sikhs."

"Panditji specifies the charge against me by further saying, 'If he (myself) wants to go into the League camp, he is welcome to do so.' So, it is clear that he is perturbed on account of my having had a talk with Mr. Jinnah. Why does the Pandit imagine that one who does not see eye to eye with him must be run down? Why does the Pandit think that one must follow either the Congress or the League and nobody has a right to choose an independent course or to express an independent opinion?

"I refuse to be bullied in this way and *woe be to me if I am at the mercy of a gentleman of the mentality of Pandit Jawaharlal.* I must and shall secure an independent position for the Sikhs in an independent India. I refuse to admit that I need a permit from Pandit Jawaharlal to see Mr. Jinnah or anybody else."

"We must be much more responsible at this most critical juncture. We shall either have independence or there will be chaos, and every responsible man must do all he can in order to secure independence and avoid chaos. But if responsible gentlemen resort to personal attacks and abuses at this critical moment, they will add another complication to an already complicated situation." Master Tara Singh's words were prophetic and three years had to elapse before he and the world realised *how woe did come to him as soon as he was at the mercy of Pandit Jawaharlal Nehru*.

Having won the elections, the Congress was now in the supreme position to dictate terms for a political compromise to the British government and the Muslim League on behalf of 37 crores of Hindus. The political map of India was going to be recast and, hence, the coming two years were considered as crucial ones in the history of this land. The presidentship of the All-India Congress Committee was going to be the key position in the new set-up of things. There were two candidates in the running, Sardar Patel and Pt. Jawaharlal Nehru. Majority of the Provincial Congress Committees had voted in favour of Sardar Patel. He had been only once elected before as the president of Congress, though Pt. Jawaharlal Nehru had had that honour several times. The result was considered as foregone. But there was considerable activity behind the Purdah (curtains). Maulana Azad saw Mahatma Gandhi in Bhangiwara, New Delhi, and somehow got sanction for Pt. Jawaharlal Nehru to be appointed as his successor in preference to Sardar Patel. It was openly said in the papers that Maulana Azad had advised Mahatma Gandhi to run down Sardar Patel's name in favour of Pt. Jawaharlal Nehru on the plea that if the former became the president, it would create difficulties for the non-Hindu elements in the Congress. Mahatma Gandhi's intervention at this stage proved a turning point in India's history as the later events clearly showed.

Mahatma Gandhi embodied in himself two personalities which are usually regarded as incompatible..... the Mahatma and the politician. The masses in India and elsewhere who admired and reverenced him believe that both personalities reached their apotheosis in him. But it had not always been easy to decide where 'Mahatma' had ended and the 'politician' begun. Was this act of Mahatma Gandhi in turning down the majority vote of the Provincial Congress Committees the act of 'the politician' or 'the Mahatma'? Apparently, it was the act of 'the Mahatma' because Sardar Patel like a faithful disciple acquiesced in it without protest.

Being the Congress president, Pt. Jawaharlal Nehru now became the leader of the interim government and Acharya J.B. Kriplani later on became the Congress President. The presidentship had now lost much of its charm. It was said about Acharya J.B. Kriplani that he was the 6th of the 7 brothers and belonged to a strange family of highly 'strung individuals'. Two of his brothers had embraced Islam. The highly strung Acharya proved true to his reputation and had to resign from the presidentship before his normal span of office had ended.

In a statement issued on 24-2-47, Acharya J.B. Kriplani said, "I would also like to caution that the country and the Congress are not identical. This fact is in a way realised by many people. The ministers are more under the influence of the members of the permanent bureaucracy than under the influence of the people. The members of the permanent bureaucracy have been trained and perfected in the art of serving and in flattery. They can easily win over the confidence of the ministers and, in fact, they have succeeded in doing so. But the ministers must regard the interests of the people as paramount."

Stories of a rift between the Congress ministers of the interim government also began to circulate in those days. But, for the dominant influence of Mahatma Gandhi, these differences would have come up to the surface and shown clearly to the people that the Congress leaders were after all human beings and not 'Gods' or 'devtas' from whom they should expect impossible things.

The White Paper by the British Labour government and the debate in the House of Lords took the Indian leaders off their guard. Till that time, they had been repeating slogans of wresting power from unwilling hands and of preparing the country for the next fight. Very few of them had ever dreamt that they would be called upon to put their professions to practice. The jail convictions to the credit of many of them had raised them to the pinnacle of leadership, without the necessary mental equipment or physical grit. Gandhian politics had made our public life an easy hunting ground for the self-seeking politician behind the shield of the Gandhi cap and the spinning wheel. Democratic ideals and healthy political principles had been smothered under the non-violent baton of the Mahatma and the 'chhota Mahatmas'. Blind obedience to persons had been given a premium over loyalty to principles and ideals under the Gandhian teachings. The White Paper now put them on their mettle. The lurking suspicion in the minds of the Indians that Britain never seriously meant to leave our country was now removed. There was a ring of honesty in the words of Premier Attlee, Lord Pethick Lawrence and Lord Listowel, who spoke on behalf of the British Labour government, that was absent in former British statements. Their statements were categorical, unambiguous and brutally blunt. India was now on the thread of a new era and the question that began to be asked by all was whether our leaders stood the test of new values and fitted in the new scheme of things. In the past, they had appeared to the world and the Indian public as the cream of India's manhood ....bold, courageous, sincere and selfless. The rank and file of the Indian masses had followed their lead unquestioningly and blindly. There was created a halo around most of them which was out of all proportions to the real worth of many. The need of the hour now was for these leaders to face facts and to grapple with the day-today problems, national as well as international, with a sense of realism coupled with responsibility. The politicians had now to become statesmen. Not many of them were qualified for this role of leading the country into the new era of freedom and progress, but party interests and party discipline necessitated that all of them should remain where they were and be rewarded suitably for their past sacrifices.

The Congress leaders, utterly surprised at the new situation that had obtained when they could not hold out threats to the British government nor to the Muslim League, now began to hold out threats to all and sundry. There was the threat to business management uttered by Morarji Desai. Pt. Jawaharlal Nehru on April 19, 1947 while addressing the All India States Peoples' Conference, warned the Indian states that if they did not come into the constituent assembly, then they would be treated as a hostile State by the country. Referring to Sheikh Abdullah, he uttered the following prophetic words: "When I think of him behind prison bars, I hang my head in shame. All I can say now is that Kashmir is like a flame in my heart. Some day it will bring forth some result." That flame has brought forth important results, though not to the exact liking of Pt. Jawaharlal Nehru, because in achieving the results, he has not followed the course of action suggested to him by his military advisers. Criticising Pt Nehru's Gwalior speech as thoughtless as he happened to be a member of the Interim government, the Muslim League leaders said, "If the spirit of arrogance exhibited by Pandit Nehru is to be the guiding principle of the Congress policy in the future, then God help those who may choose to cast in their lot with the Congress." The Muslim League members of the interim government in their turn were as indiscreet as Pandit Jawaharlal Nehru. They were making inflammatory and provocative statements in season and out of season for months without break and openly inciting lawlessness in provinces, like Punjab, the Frontier and Assam. Mr. Liaqat Ali Khan, Mr. Abdur Rab Nishtar and Raja Ghazanfar Ali were the leaders of this 'war of statements' on the Muslim League side. The Congress members of the central government, however, did not openly criticise their colleagues. That would have brought matters to a head and ended the evil. But they thought discretion to be the better part of valour and only 'discreetly' brought, it seems, such utterances to the notice of Lord Wavell.

Dr. Rajendra Prasad, who is known for the sanity of his views, made a statement as late as on May 15, 1947, "We should be prepared to save our country from division. We should be prepared at the same time to save non-violence from being destroyed in this melee. Those of us who have been serving you all these years have felt that the step taken by us is the correct one. Therefore, do not misunderstand us, but give us strength and support, which we need so badly in these critical times." There were misgivings in the country as to what the top leaders would do to preserve India's unity, but Mahatma Gandhi was doing his best to defend them. He would quote homely examples and by trying to flatter the masses keep them quiet. "If the people at the top went wrong, it was certainly open to and it was the duty of those at the bottom to remove the wrong top even as he would remove an umbrella which appeared to be at the top, but which was sustained by him. Thus, Pandit Nehru was at the top. But, in reality, he was sustained by them. If he went wrong, those at the bottom could remove him without trouble," was the counsel of perfection he gave to a group of demonstrators in Bengal.

On May 24, 1947, it was reported from New Delhi that Mahatma Gandhi had joined hands with Mr. Jayaparkash Narayan to oppose partition of India and to have informed London authorities accordingly. It was again reported on May 31, 1947 that Mahatma Gandhi was not only not prepared to acquiesce in any demand for division of the country, but was prepared to "stake his all to prevent what he considers a grave wrong" and further that there was no difference of opinion between Mahatma Gandhi and the working committee of Congress on this question. Acharya Jugal Kishore, general secretary of the All-India Congress Committee in an interview at Allahabad on the same day said, "If there were to be a choice between transfer of power to the Muslim League or continuance of the British rule, then Congress would prefer the first alternative, though it might leave dissatisfaction in the minds of those who have no more faith in the ability and intentions of the Muslim League." Acharya Jugal Kishore admitted that it might leave the country in chaos and civil war, but, in his opinion, it was better than the continuation of the British rule. Mahatma Gandhi declared in his post-prayer speech on Thursday evening (May 30, 1947) that "Even if the whole of Hindustan is burnt to ashes, I will never concede an inch of India to Pakistan if it is sought to be achieved by coercion or violence." These words of the Congress leaders were brave words, boldly uttered, but none of them including the Mahatma was now in touch with the feelings of the masses in Punjab. They were not living in Punjab and all their sermons had failed to stop the riots. The Hindus and Sikhs of Punjab were undergoing at this time, terrible physical and mental anguish, but were being sustained in their morale by the heroic words of the man whom they regarded as the greatest hero of India. Mahatma Gandhi's sudden outburst of a sentiment on 1st June, 1947 that "Every man should be his own policeman" and the advice and warning of Sardar Patel that people should not look to the police for help and protection, but depend upon themselves, however, sounded to the people as not only ridiculous, but also sarcastic, adding insult to injury. The great leaders obviously, immune from such dangers and well-guarded as they were could hardly visualise the helplessness of the common man in the circumstances to be his own policeman.

Dr. B.S. Moonje, the Hindu Mahasabha leader, alone sounded a note of warning at this time at a press conference held in Poona. He warned the country that they should take it for granted that the Congress leaders who had been granting one concession after another to the Muslim League "to achieve agreement and peace in India" would agree to Mr. Jinnah's demand for Pakistan.

The unexpected happened. Only a few days after his declaration that he would never agree to India's partition, Mahatma Gandhi had accepted it to the utter amazement of the millions of his countrymen who had come to place implicit faith in his words. Dr. B.S. Moonje and other Hindu Mahasabha leaders who had never put trust in the Congress leaders' statements alone proved to be correct. Lord Mountbatten confronted the Indian leaders on June 2, 1947 with his new proposals. At midnight on Monday, the Congress high-command was still in session at Pt. Nehru's residence drafting a reply to the viceroy to His Majesty's government's proposal. Ultimately, the Congress agreed to the vivisection of India. The Congress leaders having accepted the procedure plan of transfer of power by August 15, 1947, Lord Mountbatten emulating the example of Mahatma Gandhi very heroically declared that he will now not tolerate communal rioting in any part of India and had issued instructions to all local authorities to shoot offenders on sight! The rioting continued, no offenders were shot at sight and to the insistent demand of the minorities in Punjab for the declaration of martial law in the disturbed areas, Lord Mountbatten turned a deaf ear.

The question which every Punjabi was asking now was: "Why did not the followers of Purna Swaraj accept the dominion Status at the outset? Had they done so, the British Labour government might have seen to it, not withstanding separate electorates, bureaucratic machinations and League mischief that the unity of India was not impaired and the future greatness and glory of the country were not imperiled. Then a different type of scheme might have emerged from British statesmen's cogitations and conferences. The Congress leaders alone were satisfied because they believed that like the king, they could do no wrong. Not so were the Punjab Hindus and Sikhs who were now to be sacrificed at the altar of 'azadi' of provinces other than their own. A new 'Era of Destruction' or 'Sammat-i-Barbadi' had been ushered in for them on the 2nd of June, 1947.

The greatest surprise, however, that the country received on the evening of June 5, 1947 was when Mahatma Gandhi told at his prayer meeting in New Delhi that he would not fast unto death to prevent the division of India unless his inner voice so dictated. Mahatma Gandhi disclosed that he had been receiving letters asking why he did not undertake a fast and said, "If the Congress commits an act of madness, does it mean that I should die?" A few days later, in his post-prayer speech, he referred to another letter sent to him by a sister that he should retire to the jungle as "it was he who had spoiled Jinnah and turned his head". Gandhiji's only reply was to call upon 'Qade-i-Azam' (great leader) referring to Muhammad Ali Jinnah to make Pakistan too attractive in words and action.

The All-India Congress Committee which met in session at New Delhi passed the resolution on June 15, 1947 accepting the working committee's resolution on His Majesty's government's June 2, 1947 statement by 157 votes to 29. The opposition was led by Babu Purushottam Das Tandon. In all, 218 members were present and 32 members did not vote.

The reaction of the Hindu and Sikh masses to the division of the country, agreed to by Mahatma Gandhi and the Congress leaders was forcefully brought to their notice when the latter visited Haridwar on June 21, 1947. Pt. Jawaharlal Nehru stayed in Dak Bungalow while Gandhiji stayed in Birla House. They were received by high officers and a large number of Congress workers, but while going to Birla House, Mahatma Gandhi was confronted with a huge procession of Hindu and Sikh refugees who had been driven out of their homes owing to Muslim League terror and who now found that there was very little chance of their going back to their home-lands. For the first time, Mahatma Gandhi heard shouts of "Mahatma Gandhi Murdabad", "Nehru Murdabad", and U.P. Government Murdabad. The way was found for them with great difficulty to get out of this crowd. While visiting the Punjab Sindh Keshetra, another hostile mob shouted, "Nehru go back" and the usual 'murdabad' slogans. He was not allowed to continue his speech. There were several points brought to the notice of Pandit Nehru when a few deputations met him later on, in a quieter atmosphere. One was that if the Bihar Congress government could spend lakhs of rupees for protecting the Muslims in the riot-affected areas, why had the Congress given so far only ₹5,000/- for 15,000 refugees in Haridwar? When, in the evening, a public meeting was to be addressed in the Town Hall by Pandit Nehru and Gandhiji, the same scenes of rowdyism were witnessed there and, for the first time, Gandhiji could not hold a public meeting and had to come back to Delhi. It is said and we heard the story in Lahore, though it may not be correct, that one of the rowdy refugees inadvertently touched the hand of the daughter of Pandit Jawaharlal Nehru (Mrs. Indira Gandhi) who was with him on this trip. Pt. Jawaharlal Nehru is said to have flown into a rage and to have threatened to use violence against the culprit on which the latter humbly told Pt. Jawaharlal Nehru, "You have flown into fury simply because my hand has inadvertently touched the hand of your daughter in this large crowd. Can you imagine how deep is the anguish of my heart when I tell you that two of my daughters have been kidnapped and forcibly converted and married to goondas in West Punjab, my wife killed and my house burnt and property looted. It is all well of you to preach non-violence to others, but charity should begin at home."

The Hindu Mahasabha celebrated the 'Anti-Pakistan Day' in various parts of the country and even threatened to launch Satyagraha. There were clashes with Congress workers followed by arrests of the office-bearers and workers of the provincial Hindu Sabhas. Congress was now the government of the country and, therefore, it succeeded in easily crushing the Hindu Mahasabha opposition to the partition of the country. The Congress also turned a deaf ear to the demand put forth by the Hindu public all over the country to resign on the issue and seek re-election on the question of division of the country. Their utter failure to keep their election promises to preserve the unity of the country and their incompetency to safeguard the Hindus and Sikhs, against the well-organised Muslim League aggression, was the theme of conversation in the whole of Hindu India, but of what avail?

□

Hindus and Sikhs waiting at a camp in Pakistan for evacuation into the Indian Union. Note the expressions of fear and anxiety in their faces.

Hindu and Sikh evacuees in Pakistan waiting anxiously to be transported to India.

10

The Protectors of India Seek Protection

The dictionary meaning of the word 'Refugee' is a person who seeks asylum or refuge. The word was first applied to the millions of displaced Hindus and Sikhs who had to leave their homes and hearths in West Punjab and seek temporary asylum in the Indian dominion. Almost every one of them, who came away from West Punjab when the communal riots raised their ugly head in March 1947, had come out with the firm belief that he would sooner or later go back to his own place and, therefore, all that he wanted was a temporary refuge in any corner of India where he could make his both ends meet. The first wave of refugees from the North-West Frontier Province and the Rawalpindi division was able to bring with it, a part of their moveable property. There was at that time no restriction on taking out their cash, silver or gold and ornaments, etc. and, therefore, in the first few months of their stay in India, they kept up the high standard of living to which they were accustomed. The standard of living of a Punjabi townsman is higher than that of a fairly well-to-do person in Delhi and U.P. It is said about the Punjabis, Frontier men and Sindhis that they earn like lions and also eat like lions while the banias and Brahmins of Hindustan earn like lions but eat like jackals. The vested interests in the U.P. towns and in Bombay began to howl in a chorus of disapproval against the spendthrift habits of the refugees. Little did they realise that people being desperate as they are, who see the accumulated wealth of centuries being taken away forcibly from them, become a little reckless in spending whatever little is left with them. It is difficult also to forego speedily, the necessaries and comforts to which a person has been accustomed for the whole of his life. Cheap jibes used to be cut at their expense by the 'locals'. In fact, the word 'sharnarthi' (refugee) was coined by them more as a term of contempt for the new arrivals than as a word correctly describing their position.

The second wave of the refugees consisted of those brave people who had stayed behind hoping for the best in the Rawalpindi division and of the Hindus and Sikhs in the urban areas of the Lahore division. This second wave of the refugees started after the June 2, 1947 announcement from the Rawalpindi division. A heavy exodus of Lahore citizens took place only after the 21st of July, 1947 when, thanks to Mr. M.G. Cheema, the whole of Shahalmi Gate and Papar Mandi area was burnt and raised to the ground. The exodus became a panic flight after the 11th of August, 1947, when wholesale shooting and murder of the minorities with the active help or connivance of the Muslim Police and Balochi troops became the chief task of the Muslim League in all the districts of Lahore division. Lahore soon became empty of Hindus and Sikhs. Thousands of them now congregated at the D.A.V. College Refugee Camp awaiting evacuation through daily convoys. The instructions to the military at this stage were to bring out as many persons as possible in the shortest period of time, but not to allow their trucks to be used for the evacuation of their property except a small trunk or a roll of bed. A regular black-market sprang up both for the evacuation of the personnel and the evacuation of their moveable goods. Some unscrupulous people made fortunes. Of the drivers of the cars, the police and the military detained to protect the convoys, the liaison agency, the organisers of the camp and the custodians with whom the people left their trunks and luggage, a few were in the racket. Later on, when the luggage left behind was retrieved, the owners found that gold, silver and other ornaments had mysteriously been filched away, though the locks were still there. I have met scores of friends who lost their valuables in this way and yet who cannot account for the loss, though they openly name the suspects. The Muslim Military and Police detailed on convoy duty was more 'straightforward' in robbing the Hindus and Sikhs. Their modus-operandi was to halt the whole convoy either near the Shalimar Garden or well on Pakistan side near the border and then to organise a minute search of the whole convoy. The Balochis would get on both sides of the road and ask the people to voluntarily surrender their gold, silver and ornaments, etc., as the export of these without a permit was prohibited. There was no notification to that effect, but the pointing out of a loaded rifle towards any person who showed the least reluctance to comply with the orders was a good enough hint to submit meekly to the illegal demand. After taking away and pooling together for distribution among themselves, later on, the booty so obtained, they would start searching the rest of the luggage. The heavy trunks and beddings would be thrown on the road-side and every article scattered. The only alternative was to strike a bargain and hand over anything to which the soldiers took a fancy or to give cash concealed by the refugees on their persons or in the luggage. Pakistan Military was so bold and reasonable as to agree to accept the payment, if necessary, on arrival at Amritsar. My own man, on occasions, had to hand over money at the Khalsa College Camp for the return of a few articles which the soldiers had taken possession of. It was open loot in those days and stark ruin faced the West Pakistan minorities in the face. Some of the guardians and agents connected with evacuation lost all vestiges of the high moral sense that would have made them true servants of the people. 'Everyone for himself and the devil take the hindermost' was the formula of action, of course, with a few honourable exceptions here and there.

There were many tragic happenings to passengers of convoys of which a few can be recorded here. In early September 1947, when Hindus and Sikhs were evacuated by convoys to East Punjab, a Baloch convoy leader asked the Hindu and Sikh ladies to come in his truck quickly so that they might be kept in between the trucks loaded with their men-folk which were to leave for East Punjab. All the ladies with their belongings hurriedly sat in that truck. Their men-members had already left for Amritsar, but this truck instead of going to Amritsar was mischievously driven away via Shahidganj Gurdwara to Minto Park and then beneath the bridge of Chhota Ravi. The passengers belonged to good families and some of them were wearing ornaments. They were forced to hand over all their ornaments and cash at the point of guns and were in the process of being handed over to the goondas who had assembled there when a truck of Gurkhas which was following the deserting truck overtook it. The women fortunately were saved and brought back to the D.A.V. College Camp. The sight of these women beating their breasts, crying and weeping was pitiable. Shrimati Sita Devi who happened to be present in the Lajpat Rai Bhawan that day heard their tragic story.

On another occasion, the whole convoy was halted for no reason whatsoever near the canal bridge. The military, as if on a pre-arranged signal, retired for smoking or resting to a distant house and the convoy was suddenly surrounded by a Muslim mob armed with deadly weapons. Several evacuees were killed, scores wounded and all property looted. A friend of mine, who was an unfortunate traveller in this convoy and had gone from Amritsar to Lahore to bring his luggage from there, now came back, minus one ear and the tip of his nose and minus his entire luggage.

The fourth wave of refugees consisted of the rural Hindu and Sikh population, mainly the owners and tillers of the soil in the rich canal colonies of Montgomery, Sheikhupura and Lyallpur. They had stayed behind to the last moment firmly resolved to remain in Pakistan if they could be assured of an honourable living. But the Pakistan government had by that time decided to get rid of every one of them. The Muslim mobs organised by the police and the Baloch Military actually hunted them out from every nook and corner of these colonies and forced them to move to refugee camps set up for evacuation. This was a big task indeed and had to be organised on government level between the two governments. The Government of India for reasons best known to them agreed to accept the longer route for the evacuation of the Hindus and Sikhs and allowed the shorter route of Amritsar and Lahore to Muslim evacuees from East

Punjab. Ostensibly, it was done to avoid a clash between the convoys of refugees coming from opposite directions. But the acceptance of a circuitous and longer route by the Government of India for the evacuation of Hindus and Sikhs meant additional terrible strain on those who had to make this journey by bullock-carts and on foot. Both the governments had made themselves fully responsible for the feeding and the protection of convoys passing through their territories. The Pakistan government, however, failed to keep up their part of the bargain and the Indian government meekly submitting to it now was burdened with the problem of providing food both to the incoming convoys of Hindus and Sikhs and the outgoing convoys of Muslims. Some of the foot convoys numbered from 30 to 40 thousand-strong and had to travel a distance of 150 miles to reach Hindustan. It took 42 days for the Hindu and Sikh foot columns numbering 8,40,000-strong to cross the border into India. On the way, the columns were often attacked and sometimes suffered heavy casualties, women and children were abducted and unauthorised search here and there deprived them of the few valuables they carried with them. Next to foot columns, trains carried the largest number of refugees. About 13,62,000 Hindus and Sikhs were carried by trains between the end of August and first week of November 1947. Even the refugee trains were not spared by armed Muslim mobs, though the Government of India on their side took every care to safeguard the Muslim refugees. In addition to heavy military protection provided by them, they introduced stern measures against the villages through which the trains passed and imposed collective fine and curfew on the affected areas along the railway lines.

The fifth wave of refugees consisted of the people stranded here and there in small towns and villages and in other small pockets, who could not move to a bigger town or a railway station without danger to their lives. They were brought out by motor transport by the Military Evacuation Organisation and later on by air. By November 21, 1947, over 21,000 Hindus and Sikhs were flown out from different points in Pakistan to the Indian dominion. The result of these successive waves of refugees from Pakistan to India was that the bulk of the Hindu and Sikh population was brought out from Punjab and North-West Frontier Province thought, at present there are 50 to 60 thousand of them still left in Pakistan. These consist mostly of the Meghs, the Choohras, the Odes and other menial classes whom the Pakistan government does not allow to migrate to Hindustan or those who have since then been forcibly converted to Islam.

The evacuation of Hindus and Sikhs from Sindh had started by sea and rail when the situation in Punjab had taken a serious turn. The Sindhis had, however, ample time and though no wholesale and organised massacre of the Sindhis took place on as large a scale as in West Punjab, Pakistan Muslims made it clear to the Sindh Hindus and Sikhs that their stay in Sindh was not welcome. By hook and crook, by pinpricks, by open violence here and there and by ceaseless propaganda and hymn of hatred preached against them, they made it clear in no uncertain terms to the minorities that their stay in Pakistan was most unwelcome. Here again the looting of the evacuees, the unauthorised seizure of their property, the abduction of their women-folk and close searches of their persons became the order of the day. The Sikh settlers of Sindh were made to go first and hundreds of them were mercilessly butchered before they reached Karachi. They were attacked even in Karachi while seeking shelter in Gurdwaras and soon not a single Sikh was left in the whole of Sindh. By November 21, 1947, nearly 1,23,000 Hindu and Sikh evacuees had been cleared from Sindh by steamer and country-craft. More came by Hyderabad-Jodhpur trains. Of the total population of 13 lakhs Hindus and Sikhs in Sindh, not more than two lakhs had been left behind. The latest act of the Sindh government in arresting and deporting the Mahant of the Sadh Bela Shrine in Sukkur, the holiest of the holies of the Hindus had created fresh terror in the minds of the remaining members of the minority community.

At the time of the partition of Bengal, Shri Syama Prasad Mukerjee had given out in a statement that the partition had saved the sixty lakhs of West Bengal Hindus from utter ruin and destruction that was facing them under the Muslim League Government and that the 1½ crores of Hindus left in East Bengal would form such a substantial minority there that no fear need be entertained about their safety. The first part of the statement has proved to be correct, but all expectations of fair treatment of minorities in East Bengal have been belied. Since then as many as 20 lakhs of East Bengal Hindus had to seek refuge in West Bengal and the evacuation in trickles still goes on.

The colossal movement of the refugees would not have been possible without the aid given by the Indian Army. The army took over this duty from September 1, 1947 and it must be said to their credit that they set up a fine record of achievements in discharging their duty. For the first time, the masses realised that the army was their own. The contrast between the slow-moving, inefficient and many times corrupt civil administration of the country and the efficient and alert performance of the task allotted to the army was apparent to all. The Dogras and the Gurkhas in particular, endeared themselves to every heart. The Sikh soldiers were particularly useful in evacuating Hindus and Sikhs stranded in small villages and pockets all around Pakistan. The stories of the gallant rescue in the Baddomalli area, of a large number of young Hindu and Sikh girls who were being kept in hiding by the Muslims, are now known all over the East Punjab. An unmidful officer sent out the Hindu Military there. They paraded through the streets and knocked at every door asking the women to come out for being rescued. The Muslim kidnappers had frightened them into the belief and had even done a rehearsal with their own Balochi soldiers. Before that, the rescuring parties were not of the Hindus but of the Muslims, and their only object in bringing them into the village was to find out how many of them were traitors to Pakistan. This military party had to come back without rescuing even a single woman. But the guardians of the women left behind in Ajnala and Amritsar still insisted that their women-folk were present across the river in those very villages from where the military had come back after a fruitless search. This time Sikh soldiers were sent and they only had to make their appearance in the village and shout out to the women imprisoned in the hunters' houses when from every nook and corner of the village, out-popped the heads. In a few minutes' time, scores of women in a state of utter dejection were rescued and brought back to their kith and kin in Amritsar. There is also the story of a village near Hafizabad where the entire Hindu population of the village had embraced Islam for fear of their life. They were left in possession of their property and their women-folk were not separated from them. The Muslim League workers arrived in the village and, in order to test their sincerity, arranged for a few Baloch troops to come and shout in the village telling that they were Hindu Dogras who had come to rescue the Hindus and Sikhs left in the village. The Baloch Regiment and the Frontier Forces, before partition had companies of Muslims and Dogras whose uniform was almost alike. The red beret was common to all. All the converted Hindus came out bagging to be rescued and were all marched out and shot by the soldiers as traitors to Islam. The similarity of uniform of the Dogras and the Balochies has been the cause of several tragic slaughters of Hindus and Sikhs in many parts of the province. I know of the tragic circumstances surrounding the death of one of my friends Late Ch. Ram Dayal Sehgal, an advocate of Jhang. He was a fairly rich landlord of Shorkot and was living in Shorkot Refugee Camp with his entire family. One fine morning, a truck manned by troops who called themselves as Dogras arrived at the camp and offered to take the leaders of the camp to Lyallpur to enable them to arrange for more escort for the evacuation of the remaining refugees in the Camp. Ch. Ram Dayal Sehgal along with his son and two other rich men boarded the truck with their cash and jewellery and were butchered in a lonely place on the way to Lyallpur. Ch. Ram Dayal was carrying on his person, among other things, two drafts on two leading banks; one on a European and the other on an Indian. One draft was presented by a Mohammedan, but the other draft when presented to the Indian bank, aroused suspicion and was refused payment. The presenter disappeared, but the mystery about the disappearance of Ch. Ram Dayal Sehgal, of whom nothing had been heard for several months was now cleared. A similar thing happened at Sheikhupura after the Sheikhupura slaughter. A group of Hindu men and women who had been hiding, came out on the road after two days' starvation when a truck manned by Balochis passed by them. They mistook them for Dogras and when asked, Balochies professed to be Hindus. They told the women to deposit all their ornaments of gold and silver and cash in a pool for safe custody with the officer so that on passing the border they might not be deprived of these by Pakistan Police. As soon as the heap was collected, the truck drove away without carrying any one of the refugees, but mercifully leaving them unhurt. The matter was duly reported by the unfortunate people to their own police and military escort that came to fetch them later, but no action was taken by Pakistan authorities to recover the looted property. But for these unfortunate cases of mistaken identity, the exploits of the Indian Army in the humanitarian task have been many and varied. In view of the proved utility of Sikh soldiers in rescue operations, it was unintelligible to the masses why our government had later on agreed to the demand of Pakistan to not send them on these missions of mercy.

According to the 1941 Census, the Hindu and Sikh population of West Punjab, North-West Frontier Province, Bahawalpur, Sindh and Balochistan was 59 lakhs. This figure was an underestimate as the 1941 census was a fake census. Allowing the normal rate of increase from the period 1931 to 1941, the total population by 1947 should have been even on the basis of 1941 census 68 lakhs. Of these, about 55 lakhs were evacuated from West Punjab. There were still 4 lakh Hindus and Sikhs in Sindh on June 15, 1948 while 4,78,000 had been evacuated from Sindh. Where have the remaining gone? According to the lists given to Pakistan, there are still 28,000 Hindu and Sikh women and children to be rescued from there. But the great majority of four lakhs unaccounted for must be presumed to have been killed in Pakistan. History's first partition war was waged with an unexampled fury. No quarter was asked and no quarter was given, 'prisoners' taken or, in popular language, 'converts' were also not spared especially if they possessed property. The total loss of Hindu and Sikh manpower in West Pakistan must, therefore, be presumed to be not less than four lakhs.

Evacuation from Sindh proceeded slowly as a result of the permit system introduced by the Sindh government. Sindh evacuees were required to produce certificates from the income-tax authorities to the effect that no dues public or private, were outstanding. Sureties were demanded that no debt, either of a bank or of a private individual was outstanding and that no ornaments of Muslims were pawned with them. It was very late in the day that it dawned upon the Government of India and the people of the Indian dominion, other than Punjabis, that migration from Pakistan to the Indian Union was no longer a matter of personal choice for the non-Muslims. People were forced to migrate on account of the orgy of murder and loot connived at, if not actually encouraged and, in many cases, freely participated in by the police and the military. It took still more time for the Government of India to realise that there could be no going back of the Hindu and Sikh evacuees to their homes in Pakistan. The Hindu and Sikh population of Bahawalpur which was 2.4 lakhs in 1941 could be estimated in 1947 to be about 2.7 lakhs allowing for the normal increase. Of these, 70 to 80 thousand had to leave the state as a result of the disturbances. The number left behind was estimated by the Government of India officials, who went to Bahawalpur to be in the neighbourhood of 70 thousand. This left over one lakh of persons unaccounted for. Information with the Ministry of States showed that an overwhelming majority of those who were untraceable had been either killed or forcibly converted during and after the communal disturbances. Bahawalpur, thus, stands out as the 'Kerbala' of the Hindus and Sikhs in the whole of Pakistan.

It may be noted that all assurances of safety and security offered to the minorities by the leaders of Pakistan during this period were devoid of any reality and were made only to mis-lead the Indian and international opinion. All arrangements made with the Government of India regarding evacuation by the two dominions were being flouted in practice by Pakistan. The refugees were being searched and their personal effects like sewing machines, crockery, ornaments and even clothes were being seized. The Hindus and Sikhs were being subjected to all manners of indignities. According to the official reports received by East Punjab, "Men were separated from their families in Jhelum. Men were all herded together and cut down with axes and saws as orders were issued not to waste around on Kafirs. The women-folk were then allotted to groups of Pathans." In Gujarat area, the number of abducted girls was estimated at 4,000. At certain places, general traffic in Hindu and Sikh women proceeded and abducted women were sold in the open market at times by auction. Refugee trains were attacked, passengers killed, girls forcibly taken away and property looted practically everyday. Miss Mridula Sarabhai who did rescue work in the Punjab herself noticed quite a number of girls being taken away by Pathans from trains. In India, however, according to a government publication, while all these things were taking place in West Punjab, fair treatment of minorities continued to be the sheet anchor of the Congress leaders under the influence of Mahatma Gandhi. The Hindus and Sikhs of East Punjab were being told day in and day out not to retaliate, but to leave everything to be settled at 'Government level'. Pandit Nehru paid a visit to East Punjab on August 17, 1947. He made another tour of the Punjab on August 24, 1947 when he held a number of informal meetings and addressed small road gatherings, appealing to the people that he could fully ensure the safety of the minorities in West Punjab only if they abstained from retaliation. I was in Amritsar when the ghastly news of the massacre and looting of Pind-Dadan Khan train reached Amritsar. The gentry of Bhera, Pind-Dadan Khan and Miani, with all their valuables had left under protection of Pakistan troops for Amritsar. The train was halted beyond Kamoke railway station when the military disappeared for a while and the entire Hindu and Sikh passengers, men, women and children were murdered or seriously wounded and their belongings looted. A few wounded were transported to Gujranwala hospital and the train, when it readied Amritsar, was found to be empty except for the few refugees who had entrained on the way from Lahore to Amritsar. The compartments had splashes of blood and the floor of one of these compartments contained congealed blood almost half an inch thick. A superintendent of police who had gone to receive his aged father and mother and other relatives actually burst into tears at the sight. His mother seriously wounded and deprived of one arm was rescued several months later from Gujranwala hospital. At this time, train loads of Muslims from East Punjab were on their way to Pakistan and the Congress rulers became very anxious on their account when they heard the news of Kamoke train slaughter. Sardar Patel flew to Amritsar and addressing a huge gathering of people there exhorted them to allow safe passage to the Muslims and, in return for this, assured them that the question of meting out suitable punishment to the offenders who were attacking the Hindus and Sikhs in Pakistan would be taken at 'government level'. A few weeks later, in January 1948, inspite of assurances given by Sardar Patel, there occurred another tragedy at Gujarat. This time the victims were the Hindus and Sikhs of Bannu, my native town, from the North-West Frontier Province. The train which had started under adequate protection and had been given an Indian escort was to come via Daud Khel, Darya Khan, Multan and Montgomery. For no apparent reason, it was routed via Malakwal and Lalamusa. The train carried the richest men of Bannu, a large number of army contractors and Mohalla Chaudhries, who were reported to be possessors of a fabulous store of wealth. The train was halted in Gujarat and fired upon by a mob of Pathans. The Indian troops, every one of who was injured appeared to be brave, but inexperienced soldiers. At the first attack, they opened out bursts of fire and, in a few hours, exhausted their entire ammunition. The mob which seemed to be led by a cunning military brain held itself at a distance for hours till they were convinced that no more ammunition was left with the Indian escort. The train then became an easy prey and the fate of men, women and children at the hands of the blood-thirsty Pathans and the Muslim league goondas can better be imagined than described. According to the calculations of one of the survivors of the train, the loss of property alone amounted to ₹1 crore. The news of Gujarat tragedy stunned every Punjabi Hindu and Sikh and the only assurance that the Government of India could give was that, suitable action would be taken in the matter and discussed at 'governmental level' with Pakistan. Of course, vigorous verbal protests were lodged with that government. Mahatma Gandhi was observing a fast at this time. His followers became alarmed at the thought of any retaliatory action taken by the Hindus and Sikhs in Amritsar against the Muslim evacuee trains at this time, heading towards Wagha frontier. They were sure that any such action taken against the Muslims would mean the end of Mahatma Gandhi as, in that case, he would not break his fast. They ran to Amritsar from all corners of Punjab, went about to all people who mattered, imploring them to desist from taking revenge. The police and the civil authorities were alerted. Curfews were imposed and dire threats held out by beat of drum to all elements who would try to settle the matter at private level. Of course, the phrase 'Save Gandhiji's life' was their main slogan. The Punjabis whose blood was boiling were, however, calmed down when they were told that the life of Bapu was in danger. What action the government of Pt. Jawaharlal Nehru took about this Gujarat train tragedy is, of course, known only to his government. So far, no public announcement has been made about it nor has any compensation been paid to the victims.

While the migration of Muslims from the Indian dominion was taking place, there were about 1,25,000 Meos of Gurgaon district waiting in refugee camps for evacuation. The Pakistan government was raising a hell at this time about being inundated by a huge stream of Muslim evacuees from India. The Government of India, always afraid of the world opinion more than that of their own countrymen, gave in. It was decided on the personal intervention of Mahatma Gandhi to keep the Meos in India. In addition to the Meos of Gurgaon district, a proposal was put and accepted to settle about 15,000 Meos belonging to the states of Alwar and Bharatpur recently displaced in Punjab. The area lying in the jurisdiction of

Nuh and Firozpur-Jhirka tehsils was to be declared non-refugee area. The 10,000 Hindu and Sikh refugees from West Punjab who had been allotted some land in those areas were soon asked to vacate it. It was even announced that civil and police officers in those areas would be appointed in consultation with Meo leaders and a small contingent of troops was stationed in the areas. The original plan of the East Punjab government to settle the Hindus and Sikh refugees in the Gurgaon district was, thus, upset by the central government.

The spontaneous reaction of every refugee who crossed over to the Indian dominion was to shout 'Hindustan Zindabad'. There was a sense of joy and relief on setting foot on its soil which promised them deliverance from certain death. The first reception was always cordial—hot food served by willing hands, clothes given free and what more, a shower of sympathy and goodwill freely offered. It were their own kith and kin of Punjab that met them on their first arrival in Hindustan. A Punjabi's heart, whether he be of East or West Punjab, bleeds for the other Punjabi. But all the new arrivals could not be absorbed and, therefore, kept indefinitely in East Punjab. Arrangements for their stay had to be made outside. With that object, the main concentration areas selected outside East Punjab were in Delhi, U.P., Bombay, the East Punjab states, Bikaner, Jodhpur and Rajputana. The total number of refugees who could not find their own place or a place with their friends and relatives and therefore had to live in camps, was estimated towards the end of November 1947 at 12,50,000 including 5 lakhs in East Punjab, 2½ lakhs in Kurukshetra, 1½ lakhs in Delhi and rest in other parts of the country. By the end of December 1947, the population in 85 refugee camps in the East Punjab had swelled to 7¼ lakhs. Though those people were brought to refugee camps, the question of providing all of them with sheltered accommodation was neglected. The tents made available for the refugees in all the camps by the government could hardly provide accommodation for more than 7 lakhs persons. Many refugees, therefore, preferred to remain on the railway station platforms. On the main line from

Amritsar to Karnal, suitable arrangements for reception were never made with the result that the refugees many a time arrived at their destinations without the district authorities being informed about their arrival which caused confusion and hardship. People were simply brought and dumped here and there all over the country. The central government thought that by sending refugees to various centres, they had shifted the responsibility for the proper looking after them to the provincial and state governments concerned. But the provincial government officials, after the first flash of sympathy was over, became indifferent and by stages hostile, e.g., orders were promulgated by Mr. Pande, Additional District Magistrate Katni (C.P.) under Section 144 Cr. P.C. directing Sindi refugees not to leave the camp without permission on January 9, 1948. The refugees, however, resented this order and hundreds of them were arrested and sent to Jabalpur Jail.

The U.P. government's attitude had been a mixture of warmth and coolness. According to Goswami Ganesh Dutt's letter published in the 'Hindustan Times' of August 13, 1949, the U.P. government's hostility towards the refugees dates back to the time in 1947 when on his persuasion, Gandhiji and Pandit Jawaharlal Nehru went to Haridwar to see for themselves the conditions of the refugees from the North-West Frontier Province and where they met with a hostile demonstration from them. This is what he says: "Despite my request, the refugees put up a bad show and demonstrated against Gandhiji and Pandit Ji. We had to bear the consequences of this. The U.P. government did not accept us (refugees) with honour and sincerity. They could have easily rehabilitated 20 lakhs of them." If Goswami Ganesh Dutt's version is correct, the cause of hostility, in certain circles of U.P. to the refugees can be easily understood. Apparently, it was due to the insult offered to the Congress leaders. The U.P. government's action against the refugees took a two-fold shape. In the first place, they instructed the district magistrates of Dehradun, Saharanpur, Meerut, Muzaffarnagar and adjoining areas to try to bring back and resettle the fleeing Muslims in their homes. In the meantime, their houses and properties were to be sealed and protected. All attempts of the refugees to take possession of the vacant houses were forcibly resisted. Their second action was to prohibit the coming in of the refugees into U.P. by rail and road. Large placards boldly announcing that the entry of refugees into U.P. was prohibited were put up and road blocks manned by trusted U.P. Hindu and Muslim police were erected on all the roads from Punjab leading into U.P. The police was authorised to stop, search and send back all such refugees unless they had a regular permit for entry with them. It is on record that India's defence member, S. Baldev Singh was also stopped near the Ghaziabad barrier and unceremoniously ordered to go back. These placards remained on the roads for several months. Nothing could be more humiliating for the country than this. The protests of the East Punjab government and resentment of the refugees against this invidious distinction and show of narrow provincialism proved of no avail. The U.P. government took their own time and relaxed the restrictions only when it suited them. The unsympathetic attitude of Mr. Gobind Sahai, the conscience-keeper of the U.P. government towards the Punjabis as revealed in his book, 'Rebellion of 1917' is well-known. Perhaps that explains why the Punjabis received a raw deal at his hands in their hour of trouble.

Even the Bombay province which received refugees mostly from Sindh soon got tired of receiving more. They were kept at places distant from towns and all sorts of obstacles were put in the way of their earning an independent living for themselves in competition with the local population. The attitude of the Delhi administration soon became hostile. They fixed a deadline and refused to register more refugees after that date. They also officially announced their policy of not absorbing more than a given number of refugees in the 'economy of Delhi', though what they actually meant by the 'economy of Delhi' has never been made clear to the refugees. Driven from his home, uprooted from a settled existence and deprived of his means of livelihood, the refugee has become a wanderer on the face of the earth. He ceaselessly moves here and there in the hope that something would turn up and life would once again acquire for him some significance and some redeeming qualities. Familiarity with him has bred contempt in the minds of others. The first upsurge of sympathy for him has exhausted itself. Shelterless and homeless as the refugees are, there is nothing for them but slow and sure annihilation in the years to come. The refugees sacrificed at the altar of freedom for others than themselves would derive some consolation if grateful words in appreciation of their sacrifices were addressed to them but even that token of mercy is now being denied to them.

The change in the attitude of Delhi administration towards the refugees was signalised by the changes in Delhi administration. The Deputy Commissioner Mr. M.S. Randhawa, had proved himself as a very efficient district magistrate. It was largely due to his personal efforts that law and order had been maintained in the capital especially in relation to the refugee problem. He was a strong but sympathetic officer and was ever ready to listen to the woes of the refugees at all hours of the day. He felt for the refugees and this feeling brought out a sympathetic response from the refugees. They were always ready to listen to his advice and obey his order even when they were sometimes harsh. All the mosques in Delhi were voluntarily vacated by the people on the persuasion of the deputy commissioner. But for the presence of such a sympathetic officer in the capital at that time, the situation might have taken an ugly turn and not returned to normal so soon as the unending stream of refugees pouring into the capital was in an angry mood. If Mr. Randhawa had continued to be in charge of the capital, he might have been most helpful to the refugees in the second stage of their rehabilitation. But the seths and black-marketeers of Delhi never got reconciled to the presence of a very large number of Punjabis in their midst. They thought that there was a danger of their being swamped by non-Delhi elements, ignoring the revolutionary change that had taken place in the country. The influence of the local people of Delhi with the Government of India was considerable. There was not much love lost between the deputy commissioner and his Muslim chief and the Delhiites soon got busy in idolising the latter and scandalising the former. The political elements in Delhi, according to the special correspondent of 'Hindustan Times', got divided into two camps—one upholding the chief commissioner and the other the deputy commissioner. The compromise was struck at by making a change in both these offices. Mr. Shankar Prasad, the new chief commissioner, was a friend of the Nehru family and Pt. Rameshwar Dayal a friend of Mr. Rafi Ahmed Kidwai. The claims of Punjab services were completely ignored. The new deputy commissioner was known for his stern attitude towards the refugees. He was the deputy commissioner of Saharanpur District when Mahatma Gandhi, Pt. Jawaharlal Nehru and Mrs. Indira Gandhi had paid their visit to Haridwar and had met with a hostile demonstration. According to Goswami Ganesh Dutt, this action of the refugees had made the U.P. government and its faithful civil servants to change their attitude towards them. The subsequent doings of Pt. Rameshwar Dayal in Saharanpur District bore ample testimony to this change in his behaviour towards the refugees. Hence, when he took over charge as the deputy commissioner of Delhi, the hearts of all the refugees at Delhi sank. There was a wave of despondency in all Punjabi circles that the government should have selected a P.C.S. man for an I.C.S. post could not be explained away on the plea of shortage of I.C.S. officers and to this day, there is no explanation given for the fact that none of the two offices was given to a Punjabi, though the East Punjab government, it is reported, had placed the services of a very competent Punjabi I.C.S. officer at their disposal. The importing of the Chief Executive Head of the Police, Mr. Jia Lal Saxena, another U.P. Officer and the special recruitment of 500 armed constables from the same province were all meant to remind the West Pakistan refugees of the kind of treatment they were sure to meet if they did not timely listen to the advice given by the administration. The subsequent events that happened in Delhi—the forcible removal of the refugees, from Chandni Chowk, the confiscation of their goods in Connaught Circus, the deportation of some of them from the Delhi Province to the village Khor, the indiscriminate confiscation on a vast scale of their arms licenses and impounding of arm, the difficulties placed in the way of their getting employment in Delhi administration, etc., are enough to show that the fears of the refugees about the intentions of the new administration towards their rehabilitation and resettlement in Delhi were not ill-founded.

This is not the place to refer to the mass brutalities committed on the Hindu and Sikh women by the Muslim League goondas, first in Calcutta on the 26th of August, 1947 and, later on, in Noakhali, Tippera and the Rawalpindi division. The tales are too horrible and shameful to be put down in cold print. But one phenomenon that emerged from these brutalities must be noticed. As a result of these disturbed conditions in the country and particularly as a result of the partition of Punjab and the invasion of Kashmir by Pakistanis, a very large number of Hindu and Sikh women were kidnapped by Leaguers. The task of recovering these unfortunate women was taken in hand by Miss Mridulaben Sarabhai with the full support of the Indian government. The Pakistan government's higher officials agreed to a joint effort though the lower hierarchy refused and is refusing right upto this time to cooperate in this noble and humanitarian task. According to the statement made in the Dominion Parliament by Shri N. Gopalaswamy Ayyangar, the total number of recoveries from West Pakistan from December 6, 1947 to July 31, 1948 was only 5,510, whereas the corresponding figure for recoveries of Muslim women from the Indian dominion was 9,659. In the original lists of Hindu and Sikh women to be recovered from Pakistan, the total was 33 thousand, while according to the Pakistan's official list, the women to be recovered from India numbered 21 thousand. The Government of India passed ordinances to help in the recovery of the Muslim women from India. A belated measure to that effect was also passed by Pakistan, but owing to the lack of humanitarian zeal on the part of Muslim workers and officers and general lack of cooperation on the part of the Pakistanis, the work of recoveries in Pakistan has been most unsatisfactory. In the later stages, this task became only one-way traffic in which the duty of acting as a traffic police constable, directing traffic only towards Pakistan has been played by the organisation set up by Miss Mridulaben Sarabhai. Being the personal representative of Pandit Jawaharlal Nehru and a great friend of his family, she is in such a domineering position that nobody in East Punjab dare disobey her orders conveyed, though they may be by the slightest nod of her head. She is an untiring social worker and never allows rest to herself or to others who work with her. When she first arrived at Amritsar, her queer dress and manners aroused the affectionate curiosity of the Punjabis, but soon the district officials and others at Amritsar found that it was not with a frail woman worker that they were dealing but with an Amazon. Woe to the officer who did not do what she asked him to do. She got a high district officer transferred to another station in East Punjab where also he was not given rest. He might have been sacked but for the bold stand taken by Dr. Gopichand. She has by now quarrelled with her Hindu and Sikh women co-workers, but undaunted, she is carrying on her noble work. How does it matter if Pakistan does not cooperate? They anyhow show great lip sympathy for the cause and respect for her person. When she first arrived at Amritsar, her four, syllable name was difficult to pronounce and, therefore, the Punjabis affectionately nicknamed her Adhi Behn, Adha Bhai, 'Half-sister half-brother'. By her persistent and strong action, she has proved that she is more of a full brother—'Sara Bhai' to the kidnapped women than a weak sister.

Mr. Bhim Sen Sachar, as chairman of the Refugees Inquiry Committee appointed by the East Punjab government to report on the conditions of the refugees in the province after completing his tour of the province, said in an interview on December 14, 1948 that the condition of the refugees was deplorable. "Many were facing starvation. Widows, orphans and the unemployed refugees needed special help and care of the government and the public in general. The hardships they were facing were driving them towards moral degradation." Speaking of the agencies working for the relief and rehabilitation, Mr. Sachar said that these were themselves exploiting the refugees in different ways. No truer picture of the condition of refugees in East Punjab and, as a matter of fact, all over the country could be given than what Mr. Sachar gave in his report.

The secretary of the Relief and Welfare Workers' Association, New Delhi speaking of Sindh refugees said in December, 1948 that thousands of refugees from Sindh were kept at the docks in Bombay for a long time and some time ago were forcibly removed to various refugee camps where also they were treated inhumanly. The refugees were not allowed to remain in Bombay and earn their livelihood. They were refused licenses even as railway coolies. Lakhs of refugees could easily find means of livelihood in the city of Bombay, but the authorities were not sympathetic in this regard. About the East Bengal refugees, this is what Mr. G.R. Choudhary, the secretary of the East Bengal Minority Welfare Central Committee, after touring all the refugee camps, with a letter of authority from the Government of India said: "In West Bengal, the refugee gets only rice and dal, which are not enough for half a meal a day. I learn that the U.P. government disowns responsibility for the Bengali refugees in Banaras and other parts of the province, while West Bengal asserts that the Bengali refugees from East Bengal are no concern of theirs. In Patna, I found the refugees getting help from the Bihar government, but in Assam and the eastern state, they are left uncared for. These people, who have been sacrificed behind their back in the interest of the rest of the people of the country, hate the idea of living on charity or being even a liability to the state, and they are, therefore, desperately trying to avoid creating a situation which may embarrass the government. But there is also a limit to their patience and it is now nearing the breaking point."

Writing in December 1948, the special correspondent of a paper in Delhi observed: "Several hundred men, women and children who had come from West Punjab, the N.W.F.P. and Sindh passed the coldest night of the season on December 14, when the minimum temperature was 39.6°—the lowest recorded so far during this winter—at the railway platform. Many of them had not enough clothes to protect them from the severe cold. Besides these, a number of people spent the night on footpaths in Chandni Chowk and Queens Garden."

Writing about the fate of Haridwar refugees, the General secretary of Frontier and Punjab Riot Sufferers Committee, Haridwar wrote to a Delhi paper on December 27, 1948 protesting against the remarks of Mr. Hira Vallabh Tripathi, Chairman of the Union Board, Haridwar. The total number of refugees according to him in Haridwar was not even 1/5th of their original number and that only an insignificant number of them sat in the bazar and on the pavements near Har ki Pauri carrying on petty trade which was better than begging. "The refugees were residing in dharmashalas built by their own ancestors for the use of needy people not because they wanted to enjoy houses free of rent, water and electricity but because the government had not provided them with any other accommodation."

'If winter comes, spring cannot be far behind' is the popular title of a book which proved the bestseller after the First Great War, but there is no such hope for the refugees. There is no spring for them after the winter, but only the blazing heat of a June day in summer. A very large number of refugees even now are living in alcoves about 4 feet deep and 9 feet broad in the walls of the city of Delhi. In some of the alcoves, more than one family is living with their clothes and utensils somehow fitted in. There are no sanitation facilities for these families with the exception of a public hydrant and no light at all. They use the space outside the walls as open air latrines.

In April 1949, when the issuing of free rations to Delhi refugees was stopped, the destitute refugees were told that the government would give them relief if they joined the work centres. The refugees' demand that work centres be started in Kingsway Camp was not acceded to by the Delhi administration for reasons best known only to them. They started a work centre near Okhla, where it was impossible for the refugees staying in Kingsway Camp to go for work. The result of this was that the Okhla scheme proved a complete failure.

A census of refugees in Bombay province carried out between October 25 and 30, 1948 revealed that there were about 8,000 matriculates and under-graduates among 2,58,000 refugees living in camps in the Bombay province. Twelve hundred of these were women. There were more than one thousand graduates in arts and science and a large number of them were diploma-holders in engineering and medicines. In Kalyan Camp alone, there were 252 medical graduates including 55 women. That this should be the case when there is a universal complaint about paucity of qualified doctors the country is rather strange. Why have they not been suitably employed in the rural areas of the country if there are no places for them in the towns? The real explanation, however, is the reluctance of the various provincial governments run by Congressmen to have in their midst people other than those belonging to their own province. The refugees are looked upon as outsiders and as a foreign element. That there is open hostility on the part of non-refugees towards the refugees in Gujarat is proved by a letter published in the 'Hindustan Times' under the signatures of one Mr. S.L. Mehta. Of course, Mr. Mehta's antipathy towards Punjabis can be well understood and he is welcome to hug his provincial prejudices, but while protesting against the meagre quota of employment that was being dished out to the refugees he pleaded for those who according to him "do not have the luck of being refugees". Many a refugee would be simply too glad to exchange his place with Mr. S.L. Mehta and others of his way of thinking who got freedom so to stay in their beds. Having been uprooted from their homes for no fault of their own, cruel references to their status only add insult to injury.

That there is a new note in the dealings of the Delhi administration with the refugees was forcefully brought to the public notice when, on the 7th of July, 1949, the Delhi Police cane-charged hundreds of refugees, including women and children, who weeping and wailing, demonstrated in the compound of Delhi District Courts to protest against the conviction of 121 refugees of Kingsway Camp. The Delhi Bar Association, at an emergent meeting, passed a resolution deploring the incident. "The Association viewed with consternation and painful regret the excesses committed by the police in callously lathi-charging and manhandling innocent members of the public including women and children without any provocation or justification whatsoever within the precincts of the court and in full view of the members of the association." The cane-charge made for the first time, after August 1947, produced a feeling of such intense resentment that the men, women and children were soon heard shouting slogans of "Congress government Murdabad". The Sabzi Mandi Fruit Market incident, where a large number of responsible merchants including refugees, were detained on July 4, 1949 under the East Punjab Public Safety Act and when a collective fine of ₹25,000 was imposed on the market and realised in cash on the spot is an eye opener to the refugees as to the kind of treatment they are likely to receive at the hands of their own kith and kin. A warning was issued by the Baroda government on July 12, 1949 to Sindhi refugees who had started hunger strike in protest against stopping of free rations in Outram and Harni camps to desist from leading other people astray. They were told in plain words that the interests of the original inhabitants of the city had to be adequately protected against the interests of the refugees.

Writing about the deplorable state of tentage provided to the refugees, Mr. Radha Raman, the president of the Delhi Provincial Congress Committee, who is not known for his love of the refugees, said that either the refugee families be provided with new tents or be immediately shifted to newly constructed quarters in order to avoid further hardships. He also pointed out that cases of paralysis and pneumonia were occurring in the camps and if timely help was not rendered, there might be many more such cases.

According to the Government of India Census covering the period up to the 10th of April, 1949, five million refugees from West Pakistan are now living in India. The number of refugees from East Pakistan was estimated at 1.95 million. Of this number, the refugees living in one hundred camps in the provinces and centrally administered areas was 6,50,000. The number of refugees in sixty camps in states was roughly estimated at 1,80,000. Of the East Pakistan refugees, 52,000 were living in West Bengal. These figures were not complete as no enumeration was undertaken at places where there was no large concentration of refugee population. It was roughly estimated that 2,50,000 Hindus and Sikhs were still living in Sindh and a few thousands in the other provinces of Pakistan.

The Government of India has fixed October 31, 1949 as the deadline when all assistance to refugees in relief camps will be totally stopped. The states and the provincial governments have been asked to make arrangements for a progressive and systematic dispersal of displaced persons living at present in relief camps. No expenditure on relief work is to be allowed after October 31, 1949. On the average, the government announced that they were spending about 12 annas per day per head on refugee relief. In Delhi camps, where there are still about 42,000 refugees, no doles are distributed.

The significance of the date line fixed should be understood because if in the meantime, plans are not put into operation to train all able-bodied people in vocations by which they can rehabilitate themselves, the Government of India's decision will result in great misery for the lakhs of people who have already borne unbearable hardships. The squatting in front of the Rehabilitation Minister, Mr. Mohan Lal Saxena, on July 22, 1949 and, later on August 10, 1949 at the bungalow of Pt. Jawaharlal Nehru, has not produced the results desired by the refugees. What these refugees want and what every refugee wants is that Pt. Jawaharlal Nehru and Sardar Patel should themselves personally take up the problem of their re-settlement and rehabilitation under their own charge. Mr. Mohan Lal Saxena, speaking in the Refugee Conference and referring to the few cases of pneumonia among the refugees lying in front of his residence, made the callous remark that the Government of India had no control over the weather.

That very little regard is paid to the susceptibilities of the refugees even on minor points is proved by the agitation which the Sindhis have carried on against naming the new refugee township as 'Ulhas Nagar' and not as 'Sindhu Nagar'. The governor-general who laid the foundation stone of 'Ulhas Nagar', discovered on his arrival there that his function had been completely boycotted by the refugees for whom the town was being built. To name the town of the refugees as a 'Pleasure City' or 'City of Joy' is a cruel joke indeed against the uprooted people and though the governor general in his scholarly manner decanted upon the phrase 'what is in a name' he refused to change it to the one demanded by the refugees. If there is nothing in a name, as he said, why force it on them? The audience of eight hundred assembled on the occasion constituted mostly of non-Sindhis. Despite police arrangements, crowds of Sindhis outside were shouting, vociferating and demonstrating against the naming of the township as 'Ulhas Nagar'. An order under Section 144 I.P.C. had to be enforced soon after the governor general's visit.

Mrs. Rameshwari Nehru, director of the women's Section of the Ministry of Relief and Rehabilitation, Government of India, in a statement on the refugee problem said on the 14th of August, 1949 that she had noticed an attitude of hostility towards refugees in all the provinces and states of India she had visited. "It is evident," she added, "we cannot allow this friction to go on. We have to make room for the displaced people within the frame-work of our economy. They have been the victims of circumstances. Their sacrifices, though involuntary, have been for the sake of the country. The local people everywhere must take all this into consideration. They must share the sacrifices and burdens of their brothers. They must treat them as members of the Indian family. Their sacrifices are not over by their losses in life and property in Pakistan as they are continuing to live in misery which defies all description."

Suggesting a remedy, she wishes the Congress to take to propaganda, primarily among the local people, for befriending the refugees. But can the Congress, with the ideal of a secular state and dominated by non-refugee elements, do this?

Among the new experiences of the refugees on arrival in the Indian dominion has been the discovery that in spite of much lip sympathy with them, the provinces were not prepared to absorb them permanently in their economy to an extent greater or even equal to the vacuum created by the exodus of Muslims. They are not prepared to undergo any hardship themselves whether it be in the shape of providing them housing, accommodation or opportunities for doing business. While we were in Punjab and used to listen to the glowing speeches of the leaders from U.P., Bihar, Bombay, C.P. and Madras, etc., we always thought that we were a part of India and Indians in full sense of the word. On coming to India after partition, the Punjabis and the Sindhis soon realised that in actual practice, there was no such person as an 'Indian' here. They were either Madrasis, Europeans, Bombaywalas, Gujaratis, Biharis or Delhiwalas, etc., Provincialism was deeply rooted in the soil and the Government of India was dominated by one province. Very fortunately that province is just the one which has never suffered any uprooting or political trouble since the world began and, therefore, its nationals lack in the psychological background which would make them sympathetic towards afflicted humanity. They just don't understand your troubles much less can they sympathise with you. An under-secretary in a department, Mr. S, tauntingly inquired from a Peshawar refugee who was posted as a superintendent under him, "Afghanistan was nearer Peshawar than Delhi, why did you not go there?" "The real rulers of India are not the ministers who may come and go, but the secretariat higher officials who all come from the South and stay out here till they are not fit to work. Even then they manage to secure memberships of deputations going abroad or special jobs on still higher salaries. The first joke I heard in the secretariate here on arrival, in Delhi, was that the Government of India was suffering from an attack of 'Menongitis'. The Punjabis were conspicuous by their absence. It appears that the vacuum created by the quitting of the British and the Muslims was filled up from the South. Of course, India's Monsoon comes from South and South-West and it was no wonder that India's Swamies, Menons and Ayyangars also came from the South. A time may come when the people of Northern India, as several times before in their history, will again be required to defend India against foreign aggression and die for it if necessary in the process. Will the *novo de rich* bureaucrats stand by their office files in such a contingency or desert the ship of state at the first opportunity? Time will tell. This, however, can be said that unless the Government of India reserves due share for each province in her governance according to its importance, the mounting discontent will create a storm that will weaken its defences. The present arrangements between the North and the South, "You defend the cow, I will milch it", will not last long. How different would have been the treatment of the refugees, if they had their own kith and kin in higher places where policy is moulded."

Why has the refugee problem not yet been solved? The reason is not far to seek. Pt. Jawaharlal Nehru has not up to this time thought fit to entrust the work of Relief and Rehabilitation Ministry to a refugee. The U.P., which is known for its 'love' of the Punjabis, is the last province from where care-takers should have been drafted to look after them.

The refugees from East Bengal are even in a worse condition than the refugees from West Pakistan. They are unwelcome in Bihar and even the two districts of Bengal which had been taken away from them unjustly at the time of creating the province of Bihar, have not been returned to them. Assam has shut its doors on Bengal and unlike people of Northern India, (Bengalis) make very indifferent settlers in parts of the country other than the two contiguous provinces mentioned above. Only two million of them have yet arrived, but supposing more were to come and there are still one crore left in East Pakistan, where will they be absorbed? The Bengali immigrants and intending immigrants know this and there is very real danger that those who have come over to the Indian dominion may go over to communism and those left behind in Pakistan may go over to Mohammedanism. Madras, it will be noted, has got the least number of refugees from other provinces.

□

11

The Refugees' Last Hope: Their Properties Left Behind

People of West Punjab left their homes not because they were anxious to leave their homes, but because their government failed to give them adequate protection. They cannot be blamed or held responsible for leaving their homes. Even if they left their homes, it is difficult to grasp by what process of law or reasoning have the evacuees ceased to be the owners of their properties left behind? What justification has any government to take away such properties and treat those as their own? This was the position taken up by the Pakistan government when the exodus of the Hindus and Sikhs began from there. It was announced that the right to property, moveable or immoveable, of the evacuees would remain intact, but during the last two years, Pakistan has deliberately and, by calculated stages, gone back on its declaration. Both the history of its actions and of the doings of our own government, make a sad reading.

The refugees were full of anger and fury. They were itching for some action for the wrongs done to them in Pakistan and expected their national government to take up the cudgels on their behalf. They had suffered terrible losses, but were prepared to make even greater sacrifices for settling their account with Pakistan. Had the Government of India adopted a strong attitude then or later on when the Indian territory was invaded by Pakistan, there would have been a wonderful response to their appeal for men, money and material in the war of 'back to our homes'. But the government looked upon the problem from mathematical point of view. The total refugee population involved was not more than 3 per cent of the total population of the Indian dominion. Ninety-seven per cent were safe, happy and prosperous. Why to fight against Pakistan for the sake of just only 3 per cent, forgetting that wars are fought not according to the precentages of the people insulted and humiliated, but in vindication of the rights and honour of the people. Anyhow efforts were made to calm the refugees by telling them that action would be taken at the 'governmental level' for all the losses and indignities suffered by them at the hands of Pakistan. In order to further assuage the angry feelings of the refugees and to divert their attention in a different direction, 'claims officers' were appointed first in Delhi province and then in all the other towns of East Punjab. 'P' Block in the Delhi Secretariat soon became the 'Mecca and Madina' of all refugees. Up to this time, it has retained the reputation of being the holiest of holies of refugees as, I believe, more people have come to the 'P' Block during the last two years than have ever visited any other place of pilgrimage. Of course, there was that usual phenomenon of black-market coming to exist even in the supply of the claims forms, but as soon a refugee filed his claim and was given a receipt, in acknowledgement of having done so, he became mentally happy. The idea spread about was that you only had to file your claim and have it accepted by the registrar to get the compensation from the Government of India at no distant date. Several months passed away and the claims continued to be registered. The 'office of the Registrar of Refugees' Claims, Delhi Province' was, however, closed with effect from August 1, 1948. No last date was notified for the registration of claims and the office was closed without any notice to the intending claimants. But as soon as the office was closed, disillusionment began to dawn upon the refugees. The claims, it was now discovered, were not to form a part of any scheme of compensation. There was no such scheme and the only object was the collection of statistics for the purpose of a newly established School of Economics. People began to wonder why they had spent large sums of money in travelling all the way

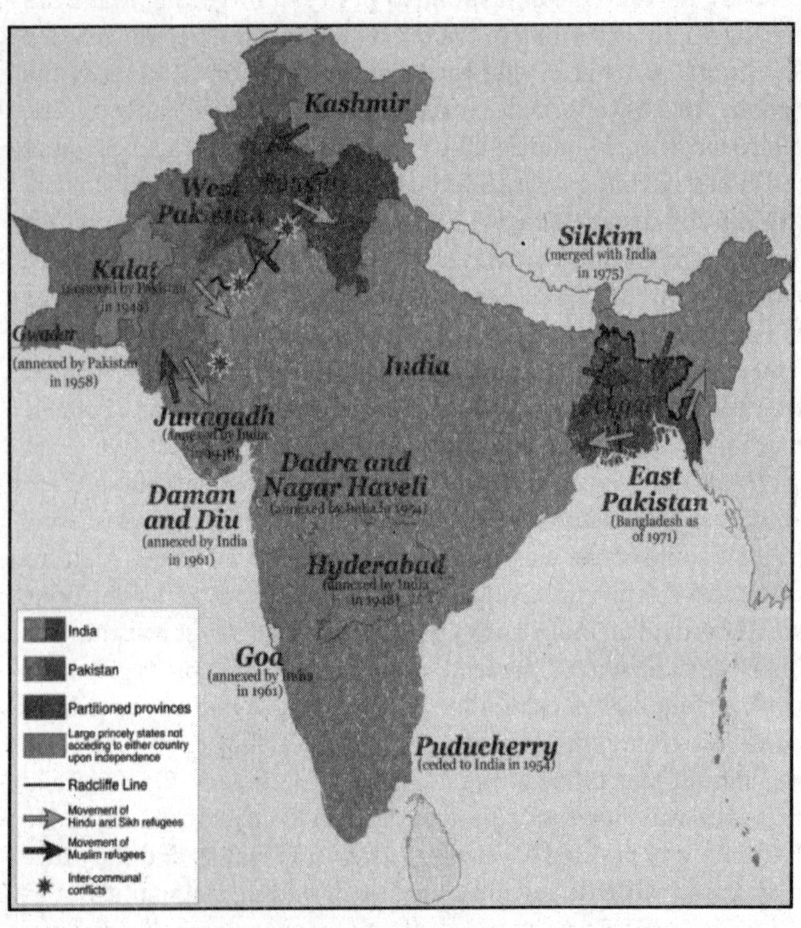
Kashmir
Sikkim
(merged with India in 1975)
Kalat
Gwadar
(annexed by Pakistan in 1958)
India
Junagadh
Dadra and Nagar Haveli
Daman and Diu
(annexed by India in 1961)
East Pakistan
(Bangladesh as of 1971)
Hyderabad
Goa
(annexed by India in 1961)
Puducherry
(ceded to India in 1954)
India
Pakistan
Partitioned provinces
Large princely states not acceding to either country upon independence
Radcliffe Line
Movement of Hindu and Sikh refugees
Movement of Muslim refugees
Inter-communal conflicts

to file the claims, if the idea was only that of academic research. The whole thing soon took the shape of a hoax that was started to side track the refugees.

The second step taken by the government was to appoint 'custodians of evacuees' property to look after and manage the properties on behalf of the evacuees. Both the governments soon became engaged in working out details relating to properties, such as the sale of property, the transfer of sale proceeds and the extent to which the exchange of property would be permitted. The custodian in Delhi was, in addition, asked to allot the houses rendered vacant by the Muslims to new arrivals in Delhi according to certain principles. Of course, as it later on transpired in the legal proceedings against Mr. Lobo Prabhu, the only principle was 'monetary consideration'. But creation of the Custodian's Department had everything to recommend it, though here again the claim of a refugee to the appointment was over-looked in favour of a Madrasi and, later on, in favour of a Gujarati. The appointment of Shri Achhru Rain as the custodian general gave joy to the refugees, but he has yet to be vested with powers and given staff to effectively discharge the duties of his high office.

With the government setting up the custodian's department and with vague speeches here and there, full of vague promises of help, the evacuees continued to live in the hope that something after all will be done for them.

When the refugees migrated from West Punjab and the Muslims migrated from East Punjab, the 'locals' both, in Punjab and in Delhi had the first choice of picking up the best propositions. Their relatives and friends were hurriedly imported from distant places and given possession of the evacuee properties. In Delhi, there were hundreds of cases where forged claims about the purchase of property were brought forward by the Delhiites. Self-styled managers and attorney sprang up all over the country for the Muslims who had left for Pakistan. Also, the refugees who were on the spot and had been the first to arrive had an easy task of marching into their newpost. But those who came behind or those who were too peaceful and law-abiding and had pinned their faith in the government's announcement that allotment would be done on merit were left in the lurch. The result of this has been that in many a case those who had little or no property in Pakistan are now the proud possessors of palatial buildings and large properties, whereas those who had big properties are now living in hovels or refugee camps. The agriculturists who first came to East Punjab similarly walked into the villages and took possession of the best lands there. In many cases, here also the 'locals' took advantage of the Muslim exodus. In practically all cases, however, so far as their standing fodder crops and moveable goods and cattle were concerned, the loot remained with the 'locals'. The tenants and landless labourers and village Kamins of West Punjab became now the landlords in East Punjab while the landlords, specially those, who did not plough with their own hands met the worst fate. Punjab was a land of peasant proprietors; 40 per cent of the area of land was owned by peasant proprietors and 10 per cent by occupancy tenants. The Punjab government, therefore, could not ignore the interests of proprietory class. They began early to formulate their plans for distribution of land on pro-rata basis to those who had been owners of land in West Punjab. Nothing gave more joy to the landlord refugees than the East Punjab government's announcement in the papers early in 1948, asking them to have their claims registered. Here was an effort at doing something r0.eal in rehabilitation and in giving back to the land owners a part of their property left behind. The credit for formulating the policy must go primarily to the Sikh M.L.A.s of the assembly who were agriculturists and the credit for evolving a workable scheme must go to S. Trilok Singh, Director General of Rehabilitation. So far as Hindu M.L.A.s from the urban areas were concerned and, particularly those who were non-agriculturists, their attitude was first of joy at the automatic abolition of landlordism of the West Punjab refugees. Not a few of them made their joy known by speeches and statements. The socialists of Bihar, Bombay and U.P. were also happy at this opportunity of abolishing zamindari without paying any compensation with a stroke of pen. They indirectly blessed Pakistan for creating a situation which had made their work of playing the samaritan at other peoples' expense, easy. Now, they proposed the distribution of land among the landless tenants-at-will. The caste Hindus who had been carrying on the work of the uplift of Harijans for several years also saw a golden opportunity of thus turning the tables on 'sajjans' by making 'Harijans' of them and lifting the latter at their expense to a higher economic status. Mr. Bhim Sen Sachar, who was in opposition then, made no secret of his views about the abolition of landlord rights and my friend, Mr. Mohan Lal of Servants of the Peoples' Society was very vociferous in the cause of the village Kamins. That abolition of proprietory right through the backdoor of Pakistan's confiscation of Hindu and Sikh properties would be an unjust, immoral and the most degrading act never entered their heads. The pressure of the Sikh agriculturist landholders was fortunately too strong for the theorists and the visionaries who put too much faith in slogans and too little in the stability of society. The Hindu land-owners of West Punjab are under a deep debt of gratitude to the valiant Sikh agriculturists who have saved them from the onslaught of their own kith and kin.

It took a long time to classify the lands and the claims received and to evolve other details of allotment, but it was a colossal task being ably done by zealous people. The temporary allotment of land was made in a haphazard way. Communalism, favouritism, nepotism and all other isms of low variety had their full sway in this. I know something of what happened in the district of Karnal. In the early days, you could find the Fourth Battle of Panipat in full swing in the district of Karnal. The contestants in this battle were the Hindus and Sikh bigger magnates who all flocked to the rich soil of Panipat to stake their claims. But as it was only a temporary allotment, the battle was not considered worth a fight by many. The results of semi-permanent allotment will only show whether the law of the soil or the law of the jungle is to prevail in the long run. The appointment of Mr. M.S. Randhawa to carry out the colossal task is, however, a guarantee that justice will be done. Had the U.P. government co-operated with the East Punjab government by making available the evacuee lands of the Muslims to be pooled together with the East Punjab Muslim evacuees' land, the scheme would have been a greater success and the refugees would have got proportionately, a little more than they are likely to get now. Or had Master Tara Singh's earlier suggestion been accepted of making Muslim evacuees' land in all parts of India available for distribution to the refugees from Pakistan, the problem of land rehabilitation would have been solved long ago.

Now that the plan for the allotment of agricultural land is well on the way of being put into execution, a question is being asked by the urban landlords as to why the Government of India is not moving along similar lines in allotting the house property to them. It is true that the task of allotting urban property is more difficult than that of allotting agricultural lands, but the difficulties are not insoluble. If there is the will to do, the way can always be found.

The inter-dominion discussions about evacuees' property have been a long-drawn-out affair in which the Government of India has always adopted a meek attitude. They called it a 'conciliatory attitude' though the refugees unanimously looked upon it as a 'callous attitude' insofar as it never cared to take into account their point of view. The Pakistan government, on the other hand, looked upon it as a sign of their weakness and, therefore, always observed the agreements entered into at governmental level more in the breach than in the observance. In fact, the Pakistanis have always been clear in their own mind about it, though they might not have openly confessed it. After the partition, they found themselves in possession of properties which they knew were worth many times more than the properties left behind by Muslim evacuees. Two courses of action were open to them. To settle or to enter into an agreement with the Government of India for exchange of property at the governmental level and, thus incur a net capital liability equal to the difference between the properties of Hindus and Sikhs left behind in Pakistan and the Muslim properties left behind in India. The liability would have amounted to say about ₹3,500 crores. And the second alternative was not to burden their young country with any such fantastic liability, but to conserve their resources for utilising them for strengthening their military defences. It was openly said by the Leaguers that they had got Pakistan as a result of their sacrifices and, therefore, they were not prepared to 'purchase' it for cash consideration from the Hindus and the Sikhs. They looked upon the payment of compensation to the latter for their properties as a kind of 'price' that they were being asked to pay for Pakistan. Their fear, however, was that the Government of India might listen to the demand of the Hindu and Sikh refugees and freeze the Muslim evacuee property in all parts of India or allot those to Hindus and Sikhs. Hence, the Government of India, as a matter of policy was not to be bluntly refused, nor was any settlement to be arrived at. Every moment that passed would be in their favour because ever since Pakistan came into existence, a flight of capital began to take place from India to Pakistan. This flow of capital from India to Pakistan, has now taken the shape of a regular and perennial stream. The stream is fed by four sources: (i) the sale proceeds of the property which is being sold by Muslims at fabulous prices all over India, (ii) the surpluses arising out of profits from trade and industry, (iii) the gradual disposal of their businesses and other circulating capital, and (iv) surplus arising out of their incomes and wages. Most Muslims who count, with a few honourable exceptions that can be counted on the fingers of one hand, want to send their wealth to Pakistan, the country which they love.

There was another danger to be guarded against—that of the new capital coming into Pakistan acquiring Hindu and Sikh property there. If the freshly arrived Muslim capital were to be invested in the purchase of valuable properties of the Hindus and Sikhs left in Pakistan, there would have been an automatic solution of the evacuee properties problem. Hence, to begin with, they stopped the purchase and exchange of all properties altogether and, secondly, they carried on an intensive campaign against such purchases. The Government of India failed to see through the game which was crystal clear to the Hindu and Sikh refugees and to which the attention of the government was being drawn by their leaders now and then.

Even from the larger point of view of the country's welfare, it was and is a sad thing to note that while every other country of the world is trying to conserve its gold and foreign exchange, India alone is permitting free remittance to Pakistan. No steps have been taken by our government to prevent this serious and irreparable harm to the Indian economy. In the absence of a regional control over the tied and circulating assets of the Muslims of India who have gone to Pakistan, their realisation and earnings cannot be prevented from reaching Pakistan. For this, an overall control on all-India basis of all forms of property of the Muslim evacuees is essential. It is in Pakistan's interest that the control over Muslim Evacuee properties and control over exchange remittances between the two dominions should be delayed for as long a period as possible. With a clear picture of the situation in their mind, Pakistanis followed a policy of protracting negotiations and delaying decision on one pretext or the other. The result of all this has been that now when Pakistanis find that the Government of India is after all going to take some action in the matter they have abrogated all agreements entered into with them.

In March 1948, the West Punjab Governor, Sir Francis Muddy addressing a gathering of Lahore Rotarians referred to the question of the exchange of refugee property between East and West Punjab. He said that two courses were open to Pakistan—the 'Do Nothing' Plan which suited the government most or 'Rigid control and Active assistance' in the exchange of property. He made it clear that they must take into account the existing and future economic conditions and the state of public psychology. Conscious of the fact that the amount, of property left by the Hindus and Sikhs in West Punjab far exceeded the amount of Muslim property in East Punjab, the governor made it clear that no compensation was possible without landing Pakistan in economic difficulties. The Pakistan government has been acting upon the 'Do Nothing' Plan so far and now they have launched upon 'Do Everything Plan' to confiscate the entire property, not only of the evacuee Hindus and Sikhs, but also of the Pakistani Hindus and Sikhs. India's representatives on the various inter-dominion conferences have come back always with the impression that Pakistan was a hard nut to crack. They never listened to the advice of the Punjabis who know their brethren across the frontier very well. Pakistan is not such a hard nut if you begin to crack it. The Government of India, if they have the will to do so, have hundred and one ways to compel Pakistan to do justice to the Hindu and Sikh evacuees. There is no national or international law and no social and moral justification whatsoever for confiscation of the properties of any person or group of persons on the sole ground of their being followers of another religion. To do so amounts to a religious and racial persecution of the worst type. The Nehru government, like the Bourbons of France apparently will not learn a new lesson and not forget the old one. They will hug on to their policy of the League appeasement which now has taken the shape of appeasement of Pakistan and shut their eves to the vast changes that have taken place in the country.

There are several practical courses of action open to the government to solve this problem: (1) To take possession of all evacuee property in the whole of India without exception, (2) To enlarge the definition of an evacuee as suggested by Sir Bakshi Tek Chand's Sub-Committee, (3) to impose a rigid exchange control between India and Pakistan on the lines suggested by Lala Yodhraj in the Refugee Conference, (4) either to allot the whole of this property to the Hindu and Sikh refugees from Pakistan according to their claims or to sell it and distribute the sale proceeds among the refugees allowing them the discretion to settle anywhere in the Indian dominion by investing the money so obtained in property or business, (5) to bring the entire agricultural land of evacuee Muslims in the common pool for distribution to the Hindu and Sikh refugees, in accordance with the amount of land left behind by them. If these measures are taken, it will be found that there would be very little difference left between the value of evacuee properties left on both sides of the frontier. Another course of action open to them and which will be acclaimed with satisfaction by all refugees to claim additional space from Pakistan in the shape of accession to the Indian dominion of the districts of Lahore and Sheikhupura in West Punjab and the district of Tharparkar in Sindh which are contiguous to the Indian dominion territory. The largest number of agriculturist landlords holding the largest amount of land, come from Lahore district. The urban property of Lahore would go a long way to compensate in value the properties left in Pakistan.

After all, what is the remedy left open to a country if it finds that its neighbour was not only invading its territory without any declaration of war and confiscating unilaterally the entire property, movable and immovable of lakhs of its nationals. Wars have been fought on a much lesser provocation before and it is the considered opinion of all, except a handful of people who surround Pt. Jawaharlal Nehru, that some such strong action will have to be taken against Pakistan sooner or later. In the opinion of the refugees and their well-wishers, the sooner it is taken, the better.

The Government of India, realising their utter failure to bring around Pakistan to a reasonable frame of mind, convened a conference of refugees at New Delhi on July 21, 1949. Important decisions were unanimously taken at the conference with the concurrence of the representatives of the government who attended the session were to be considered by the Indian cabinet and put into execution. What those unanimous decisions were is confidential beyond a short summary published in the papers. But the following resolutions passed by the All-India Refugees Association faithfully sum up what is uppermost in their minds:

Resolution No. 1: In the opinion of this Conference, it is now patent that the Pakistan government is not prepared to restore evacuee property or to make any compensation to the displaced persons or even to pay them rent of the properties left by them in Pakistan, but puts impediments even on sale or exchange thereof. In the opinion of this conference, therefore, it is utterly futile to carry on any further negotiations with the Pakistan government and it is apparent that the only way of solving the present difficulty is by unilateral action by the Government of India.

Resolution No. 2: This Conference urges upon the government:

(a) That the evacuee property ordinance should be amended as to apply to all parts of India including the acceding states and Hyderabad except West Bengal and Assam. This should be done forthwith by means of comprehensive ordinance.

(b) That the definition of 'evacuee' should be extended to cover those persons also who though residents in India have transferred wholly or partly their families or business or any assets directly to Pakistan since March 1947, and also those persons who are attempting to dispose of their properties in India in furtherance of their intention to migrate to Pakistan.

(c) That Sections 8, 14 and 25, Ordinance No. XII of 1949 should be amended as not to leave any loopholes for the evasion of the ordinance.

(d) That the definition of 'evacuee property' be so amended (1) as to include Wakf Property also with the exception of places of worship, graveyards and tombs, (2) shares and stocks held by the evacuees in the joint stock companies who have head offices in India, (3) properties of those persons who have acquired any interest in any property of any person in Pakistan after the partition or who have started a business of theirs in Pakistan after partition.

(Note: The restrictive condition that the property of only those persons be considered evacuee property, who have acquired any interest in property which is declared evacuee property by the Pakistan government should be removed).

Resolution No. 3:

(a) This conference resolves that the displaced persons from western Pakistan be paid by the Government of India full compensation for their properties in Pakistan.

(b) This conference is of the opinion that to start with, it is imperative that the displaced persons from western Pakistan be immediately given a reasonable percentage of the value of the property in western Pakistan, so that they might take steps to rehabilitate themselves without any further delay. In view of the fact that already two years have elapsed in the fruitless efforts for settlement with the Pakistan government and during this long period, most of the displaced persons who had some savings in cash or ornaments, etc., have nearly exhausted all their resources and on top of it, the Government of India has started liquidating refugee camps and issued orders to complete the liquidation of refugee camps and to stop free ration before 31-10-49.

(c) This conference, therefore, emphatically begs that effective and immediate measures be taken to secure all the remaining evacuee properties throughout India including Hyderabad Deccan and excepting West Bengal and Assam and disposal of the evacuee property already secured or to be secured hereafter by sale or otherwise and distribute the proceeds between the displaced persons in graded proportions of the value of their properties in Pakistan, ensuring the payment of greater proportion to the people of lesser assets.

(d) This conference further resolves that, in the case of widows, orphans, poor and deserving students, aged, sick and disabled persons who have no resources, monthly allowances be given towards the account of compensation.

(e) This conference also urges that owing to the disposal of evacuee property, the Government of India should issue bonds in favour of displaced persons entitled for receipt of compensation, on the strength whereof, the displaced persons may be able to bid for the evacuee property or to raise loans by mortgaging them as collateral security.

(f) With the above objects in view, the government should, without delay, set up the requisite machinery mostly consisting of refugees for determining the value of the property of each displaced person in Pakistan and also of the evacuee property in India.

(g) This conference resolves that responsible advisory bodies composed of displaced persons be formed to assist and advise the custodian of evacuee properties in the centre and the provinces.

(h) This conference urges that the Government of India should ensure full co-operation between the centre and the provinces and states with effective control from the centre.

Resolution No.4: In view of the suffering and distress of the immigrants from Pakistan and also in view of the irresponsible attitude of the Pakistan Government towards settlement of the question of the properties left behind by Hindus and Sikhs at governmental level and adjustment of the difference thereof, this conference urges the government to levy a 'freedom tax' in recognition of the sacrifices of the refugees on graded scale on all nationals of India, from the commonest to the richest, as this will also be an appeal of new national aspirations of patriotic feelings for the growth of healthy nationhood.

If the resolutions are to be executed, Pt. Jawaharlal Nehru will have to change the stand he took up some months ago, when in answer to a question put by Mr. H.V. Kamath regarding the property belonging to Pakistan nationals in the Indian dominion, he said that it was impossible to define the legal or constitutional position of people moving from one side to the other till things settled down. The things have fairly well settled down now when the Pakistan government has abrogated all its agreements and promises made with India.

The Punjab government has done wonders in classifying and evaluating claims of Hindu and Sikh landlords of agricultural lands numbering about eight lakh families from ten thousand villages and two hundred towns and cities of West Pakistan. Surely, the Government of India with its vast resources could do much better than the Punjab government if only the will to do was there.

According to an official announcement made by the West Punjab government on June 5, 1948, the Hindus and Sikhs abandoned 1,54,000 houses in that province and 51,000 shops. One thousand (1,000) factories were left behind and they out-numbered by thirteen to one factories abandoned by the Muslims in East Punjab. The published estimates based on claims put forward by the Hindus and Sikhs, by the Hindus and Sikhs (cannot be taken as correct in the absence of an offical announcement) by Punjab government. The figures published, however, give some idea of the vast urban property left behind by the Hindus and Sikhs.

The Government of India figures of Hindu and Sikh properties left in Pakistan are yet to be published. In Delhi alone, 94,000 claims have been registered. Of these, 66,000 had been classified up to July 22, 1948, which give a total value of over ₹800 crores.

Writing about the Inter-Dominion Agreement about movable property, the 'Hindustan Times' in its issue of August 27, 1948 wrote:

"There are evidently optimists in the Goverment of India. In Pakistan, the optimism must be something in the nature of pretence, with a tinge of cynicism. Twelve months after partition, none but a super-optimist can believe that the refugees can go back to Pakistan to salvage their movable property. Most of it must have been looted and the rest either sold, removed or destroyed. And as regards goods not disposed of in this manner does anyone in the Government of India believe that the owners can get fair compensation for such goods from refugees who are using them or even the provincial government which has the right to requisition such goods?"

Emboldened by the Government of India's announcement, many refugees sent their claims to their friends or agents in Pakistan and some of them even actually went there to claim their goods. I was one of those who long before the announcement sent a detailed list of goods left behind in my bungalow on Sanda Road, Lahore to the deputy commissioner of Lahore, the deputy high commissioner's office there and some Muslim friends. I also arranged on three different occasions to send my man to claim these goods. But, apparently, the lists had been passed on to the occupier of the house because everything had disappeared from the house when my men arrived there. The only thing I got back was two or three books, one of which was on Hinduism written by Dr. G.C. Narang and contained his photo. The young son of the occupier had written across the photo: "He has since become a Muslim." My offer to give handsome cash reward if my copy books and manuscripts, typed and hand-written, about my economic research on various subjects were handed over to me, as met with the reply that owing to shortage of fuel these had been burnt to provide fire for the *hooka*. Apparently Pakistan proposes to do a similar thing to the properties of the Hindus and Sikhs left behind. These are to be used for providing her army with arms and ammunition for a war against Kashmir and India. The Maulvis of the Jamiat-ul-Ulema-i-Hind in the meantime will see to it that India does not retaliate.

The high hopes raised in the evacuee conference by the favourable and changed attitude of the government in the conference were all dashed to the ground when it came to be known that the prime minister was once in the role of Hamlet and could not make up his mind when all the possible committees and the officials of the Law Ministry had completed their task of preparing the new ordinance. Speaking of this, the 'People', in its issue of October 23, 1949, wrote:

"The Education Minister, Maulana Abul Kalam Azad was specially invited to the meetings of the Cabinet Committee dealing with rehabilitation—hitherto he had never been known to have shown any interest in rehabilitation, but when the Jamiat leaders engineered an agitation against evacuee law on the lines chalked out by the Jamiat, finally the prime minister gave in. The draft had previously been prepared by the officials of the ministry concerned and those of the Law Ministry. The main provisions of the draft had been scrutinised and endorsed by the Evacuee Law Committee on which 'refugees' were represented through their spokesmen. But at the final stage when the vital provisions of the proposed law were revised and Jamiatised, no heed was paid to the commitments made to the 'refugee' leaders—they were not even told about it."

Speaking of the new Evacuee Law, "The Indian Finance" of Calcutta wrote:

"In India, there are a large number of families who continue to be in full enjoyment of family wealth, inspite of the fact that some members from their families have become land-owners in Pakistan. Unless the Indian Union takes its stand on strict reciprocity in financial dealings with Pakistan, the latter will gleefully be eating the cake and having it too."

Dr. Choithram P. Gidwani addressing a press conference in Bombay on October 22, 1949 called the Government of India's ordinance on evacuee property as an 'unpatriotic one' which would not only completely fail to rehabilitate displaced persons, but would do positive harm as it conferred a license on Muslims of doubtful loyalty to continue further transfer of India's wealth to Pakistan. Dr. Gidwani added:

"It is now an open secret that Jamiat-ul-Ulema and other Muslim organisations immediately carried on an intensive agitation and they received the fullest support from Maulana Azad. The cabinet thereafter appears to have succumbed to Muslim agitation with the result that the ordinance that has emerged after a lapse of three months is even much less effective than the one that existed in July last."

The protests of the accredited representatives of the refugees have had no effect on Pt. Jawaharlal Nehru who has now brought in to this purely domestic affair of India, "International obligations and laws" which in his opinion cannot be ignored without great discredit in the international sphere. The latest to defend the new Evacuee Law is Shri M.L. Saksena, Minister of Relief & Rehabilitation, Government of India. He now wants to take the question to the International Debating Society, euphemistically known as the U.N.O. sitting in lake failure or success. Apparently, the Government of India has not learnt the bitter lesson of their earlier action in taking the Kashmir issue to the international busy bodies.

□

12

A Friend in Need is a Friend Indeed

During the one month of their civil disobedience campaign in Punjab, the Muslim League scrupulously refrained from giving any provocation to the Hindus and Sikhs. They concentrated all their venom on Sir Khizar Hayat and the Muslim members of the Unionist party. The government was strong enough to have called off the bluff, but it would have taken the shape of a Muslim premier attaching the Muslim League for his own personal ends and not for the maintenance of law and order. The Muslim League broke all law and order so far as the holding of the meetings, taking out of processions and shouting offensive and highly provocating slogans, etc. were concerned, but there was no life taken and no limb broken and, therefore, interpreting law in the broad sense, there was no case for suppression of the Muslim League disobedience. During this one month, the League perfected its technique of an offensive against the minorities, enlisted the help of the 'Maulvis and Maulanas' for their campaign exactly on the lines on which Mahatma Gandhi and the Congress leaders had enlisted their help at the time of Khilafat agitation. Had the Hindus and Sikhs seen through the game and known that it was nothing but a full-dress rehearsal for a war to the finish against them, their line of action would have been different. As soon as the Khizar Government collapsed by Sir Khizar Hayat's resignation, the fanatical fury was overnight transformed into fanatical praise for his action. I remember seeing a procession passing by near Nawankot that day which now began to shout "Taza Khabar Ai Hai Khizar Sadda Bhai Hai" (a fresh news has been received that Khizar is our own brother). The Muslims in

Shri Madhav Sadashiv Golwalkar 'Shriguruji'

Mozang were more effusive because there the shouting was "Rupai Ser Ghiu Hai Khizar Sada Piu Hai" (Ghee will sell at one rupee a ser and Khizar is our father). These slogans had hardly died down when their echo was heard in a different tone in the Rawalpindi division: The Muslim Leaguers began to form themselves into regular military formations and armed with deadly weapons, began a wholesale massacre of the Hindus and Sikhs in that division. It was later on discovered that in some of the districts, the leadership of these mobs was in the hands of the Muslim members of the I.N.A. for whose help, the Hindus and Sikhs under the lead had poured out money like water. The first victims of the holocaust were the Sikhs. Most of the Sikh population of Rawalpindi district consisted of Hindu Khatris, Brahmins, Arorbans, etc., who had during the last four decades embraced Sikhism and who with some exceptions were mostly engaged in trade and commerce and had made a good deal of money as a result of the two Great Wars and continued peace in the country. The Jat Sikhs of Punjab were concentrated in the central districts of the Lahore division and in the Lyallpur and Montgomery districts of Multan division. It was feared by the Muslim League leaders at this time that if the Jat Sikhs of the Majha became restive, there would be nothing to stop them from taking revenge on the Muslim population of that tract or even by marching forward to help their brethren in Gujarat, Jhelum and Rawalpindi districts. Therefore, they began an insidious whispering campaign the aim of which was to create a gulf between the agriculturist and the non-agriculturist Sikhs. As no retaliation came, the Muslim Leaguers became emboldened and now began to jeer at the fleeing Sikh population from those places. They even went to the length of blaspheming the Sikhs greeting 'Sat Sri Akal' as 'Nath Siri Akal' (Run away Siri Akal). They also tried to wean away the Hindus from the Sikhs by saying that their quarrel primarily was with Master Tara Singh and the Sikhs and not with the Hindus. Many Congress-minded Hindus began to believe in this. But the assassin's knife in actual practice did not spare either the Hindu or the Sikh. Mr Niranjan Dass Bagga, a well-known Congress leader of Gujranwala, was not spared because he was a Congressman or a Hindu and so was also the fate of a large number of other unknown Hindus in the rural and urban areas of the province who fell victims to Muslim League fury.

The insistent demand of the Hindus and Sikhs about the declaration of martial law in the province was studiously ignored. The police was mostly League-minded, particularly in the lower ranks with whom the public came into contact. Non-violence and the advice given by Mrs. Sucheta Kriplani, Mahatma Gandhi and Dr. Rajendra Prasad, etc., to stay out where they were with a firm trust in God appeared to most of the victims as a counsel of perfection which could only be given from a safe distance. Who else came to the rescue of the people at this stage, but a band of young selfless Hindus, popularly known as the R.S.S.? They organised in every mohalla (area) of every town of the province, the work of evacuation of the Hindu and Sikh women and children from dangerous pockets to comparatively safe centres. They organised for their feeding, medical aid, clothing and care. Parties for the protection of institutions were organised. Even fire engine brigades were formed in various towns. Arrangements for transport by lorries and buses and provision of escort on the trains carrying the fleeing Hindus and Sikhs were organised. Day and night vigils in various Hindu and Sikh localities were kept and people were taught how to defend themselves when attacked. When the situation on the eve of partition became very serious and law and order utterly broke down or, it would be more correct to say, was now used only to suppress the Hindus and Sikhs, several members of the R.S.S. showed their proficiency in the use of fire weapons. It almost became a tit for tat. These youngmen were the first to come to the help of the stricken Hindus and Sikhs and were the last to leave their places for safety in East Punjab. I could name several Congress leaders of note in various districts of Punjab who openly solicited the help of the R.S.S. even for their own protection and the protection of their kith and kin. No request for help from any quarter was refused and there are cases which came to our notice where the Muslim women and children were safely escorted out of the Hindu Mohallas (localities) and sent to Muslim League refugee centres in Lahore by the R.S.S. men.

While in Lahore, I had no means of knowing what was happening in East Punjab after partition. I only know this that on my way to Delhi from Amritsar by car, I came across convoys of refugees, several miles long, wending their way peacefully to Wagha border and even carrying spears with them unmolested by the police. In Karnal, I found the Muslims living still in their own Mohallas (localities) and carrying on their normal avocations. How far the R.S.S. was responsible for driving out the Muslim population from East Punjab can never be ascertained. But it is a safe bet to make that it was mainly the angry refugees who had lost everything and had seen their own men, women and children being looted and butchered before their very eyes, who ended up taking the law into their own hands. I also found during my tour of East Punjab, a deep sense of gratitude and gratefulness to the Sikhs and the Sanghis among the masses. They were considered the saviours of the people and it was a universal belief that they had made the rehabilitation of a part of the Hindu and Sikh refugees possible in East Punjab. A few lakhs of them had at least found a temporary shelter in the vacated houses and lands. Judging in the light of subsequent history of rehabilitation of refugees, one shudders to think of what would have happened to these refugees if, like the other unfortunate refugees, they also had to seek shelter in refugee camps and on road side. Pandit Nehru's Government had utterly failed so far, to rehabilitate the few lakhs who became its direct charge. How would the government have floundered if they had been burdened with the additional responsibility of having to look after lakhs of more refugees can better be imagined than described. Pt. Jawaharlal Nehru in his Kanpur speech had accused the Sangh of creating disturbances in Punjab without adducing any proof. Apparently, he thinks that any stick is good enough to beat a dog with, but a person in his responsible position should have carefully weighed his words before uttering them. And what defence would be put up if his own words were quoted against India by Sir Zafarullah Khan in the bar of world opinions? Did not Pakistan quote extensively from Mahatma Gandhi's speeches and statements on a previous occasion, in support of their genocide charge against India?

The R.S.S. was known and respected in Punjab for the love of physical exercise which it encouraged among the Hindu youth of the towns. The physical degeneration of the Hindus was a common theme of propaganda among the Singh Sabhas, Sanatan Dharma Sabhas and Arya Samajis. All these bodies had done their best to stop it by preaching the love of exercise, but they could do this through their school and college games in which only a small percentage of young men could take part. The Sangh, on the other hand, carried on day in and day out and every day of the week and every week of the month and throughout the year, a regular physical training programme, combined with games and songs. The average Punjabi loves physical exercise and, therefore, this aspect of the R.S.S. activities did more to win the people's esteem for them than any other thing. Their discipline, their physical fitness and their selflessness in face of dangers came to the rescue of the people in Punjab when the whole province was burning and when the Congress leaders were helplessly fiddling in New Delhi, not being able to overcome the opposition of the Muslim League and the obstinacy of the governor-general to their proposal for stronger action for the maintenance of law and order. If now somebody from a place outside Punjab were to call upon the Hindus and Sikhs of Punjab to disown the Sikhs and R.S.S. heroes who defended them gloriously, his advice is sure to fall on absolutely deaf ears.

The Rashtriya Swayamsewak Sangh was founded in 1925 on Vijayadashami (Dussehra) day by Dr. Keshav Baliram Hedgewar who drew his inspiration from the ancient and glorious past of the Hindus, but its main emphasis was on character-building. He died in 1940 and leadership devolved on Shri Madhav Rao Sadashiv Rao Golwalkar who was once a professor of science in the Banaras Hindu University. The movement gained popularity in 1935 when it assumed an inter-provincial status. As the Hindus realised the growing strength of the Muslim League and its insistence on

Pakistan and the perpetual weakness of the Congress in resisting this demand, the Sangh became more and more popular among the Hindus. The appeasement policy of the Congress, in other words, has as much to do with the growing popularity of the movement among the Hindus and the Sikhs as the Muslim League's unreasonable attitude to the political progress of the country. Apart from popular support, it is the organising ability of its leaders which holds thousands of its branches together. The organisation suits the Indian genius, and yet is most scientific and up-to-date in its discipline and effectiveness. The movement is organised from the smallest unit.

The movement is not puritanical in the sense that members can eat meat or remain vegetarian according to their disposition, but smoking and drinking are discouraged because they interfere with physical training and character-building. All the provincial organisers and provincial sanghchalaks presidents are directed by the All-India Baudhik-Karyawah and two Sarkaryawahas (General Secretary). There is an extra post of Sah-Sarkaryawah (Joint General Secretary) who is under the two Sarkaryawahas. Above all is the Sarsanghchalak who controls the whole organisation.

The Sangh treads across religious divisions and does not put bar to any Sikh joining it, as the Sangh and its leaders have the highest praise for the Sikhs and the Gurus for their fight against the foreign rulers. They firmly believe that Sikhs and other sects are a part and parcel of the whole Hindu society. Similarily, the present provincial boundaries are also ignored. The aim of the Sangh is to bind all the Hindus in the common ideology of the country and its culture, irrespective of its provincial angularities. A Sangh member from Madras is fired with the same inspiration as a Sangh member from Peshawar. If it were left to Sanghis alone, the problem of the rehabilitation of refugees from West and East Pakistan would have been solved long ago. The principal aim of the Sangh is to do away with the fissiparous tendencies that are raising their heads again in the country after the partition. Though the constitution of the Sangh was not published, it did not mean that the Sangh was a secret body. Its aims and objects, its method of work and its organisation were very well known to all except the die-hard Congressmen of the type of Shri Govind Sahai, parliamentary secretary to the U.P. Premier, Shri Govind Ballabh Pant. All other sections of the Hindus and Sikhs have always had silent sympathy for it. That this sympathy was not alienated even when the Congress machinery of propaganda went full blast against the movement was proved by the huge crowd that greeted the Sarsanghchalak during his tour of towns of Northern India after his release. Not even in the heyday of their glory could Gandhiji and Pandit Jawaharlal Nehru get such huge audiences to listen to their tirades against the British government. That the Sangh has taught its members and those who come in contact with it, the virtue of discipline is proved by the fact that everywhere, inspite of lakhs of people assembling, there has not been a single untoward incident.

That some of the leaders of India started with preconceived notions against the Sangh is proved by their utterances. Speaking on June 3, 1948 in Nainital, Mr. Govind Sahai accused the R.S.S. men of news-mongering in an organised manner about the outbreak of communal riots on an unprecedented scale with the departure of Lord Mountbatten. He further expressed the opinion that R.S.S. men could only thrive on communal tension. He also, in the same interview, disclosed the fact that sympathy for the refugee in the western districts of Pt. Pant's refugees' province was rapidly changing into apathy and even hostility.

That there is bound to be a clash between the Hindu culture and Russian communism is, of course, known to all, but that a few members of the Government of India should extol the principles of the latter and denounce the votaries of Hindu culture as fantastic, has taken the country by surprise. The Communists and other leftist parties including the Socialists in the early stages, spread rumours that tension existed between the Socialistic Nehru and his Deputy Prime Minister Sardar Patel. They regarded Patel as a reactionary and accused him of leaning too heavily on the side of Sikhs and the R.S.S. It was the Communist periodical that first started attacking the Sikh princes led by the Maharaja of Patiala and the Sangh for starting riots in northern India. Pt. Jawaharlal Nehru, in his recent speech in Kanpur had done nothing but to repeat the same charge against the Sangh. That Sardar Patel had nothing but praise for the work of the Sangh is proved by his earlier speeches. But Pt. Jawaharlal Nehru whose personal following was very small in the beginning became a national hero after Mahatma Gandhi's death, eclipsing Sardar Patel altogether in the process. In the beginning, in 1947, after independence, the meetings of the Indian cabinet were not always occasions for exchange of court proesies and unanimous decisions. The members were fairly well split into two parties and Pt. Jawaharlal Nehru did not always command a majority. No strong action against the Sangh could, therefore, be taken by Pt. Jawaharlal Nehru as was demanded by his supporters of the leftist parties. Had he proposed this, an open rupture between the two would have taken place. In fact, the Punjab question and the Kashmir problem had already created a sharp difference of opinion between the two and the rumours were current in the capital that Mahatma Gandhi had not succeeded in bridging the gulf between the two. Altogether, Sardar Patel's meeting with Mahatma Gandhi before his assassination was not a pleasant one.

The Socialist leaders tried to exploit the situation and brought all their batteries of propaganda guns to bear upon S. Patel and Dr. Syama Prasad Mukerjee, with a view to remove Sardar Patel from the seat of power. During all thc years of the Congress struggle, the work of party management had been left in the charge of S. Patel who, thus, controlled the Congress machinery including the provincial governments. But that Sardar Patel gave way now to Pt. Jawaharlal Nehru is proved by his subsequent actions. His well-known speech in which he conceded readily that Jawaharlal Nehru was the moon on the sky of India and the others only the stars amply proves this.

The Government of India struck strong and struck mercilessly after Mahatma Gandhi's death at the workers of the Hindu Mahasabha and the Sangh. According to a report published in the New Delhi paper 'The Hindustan Times', as many as ten thousand persons were arrested in the country after Mahatmaji's assassination, thereby establishing a world record arrests following a political murder. A mass hysteria overtook the non-violent Congress workers and supporters. According to the government's own admission in the Parliament, as many as 1,000 houses were burnt or razed to the ground, hundreds of people attacked, killed and injured in Maharashtra and the rest of the country.

A ban on the R.S.S. was imposed and the leaders were put in jail. Even the Samadhi of the founder of the Sangh at Reshimbagh, Nagpur was not spared by the Congress mobs. The restrictions on the R.S.S. chief were removed in October 1948, but the ban on the organisation prevailed and Pt. Jawaharlal Nehru even refused to see Shri M.S. Golwalkar when he was in Delhi. Failing to get redressal from any quarter, the Sangh decided to adopt the same methods which the Congress had always been adopting in its struggle with its opponents. But the Satyagraha of the Sangh took only a mild shape of going about in processions, holding meetings, etc. It was unlike the Congress' methods of organising *Sayapa* parties or fasting at the doors of their opponents or shouting offensive slogans like 'Todi Bacha Hai Hai'. The Satyagraha of the Sanghis was a commendable example of gentlemanliness and complete non-violence. They just technically disobeyed the law and courted arrests. The press dominated by the Congress, Socialists and Communists was hostile. Even the independent leaders of liberal view were afraid of calling a halt to government's repression. The Government of India, on their part, began to send to jails not only the members of the Sangh, but also what they called their 'sympathisers'. There were also 'preventive' arrests of Sanghis, that is the arrests of unknown people who had not broken any law but 'who might break law'. Lists of government employees suspected to be in sympathy with the R.S.S. Satyagraha were prepared and all such employees were dismissed from government service. The 'true' Congressmen did a good deal of informers' business during these days. Bidding good-bye to all moral ideas of neighbourliness, they informed the police authorities about mohalla people of their own localities, who were in sympathy with the R.S.S. movement and made secret reports about them. The use of tear gas and lathis was not uncommon and reports of indiscriminate beating began to be received from several jails and cities. The Congress government used all those methods that had been brought into play by the British government against them. The figures of the total number of Sanghis taken into custody have never been published. But adding the figures of persons who courted arrest in several provinces, the total well exceeded the figure of sixty thousand. Without the fanfare of publicity, the support of the press and the inspiration that they were fighting against the foreign rule, the R.S.S. organisation was, thus, able to send to jails on the first occasion, more persons than the Indian National Congress could ever do in her history. To everyone else except the die-hard Congressmen, this should have been an eye opener. But the government construed it in another way.

Pt. Jawaharlal Nehru disdainfully dismissed the whole show by calling it a Satyagraha of *Chhokras*.

On December 7, 1948, Mr. Govind Sahai gave a statement that information about the detailed working of the Sangh which had come into his possession would amaze them, that the Swayamsevaks were being daily inspired to fight for Ram Raj against the Ravan Raj; but the government was prepared to take strong action against them. Two days later, the Satyagraha had started. The only English paper in India still owned and edited by an Englishman 'The Statesman' in its editorial of December 10, 1948 congratulated the Congress government on the ban imposed on the R.S.S. The editor gave the Nehru government a certificate of having acted with exemplary impartiality and skill, and having enhanced their repute for fair and capable rule. He further congratulated them on their foresight in taking this action during an important, 'Inter-Dominion Conference' in Delhi and calling their action felicitous, expressed the opinion that it might indeed indirectly help the negotiators in their task. That a certificate of good conduct should come from an Englishman would have aroused suspicion about its bona-fides in the minds of the Congress leaders in normal times, but now they were happy with the thought that the Pakistanis and the Englishmen had all been pleased at their action. The transformation of the Congress from jail to jailor was now complete.

The Delhi administration, which had failed to achieve any constructive success so far in settling the refugee problem showed unusual zeal in suppressing the R.S.S. movement in Delhi. The administrators also turned lecturers. Pandit Rameshwar Dayal now began to address meetings, holding out promises to informers and threats to would-be Satyagrahies. This campaign against the R.S.S. and the Hindu Mahasabha was launched by him. It was reported later on under instructions received from the Government of India.

No heed was paid to the statements of Mr. L.R. Bhopatkar, President, All-India Hindu Mahasabha, Dr. Gokal Chand Narang, Capt. Keshab Chandra and Mr. Indra Prakash that the government, instead of falling a prey to falser notions of power and prestige, should at once lift the ban imposed upon the Sangh and enable that organisation to carry on its social and cultural activities as before.

Even the 'Statesman' which was so jubilant over the Government action had to reluctantly confess that the R.S.S. was not lacking in qualities. 'It inculcated discipline and sacrifice among Hindus, fostered physical culture and with often admirable gallantry, succoured the stricken.'

Master Tara Singh was the only leader in India who very bravely paid a tribute to the Sangh and pointed out to the Government of India, the urgent need of allowing Hindu unity and Hindu and Sikh unity to be promoted in the country by the Sangh. In a lecture delivered on December 13, 1948 at Amritsar, he said:

"We have crossed the stage of getting independence for the country, but two stages have yet to be crossed before we become really free; one is the stage of conquering Pakistan and second that of restoring peace in the country in which the Hindu unity promoted by the Sangh and Hindu-Sikh unity will be essential." Master Tara Singh expressed the view that in a way even the private armies of the Sangh or the Akalis would be a source of strength to the government and, therefore, he did not see any reason as to why the government should be frightened of them. He offered his services in bringing about a settlement between the government and the R.S.S. as he strongly believed that the influence of the government should not be undermined nor its energies wasted in internal squabbles.

The U.P. government in addition to taking disciplinary action against government servants who participated in R.S.S. activities also declared that watching of such demonstrations would amount to a gesture or expression of sympathy with the R.S.S. rendering them liable to departmental action (Lucknow, December 16, 1948) thereby giving a new meaning to the word 'watching' in the English dictionary. It may be noted that in spite of wild charges against the R.S.S. by Mr. Govind Sahai and others right up to the last moment of lifting the ban, no proof whatsoever was given by him and the Government of India establishing the truth of their allegations. I believe more significance attaches to what Pt. Rameshwar Dayal, the Deputy Commissioner of Delhi, told the municipal commissioners and trade representatives assembled in the Old Delhi Town Hall as reported in papers of December 22, 1948 than to what the Congress ministers said in this connection. Pt. Rameshwar Dayal was speaking under instructions received from the Government of India and he made it clear that it was not the murder of Mahatma Gandhi which had led to the ban on the R.S.S. not because the country was passing through a critical phase at the moment, but simply because of ideological reasons. As he said, the government had always been opposed to the existence of fascist bodies because democracy could not at any time exist side by side with Fascism.

The murder of Mahatma Gandhi had only provided the Government of India with an opportunity to bring their iron hand down on the movement. Through a whispering campaign carried out in the country by the Congress and the Socialist workers, the Sangh was accused of having a hand in the murder. How this propaganda that Sangh had a hand in the murder of Mahatma Gandhi was carried on in the country is incidentally proved by what Sardar Patel said after he had ordered the arrest of Shri M.S. Golwalkar. The following passage from S. Patel's statement published in the

'Indian News Chronicle' of December 17, 1918 proves it. Referring to Shri M.S. Golwalkar, S. Patel is reported to have said, "He did not meet Pt. Nehru because he was directed to go to S. Patel in the home ministry. Meanwhile, he had further intelligence that 500 people were coming from Gwalior at the behest of the R.S.S. Chief to meet him in Delhi. Sardar Patel recalled that the revolver which killed Mahatma Gandhi came from Gwalior and he immediately asked Mr. Golwalkar to return to Nagpur. But he wrote back to say that he was not going back. Sardar Patel said that the law would take its own course and he had directed the police to send him back to Nagpur". Any connection between the revolver coming from Gwalior and the volunteers coming from the same place is difficult to see because it happened to be so that Shri Golwalkar was ordered to go to Nagpur and was taken into custody on his refusal to do so. The impression left on the minds of the unsophisticated public is that there was some direct or indirect connection between the R.S.S. and Mahatma Gandhi's murder.

All news about the treatment meted out to the R.S.S. prisoners in jails was suppressed, but the enterprising correspondent of an English paper here and there would some-times ferret out the news. In the Statesman of December 22, 1948, it was given out that at one time in the Delhi District Jail, there were as many as 1,807 prisoners as against the jail's normal capacity of 677. Speaking of the treatment meted out to political prisoners including the R.S.S. detenus in the District Jail, Delhi 'The Statesman's' correspondent said, "The food was bad, sleeping space was cramped and they were made to work from 10 to 12 hours a day. Physical punishment was widely resorted to by the jail officials and even boys in their teens were caned." There were also allegations about lack of medical treatment and about a number of lunatics being kept in the same jail. It was the depth of winter and yet sufficient bedding was not issued to the prisoners nor were they allowed to bring their own. Mostly, one blanket was shared between two men.

According to official estimates, the R.S.S. agitation had spent its force within a fortnight of its start and the government praised the provinces for their faithfully carrying out a policy set up by the Centre, in spite of the fact that the personnel of both the central and the provincial governments was not always unaffected by R.S.S. influence. Like the British government in the early stages of Congress agitation, the Congress government now began to say that the R.S.S. represented only the movement of the town people and was led by a small section of the Hindu community, the Brahmins. The rest of the country and all other sections of the Hindu society were unaffected. The obvious conclusion drawn was that the R.S.S. had a very small following. The lifting of the ban and the enthusiastic receptions accorded to its workers in all the cities and small towns of the countryside have amply shown now that the movement has its roots, deep in the soil and that all sections of the Hindu society have reverence for its ideals. It was particularly unfortunate that of all people, a Congress leader of S. Patel's standing should come out with a sneer at the Brahmins who according to him, were the arch movers of the Sangh. An R.S.S. man could very well retort 'Physician heal thyself'. On India's attaining independence, what did people find but that the Brahmins had taken possession of all post of power and vantage in all the provinces of India and at the Centre? Among the premiers of the provincial governments, there were as many as ninety per cent Brahmins, a Brahmin in East Punjab, a Brahmin in U.P., a Brahmin in Bihar, a Brahmin in Orissa, a Brahmin in Madras, a Brahmin in C.P., a Brahmin in Bombay and a Brahmin in Assam. Among the governors, there were, at one time, 7 Brahmins out of 8 Hindus appointed to the job—a Brahmin in East Punjab, a Brahmin in Assam, a Brahmin in the U.P., a Brahmin in Bengal, a Brahmin in Bihar, a Brahmin in Orissa and a Brahmin in C.P. The prime minister of India himself was a Brahmin. So also the governor general. In face of these facts, to say that the Sangh Movement derived its inspiration from Brahmins was like a pot calling kettle black. If Brahmins were so dangerous, Sardar Patel should have begun by making a clean sweep of them from the Congress governments in the country and truthfully speaking, he would have had with him, the sympathies of the majority of

India's population who were all tired of this Brahmin rule in the new set-up of things since independence. A person of Kshatriya, Jat or Rajput clan would have proved a far better leader of his country than Pt. Jawaharlal because he would have had the mentality of a Kshatriya or Rajput who have traditionally provided rulers of India from their ranks, since history began. Pandit Jawaharlal Nehru, in a speech published in the 'Indian News Chronicle' dated December 26, 1948, strongly condemned the R.S.S. and called upon the country to fight the enemies within. Speaking of the influence of the Congress, Pt. Nehru boastfully said that the nominal members of the Congress were no more than about five lakhs, but they could achieve what they did because of the confidence and support of 400 millions. Of course, the Congress never had the support of 40 crores, as this figure included 9 crores of Muslims who had been fighting for Pakistan. But the main point in his speech was that the Congress party with only five lakhs of members was ruling now over a country of 35 crores. It was not much to boast about. An organised minority can always rule over a majority if it adopts fascist methods. The British government, with only 1½ lakhs of Englishmen which included their military, ruled over the country for over a century and a half.

The total Communist party membership in India is estimated at 60,000. If the Sangh were to publish the figures of its members, past and present, that would give Pt. Jawaharlal Nehru many a sleepless night. The Sangh has scrupulously avoided taking part in politics or converting itself into a political party, but that did not mean that they would not beat the Congress hollow, if like the Congress, they also seek the sufferage of the masses in a future election.

Mr. Govind Sahai, Parliamentary Secretary of the U.P. Government's Premier, went on a tour in the U.P. towns and also came to Delhi on his propaganda campaign against the R.S.S. during the Satyagraha days. He must be a learned man indeed. But some of the statements he made are difficult to understand or were unhappily worded. In a news report of his speech (uncontradicted till now) published in the 'Indian News Chronicle' of December 30,

1948, there occurs the following sentence among other. "Fortunately for the country," Mr. Sahai added, "democratically minded people had been shaken out of their apathy by the assassination of Mahatma Gandhi." It is an example of unhappy wording of one's sentences and it reminds me of the story of a relative who went to condole the death of another relative and said: "It is fortunate that I am in Lahore when the death took place, otherwise I would have had to come back from Chak Joya for condolence." Like Mr. Govind Sahai, he did not understand why the people assembled in the condolence meeting burst out laughing. Warning the R.S.S. in another speech in December 1948, Pt. Jawaharlal Nehru said that he would never allow the Sangh to rise again. But the Sangh appears to have risen again to his utter disgust, as soon as the Government of India lifted the ban. Shri M.S. Golwalkar, the R.S.S. Chief, after his release on July 13, 1949 in Nagpur, said that he had given no undertaking of any kind to the Government of India. "The Government of India might be right from its point of view in what it has said in its communique of July 12, 1949 lifting the ban on R.S.S., but I can assure you that I have done nothing either by word of mouth or in writing which is derogatory to the principles of self-respect of the R.S.S. organisation." So far as the refugees from the West Pakistan are concerned, all of them, without exception wherever they were living in India, heaved a sigh of relief when the ban on the Sangh was lifted. To a man, they are grateful to thc moment for coming to their help at the time when they felt deserted by all.

□

13

India Invaded

The history of Jammu has been traced back for about five thousand years. The importance of Jammu (ancient name Jambu Lochan) rose and fell alternately, until, in the middle of 18th century, Raja Ranjit Deo brought his kingdom to the zenith of its power. Gulab Singh, Dhian Singh and Suchet Singh were the great-grandsons of Surat Singh, a younger brother of Ranjit Deo and these three brothers distinguished themselves in the Court of Maharaja Ranjit Singh, who made Gulab Singh the Raja of Jammu in 1820. Dhyan Singh obtained the principality of Poonch and Suchet Singh of the Ram Nagar Ilaqa. Raja Gulab Singh soon entered upon a policy of consolidation and expansion. Basohli, Bhaderwah, Kishtwar and Rajouri were conquered and absorbed one by one, and the Dogra power travelled across the heights of the north-eastern hills until it reached Ladakh—the roof of the world—in 1840. The Buddhist King of Ladakh was defeated by the Dogra forces led by Wazir Zorawar. Kings of Kharmang, Skardu, Khaplu, Shigar and others in Baltistan were beaten one after the other and there remained only Kashmir with its appurtenances to be incorporated so as to make the extensive State of Jammu and Kashmir complete. Thus, even before Kashmir was acquired from the British by Maharaja Gulab Singh, the Dogra rule was firmly established in a considerable part of the Jammu and Kashmir territory. Therefore, to regard the whole Jammu and Kashmir state as the gift of the British to Maharaja Gulab Singh was a mistake in history. On March 16, 1846 was signed the 'Treaty of Amritsar' under which the British recognised Gulab Singh as the Maharaja of Jammu and Kashmir. Kashmir had been conquered by Maharaja Ranjit Singh in 1819 and in that conquest, Raja Gulab Singh was the right-hand man of Maharaja Ranjit Singh. There was peace and prosperity in Kashmir during the Sikh rule. This peace and prosperity continued uninterrupted even when the Dogra rule was established in the valley. Maharaja Gulab Singh died in August 1857 at the age of 66 before he was able to consolidate fully, the newly created state or even before the Indian War of Independence against the British had been finally settled. Maharaja Ranbir Singh reigned for 28 years (1857-85), and he carried out many reforms in the administration. Regular departments were set up. Several taxes were abolished and a number of schools were opened. A telegraph system and a postal system were established. A great patron of letters and art, Maharaja Ranbir Singh established a translation and research office. As early as in 1867, when the idea of founding a university in Lahore was first mooted by Sir D. Mcleod, the then Lieut. Governor of Punjab, a gift of ₹62,500 out of one lakh, which was collected for the promotion of the scheme, was made by Maharaja Ranbir Singh. When, in 1882, the university became an accomplished fact, in the Act of incorporation, the name of His Highness Maharaja Ranbir Singh was entered as the first fellow of the university. He was succeeded by his son Maharaja Pratap Singh (1885-1925). There existed abuses in the land revenue system which was without records and statistics. The Maharaja appointed Mr. Wingate, I.C.S.C.I.E. as Settlement Commissioner in 1887. Mr. Wingate carried out preliminary investigations and was followed by Mr. Walter. R. Lawrence, I.C.S.C.I.E., who completed the settlement operations later on. All land was carefully evaluated on the basis of the net produce, previous collections and the possibility of irrigation. Permanent but non-alienable hereditary occupancy rights were granted to those who accepted the first assessment so long as land revenue was paid by them. Among other reforms introduced by Maharaja Pratap Singh, mention may be made of the completion of the motor roads from Kohala to Srinagar and from Jammu to Srinagar, the opening of the Sialkot-Jammu Railway, the opening of two first-rate colleges, nearly 50 secondary schools and over 600 primary schools and re-organisation of the administrative machinery and the military forces. Maharaja Pratap Singh was succeeded by Maharaja Hari Singh in 1925. Maharaja Hari Singh may be rightly called the maker of modern Jammu and Kashmir. Mainly owing to his efforts, the Kashmir State acquired an honourable place among the modern advanced states of India, whose administration compared favourably with that of the British India provinces. But Maharaja Hari Singh failed to take a far-sighted view of the broad aspects of his rule over a vast territory sparsely inhabited. Punjab had contributed a good deal to providing the Dogra rulers with sinews of administration. The Sikhs and Hindus of Punjab had shed their blood in the consolidation of the state, but under the influence of his advisers, Maharaja Hari Singh now turned anti-Punjabi. His laws of settlement and acquisition of property, agricultural or urban, were all intended to keep the Punjabi Hindus and Sikhs away from the state. The Maharaja, thereby, weakened the only element that could rally to his support in times of trouble. Even in the recruitment of the army, his liberal mindedness in enlisting Poonchi and Dogra Muslims in preference to Punjabi Hindus and Sikhs proved a bane for Kashmir in 1947. Of the small army of about ten thousand or so, one-third consisted of Poonchi and Muslim Dogras who, at the call of the Muslim League, went over bag and baggage to Pakistan and proved to be staunch opponents of the Indian Army. It was mainly due to the desertion of his Muslim troops that the so-called Azad forces were able to make a clean sweep of the Jammu territory adjoining Jhelum and Gujarat. Their grip over this area is still strong. The Maharaja was the titular head of his forces, but in actual practice, he had left in recent years, the entire direction of the Army to Major General Scott who either proved to be a weak and short-sighted General or who wilfully so arranged the disposition of his troops that being scattered in tiny detachments here and there, these proved of no avail in stemming the tide of invasion.

Be that as it may, nobody in India, much less Maharaja Hari Singh could ever foresee the revolutionary changes that took place in India in 1947. That the British government would voluntarily withdraw from their prize possessions in the east, could never have been believed by anyone in 1946. The seeds of trouble for Kashmir, as for India, were sown by the Muslim League as early as in 1945. The year 1946 had been a year of war of nerves and, at one time, it was impossible to distinguish between the Muslim League and the National Conference ideologies so far as Kashmir administration was concerned. When it was known that the British were finally leaving and the choice of accession to either dominion would be left to the rulers of the states, things began to move fast. Maharaja Hari Singh wanted to be left alone, forgetting that with a handful of troops, it was not possible for him to police the entire frontier of Kashmir running into thousands of miles. He stopped Pt. Jawaharlal Nehru from entering the state territory. It is true that he also turned down the request of Mr. M.A. Jinnah later to visit Srinagar, but he should have known how to distinguish between a friend and a foe. His prime minister, Pt. Ram Chand Kak, with his English wife made strange proposals about the future administration of Kashmir at this stage. At one time, it was given out that Kashmir would hand over her north-west frontier running with Pakistan to the Indian Union for defence and, in exchange for it, obtain from them, the valley of Kangra. Pt. Ram Chand Kak was credited with having sent a memorandum to that effect to Lord Mountbatten. It was also given out from Muslim League quarters that on 1-7-47, Mr. Jinnah, on the demand of the Muslim Conference, was requesting Kashmir Darbar to hand over the strip of frontier territory of Kashmir to Pakistan and get in its return, the districts of Gurdaspur and Sialkot. No such thing, however, happened and even the visits of Mrs. Sucheta Kriplani and Mahatma Gandhi had failed to make the Maharaja see the right path.

What was not done by arguments was now done under the force of circumstances. The small Dogra army scattered all over the state and having traitors in its rank was overwhelmed at the first impact with Pakistani troops disguised as Azad forces. It was now a question of touch and go. Under the advice of Mr. Mehr Chand Mahajan, the new Dewan, the Maharaja agreed to accede to India.

The request for accession was received on the 24th of October, 1947. The Indian government lost two valuable days in framing up the conditions under which they would accept the accession and by the time the Indian air-borne troops reached Srinagar, the tribesmen had swarmed into the valley and were just a few miles off Srinagar. The subsequent history is very well known. How the Indian troops working against time and in the most unfavourable circumstances at the end of a very long line of communications were able to free the valley of invaders and recover towns has won the acclaim and admiration of all. Though the valley of Kashmir was saved and Jammu itself was unmolested, Pakistan had a free play in other outlying parts of the state. Untold havoc was wrought. Territory after territory were seized by them, looted and laid waste. It took time for India to have a sufficiently strong build-up of the army to be able to drive out the invaders from the state. This long time was an opportunity for Pakistan. Her government was at first, not sure whether an invasion of Kashmir would be construed into an invasion of India and met by a counter-invasion. Therefore, they adopted all sorts of subterfuges to create an impression that the work of invasion of Kashmir was the work of tribesmen from across the Indus, whom Pakistan government could not easily oppose. It was given out that it was a spontaneous movement of the Muslims in aid of their Muslim brethren suffering under Dogra tyranny. Pakistan even brazen-facedly told the Security Council later on that Pakistan had no hand in the matter. The Indian government, on the other hand, had the fullest evidence in their possession to prove that it was directly the work of Pakistan. The proper course of action for them should have been to give an ultimatum to Pakistan and then save Kashmir via Lahore and Sialkot and not via the tortuous and long Pathankot-Kathua-Jammu-Srinagar Road.

The partition decision of the British government had already been violated in practice by Pakistan. She had turned out and was turning out, all her Hindu and Sikh minorities and confiscating their movable and immovable properties. Pt. Nehru's government accepted partition of the country subject to other things being equal.

The other things were now not equal and the invasion of Kashmir, after her accession to the Indian dominion was another breach of the partition agreement. Therefore, there was no earthly reason whatsoever for the Indian government, not to adopt the only and the obvious course of action for the defence of India's interests—that of directly attacking the enemy concentrations in West Pakistan. Non-violence as a creed for individuals in their relations with their fellow-citizens or with the State is excellent. Non-violent action in all internal affairs, even when there is a sharp difference of opinion is very good, but non-violence as a sheet anchor of foreign policy in the face of foreign invasion is difficult to understand. But this is what Pt. Jawaharlal Nehru's government decided to do. They would not touch Pakistan. After giving thundering speeches and openly accusing Pakistan of aggression, what Pandit Nehru's government did was to submit a humble petition to the United Nations requesting their speedy intercession in the matter. That surprised the country. The Hindus and Sikhs of Punjab and North-West Frontier Province and Sindh were particularly shocked. Indian leaders' utterances and actions were poles apart. While everybody was expecting a swift action in accordance with the dictates of military strategy, what happened was a mere petition for help to outsiders. Pakistan naturally construed this as a sign of weakness on the part of India. Her leaders were now fully assured that India would not invade Pakistan, no matter what she did in Kashmir. The subsequent history confirms this view. Pakistan, after denying the charges flatly and delaying the decision for as long as it could, ultimately confessed openly to being a party to the invasion of Kashmir. So long as the U.N.O. was seized of the matter, Pakistan was sure that there would be no direct invasion of her territory by India. There are people who believe that the Pakistan leaders had well thought out in advance, their course of action and India's reaction was exactly in accordance with their reading of the situation. In other words, Pt. Nehru's government did exactly what Pakistan wanted her to do, though she made a big noise about it when the matter was first referred to the U.N O. Her task now became easy and she launch upon a war on various fronts in Kashmir, the sole object of which was to weaken the Indian army and its resources till India's superiority in men and material was sufficiently weakened to enable the shock troops of Pakistan to come into action at the appropriate moment. Their English commanders who had drawn out the plan of action for Kashmir, had advised the Pakistan government that Kashmir War must be turned into a war of attrition for India and protracted by all means. That plan is still unchanged and though it may not be clear to our government, it is crystal clear to all Pakistanis and those Punjabi Hindus and Sikhs who come from West Pakistan. Kashmir problem will never be solved except through a total war against Pakistan and it can be solved in the same short period of time in which the Hyderabad problem was solved. A question that is being asked by every man in the street is why does not Pt. Jawaharlal Nehru handover the direction of Kashmir policy to S. Patel, who has solved so many other problems confronting the country pretty successfully. Pt. Jawaharlal Nehru's handling of the Kashmir affair has been a complete fiasco so far. The best service he could do to the country was to retire from active politics and go over to Moscow or Washington as an ambassador to do the speechifying for India of which he is so fond. Practical and level-headed S. Patel knows how to call off the bluff of Rizvies of Pakistan.

In spite of the intervention of the U.N.O., the war in Kashmir continued. The Pakistan raiders had attacked Hindu and Sikh refugees in the villages of Jammu on September 3, 1947. Regular attacks on border villages by raiders started in the last week of September 1947. Regular fighting between the raiders and State forces began on October 4, 1947 and by October 24, 1947, when the Government of India received request for military aid from the Government of Jammu and Kashmir State, Pakistan had captured a large slice of Kashmir state territory. Telegrams and protest notes between the two governments began to cross the Indo-Pakistan borders while Pakistani troops in larger and larger numbers were crossing over to Kashmir. On December 31, 1947, Indian government referred the Kashmir issue to U.N.O. and Pakistan formally requested the latter to delay placing Kashmir issue before the Security Council. The Security Council continued to debate the issue while fighting continued in Kashmir. Mr. Gopala Swamy Ayyangar's speech in the Security Council about U.N.O. fiddling while Kashmir was burning, fell on deaf ears and the proposals made by the president were so unjust to India that, for once, even Pt. Nehru did not accept them. The Indian troops by April 1948 had taken the offensive in Jhangar and Rajauri areas. Pakistani troops were being driven out over a large area. In Uri, Naushera and Poonch sectors, the Indian troops' advance on Uri-Domel Road was a major strategic victory and our troops had finally succeeded in dislodging raiders in Tithwal area. On July 3, 1948, Srinagar reported the use of 25 pounder guns for the first time by Pakistani troops. The Kashmir Commission of the Security Council arrived in Karachi on July 6, 1948 and in New Delhi on July 10, 1948. The members of the commission found Kashmir in the summer, the most pleasant place to go about. They liked it so much that right up to September 1949, they are still there. By saying one thing to Pakistan and quite the opposite to India, they have proved themselves experts in the art, which in modern parlance is known as 'diplomacy'. No more incompetent group of persons could have been deputed for this purpose. But they must have mapped out the entire Kashmir and informed their respective governments about the disposition of troops and armaments on both sides of the fighting line in code. Even if they have not done so, the spectacle of a large number of outsiders prying into our military and other affairs is not exactly edifying.

Pakistan in summer, organised a strong offensive and the Indian Army which was at first, taken by surprise by the enemies' use of heavy artillery, soon took up the challenge. By December 1948, the situation had become critical for Pakistan. A few weeks' continued operations on the major scale on which they were being conducted then, would have liberated a still larger portion of Kashmir territory from Pakistani invaders. But when things were going bad for Pakistan, fortunately for her and unfortunately for India, Pt. Jawaharlal Nehru went to London in connection with the

Commonwealth Premiers Conference. What happened behind the curtains between Pt. Jawaharlal Nehru, Mr. Liaquat Ali Khan and Mr. Attlee is not known, but the first proof of something having been settled in London was forthcoming with the announcement of ceasefire agreement between India and Pakistan. Pt. Jawaharlal Nehru's government directly recognised the belligerent status of Pakistan. The news of 'ceasefire agreement' was greeted in foreign countries as evidence that Asia was taking the initiative in setting high standards for international morality. The U.N.O. had utterly failed so far to achieve any important result anywhere, either in Europe or in Asia. It had been reduced to the status of a debating society and was expected to meet with the same fate as its predecessor, the League of Nations. Its achievement in bringing about ceasefire in Kashmir was its first important success. Pakistan greeted the ceasefire agreement with a sigh of relief. They were in a tight corner and the ceasefire agreement would enable them so long as it lasted, to consolidate the areas she had already captured and make preparations for a final offensive later on. The Congress leaders and other votaries of non-violence were very effusive in their utterances and statements and vied with one another in sending affectionate greetings to Pakistan. They had, however, counted without their host. No one but a Punjabi Hindu and Sikh knows the mentality and tactics of the Muslim League rulers and they were all dismayed at the new turn of events. They knew that there could never be a peaceful solution of the Kashmir problem. Much as British and American governments would like to bring about a partition of Kashmir on the lines of the partition of Punjab and Bengal and much as Pakistan would like to accept this decision, India would be committing another great blunder by acquiescing in such an agreement. Our prime minister's frequent announcements about India's desire to not get embroiled with Pakistan on Kashmir or any other issue had only given Pakistan the much-needed assurance that they wanted. In an answer to a question in Indian parliament, the prime minister had made it clear that India would continue her activities in the Kashmir territory and as far as possible, avoid crossing over into Pakistan territory. The Pakistan government even now, twelve months after the cease-fire, still has faith in our prime minister's words. She has utilised the intervening period in constructing military roads, piling up supplies and building ammunition dumps here and there. She has also in the meantime expanded her airforce, given Pakistan nationality to European adventurers, and considerably expanded her army. The total amount of money spent on her army and on capital expenditure on military installations well exceeds her total budget. She has proved to be a heavy buyer of arms and ammunitions from anywhere in the world. Her earnings of dollar currency of which she has a surplus, have been used for the import of arms and ammunitions. While India has been spending almost her entire foreign exchange on purchasing wheat and millet (Gandam and Jao). Pakistan has been using her resources on import of guns and tanks. If the war breaks out again in Kashmir, and Pakistan will force the issue only when it suits her, she will be a much more formidable foe now than before. The intervention of Mr. Truman and Mr. Attlee must have been stage-managed by Pakistan. If it misfires, she will bend all her energies by propoganda and parleys to ensure that Pt. Jawaharlal Nehru sticks to his gentleman's agreement of confining the war to the territory of Kashmir only. Of course, the initiative rests with her. She will choose the time and the place for a renewed offensive. India will only be called upon to defend the wicket.

□□□